The Science of Criminal Justice

by
James R. Davis

McFarland & Company, Inc., Publishers
Jefferson, North Carolina, and London

Library of Congress Cataloguing-in-Publication Data

Davis, James R., 1928–
The science of criminal justice.

Bibliography: p. 159.
Includes indexes.
1. Criminal justice, Administration of.   2. Criminal
justice, Administration of—United States.   I. Title.
HV7419.D38   1986   364'.01   85-43575

ISBN 0-89950-202-4 (acid-free natural paper)

Manufactured in the United States of America.

McFarland   Box 611   Jefferson NC 28640

Acknowledgments

I wish to thank my editor for doing an excellent job of revising the manuscript; my typist, Gaye Leslie, and her assistants for doing a superb job of typing the final draft of the manuscript in spite of my poor penmanship; and especially my wife, Roberta, for being so patient while her husband, the author, spent so much time in the library and at his desk writing and revising the manuscript.

I can thank these people directly. However, I believe that many people are indirectly responsible for any success I may have with this book. These people are all the teachers I had at graduate school and the speakers at conventions who directly or indirectly gave me insight through their brilliant lectures on criminal justice. I also wish to thank the authors and researchers of the many books I read in criminal justice throughout the years. Their brilliant writing style gave me insight in how to write.

These acknowledgments show that no one is entirely responsible for his or her own success. Any creation is a synthesis of many contacts, many suggestions, and much knowledge from others.

Table of Contents

Preface

From the beginning days of my career as a probation officer, I used to question certain assumptions and argue with fellow employees about the soundness of certain procedures. For example, early in my career, most probation officers believed that defendants were in remand simply because they couldn't afford bail, and I used to argue that defendants were in remand because they belonged there. Supervisors and branch chiefs would insist that probation supervision was strictly rehabilitation, and I would point out the punitive aspects of probation supervision. Supervisors and branch chiefs constantly emphasized at meetings that sentencing recommendations followed logically from the body of the probation report, and I would always question the concept of logic in relation to a recommendation. I never received a clear answer on this questioning. I very often insisted that much of what we did in probation was guesswork, yet one branch chief insisted that our work was analogous to medicine in that the right punishment had to be prescribed for each defendant.

Probation officers write a two-page report on defendants and make a sentencing recommendation. These reports are constantly being evaluated by supervisors and branch chiefs. Although report writing and reviewing is partly political — that is, workers must please supervisors who must please branch chiefs who must please higher officials in order to retain their power — I often wondered why so much emphasis was placed on a two-page report.

All this questioning and arguing led me to believe that perhaps some workers in criminal justice really don't see the crux of the criminal justice system. They seem to believe strongly in their decisions and actions. Some workers vehemently defend their positions — for example, acting as if probation were the most important part of the criminal justice system, without seeing the relation of probation to other parts of the system.

I have performed much research in criminal justice, and perhaps this research, together with my education in criminal justice, has led me to see things others don't see. However, I have constantly wondered if criminal justice does obey the kinds of axioms, theorems, and theories found in other sciences. I have been heavily influenced by my knowledge of statistics, particularly by mathematical proofs which show that most distributions in statistics approach the normal distribution as the sample size increases. It seems to me that probability and normality are the crux of statistics, and in like manner, I believe that certain concepts in criminal justice, e.g., punishment, arrest record, are the crux of criminal justice.

The most impressive thing to me about criminal justice is that the system proceeds relatively smoothly and never really breaks down. Criminologists seem to take this for granted. There really has been a dearth of research on why defendants seem to accept their fate so nonchalantly and why the system maintains itself so well in spite of numerous problems and obstacles in the system.

It seems to me that something underlying and unchanging is at the center of the system — something having to do with free will, values, and punishment. Although these constants, as I call them, have been discussed many times in criminal justice, they can be a starting point for a system of theories for the science of criminal justice.

I certainly do not believe that my analysis is beyond criticism. However, I believe a beginning has been made. I also believe that this analysis has implications for other disciplines. If knowledge in other disciplines can be evaluated and systematized into axioms, theorems, theories, and even laws, real progress can be made in the development of science.

James R. Davis

Chapter I
The Nature of the Problem

Although numerous books have been written in criminal justice, very little has been done to determine whether criminal justice is a science. Most criminologists seem to bypass the question, either taking it for granted or thinking it is not worthwhile to discuss.

This book is about the science of criminal justice, a very complicated and very important issue. Unlike other books, in this book there is an attempt to focus on the scientific aspects of criminal justice and to answer the question of whether or not criminal justice is a science.

Before answering the question, both criminal justice and science have to be defined and analyzed. This will be attempted in this chapter and in subsequent chapters. Although definitions of science will be given in the next chapter, science is equated with logic. Therefore, this book is also an attempt to find out if there is any logic in criminal justice.

Importance of the Problem

The issue is important for many different reasons. The criminal justice system has survived for hundreds of years both in American society and in other societies of the world. Although critics argue that the system is overloaded and will break down, this has never happened. A good example of the system's sturdiness was during the racial riots of the 1960s in American cities, when thousands of rioters throughout the country were arrested for participation in the riots. These rioters had to be arrested, arraigned, charged and sentenced the same as other offenders. In spite of the overload, the system survived. The system did not break down.[1]

There are other criticisms of the system. Some claim that if it weren't for plea-bargaining, the system would be overloaded and break down. Many believe that offenders don't get justice; they are dissatisfied with the system and the treatment offenders receive. The police are attacked by various sectors of the public: offenders, victims, prosecutors, and judges. Judges are being criticized today in the mass media for letting offenders off too easily with light sentences. If an offender is paroled and kills somebody, the judge very often is criticized and punished. Probation officers are overwhelmed with excessive caseloads, cutting down on the time spent to supervise each defendant, preventing efforts at rehabilitation. Prisons are overcrowded and critics warn us of impending prison riots, which sometimes do occur.

Criminal justice agencies are suffering from lack of funds needed to carry out their work. Politics pervade the appointments of some judges and other important criminal justice agents, thus disqualifying other suitable personnel from entering the system. Yet the system survives.

Certainly critics can use a sociological argument, even a Marxist perspective, to attack the above-mentioned statements. After all, they can argue, this is simply a structural-functional argument. Structural-functionalism emphasizes the status quo: There is a minimal amount of change. All parts of the criminal justice system are functional to the system as a whole, and thus continue to survive. The structure, the organization, the institution, all continue because they contribute to the maintenance of society itself. This is true for all institutions. A radical perspective would see the need for political change in the system in order to improve the functioning of the system. Between the structural-functionalist perspective and the Marxian perspective which proposes the overthrow of our capitalist society, there are all degrees and prospects of change.[2]

There are many types of personnel in the criminal justice system. They include academics, correctional officers, guards, judges, lawyers. paraprofessionals, police, prosecutors, psychiatrists, social workers, volunteers, etc. There are all degrees of education and skill in the system. Some personnel do their work quickly with little effort, and others take more time and effort. Is this difference due to ability, education, motivation, training? This is an empirical question. However, if one works in the system, as the author has done, one would notice that there are some personnel who don't understand what their work is all about. They cannot perceive their role in relation to other parts of the system. For example, there are judges who are ignorant of human behavior and will sentence a defendant in a mechanical fashion.

There may be different skills required for different jobs. One skill (for example, the ability to deal with people), although important, may not be the primary skill required in criminal justice.

Carney states that the public has a low regard for corrections, which, among other things, can be blamed on inadequate preparation and ignorance. He states that in 1966–67, only 640 undergraduate and 89 graduate degrees were granted in criminology and corrections, and these mainly in departments of sociology. (During the early part of the century, criminology was excluded from departments of sociology.[3]) Therefore, he states, criminal justice is having a difficult time in establishing an identity.[4] Becker and Whitehouse state that there are only nineteen doctoral programs in criminal justice in the United States.[5]

Misner believes that there is no general agreement on the educational objectives of criminal justice and that there has been a scarcity of learning materials. He poses the question of whether criminal justice education should become a unifying force in criminal justice.[6]

There are over a million people in criminal justice.[7] How many of these can be considered professionals? If scientific aspects of criminal justice can be located and analyzed, this would enhance the professional status of many personnel. There is a difference between a profession and an occupation. If criminal justice is to be considered a profession, then its connection to science is very important. It is true that criminal justice education has experienced an expansive growth in the last two decades.[8]

Generalizations

Like other disciplines, criminal justice is pervaded with generalizations. Many of these generalizations are based on empirical studies. The following are just some of the generalizations applicable to criminal justice.

1. Street crime is a lower-class phenomenon. Most offenders who are punished in the system are poor, lower-class, and members of minority groups, e.g., blacks or Puerto Ricans. White-collar criminals are very rarely detected or punished; therefore, there is much discrimination in the system.

2. The majority of offenders plead guilty to their offenses. If this weren't true, the court system would break down because of the overload to the system.

3. Offenders who are in remand before sentencing generally have a more difficult time with their cases than those who are not in remand. They usually receive more severe charges and sentences than others, because they don't have the time or resources to fight their cases, they have serious prior records, or because remand has a negative effect on legal actors.

4. The more serious a defendant's record — e.g., the more arrests and convictions, and the more serious the prior arrests and dispositions of prior convictions — the more severe the disposition of the present offense.

5. The more severe the charge facing the defendant, the more severe a sentence the defendant receives.

6. Rehabilitation doesn't help. Defendants still get rearrested after years of therapy.

7. Prison doesn't deter. In fact, prison sometimes makes defendants worse. Many defendants get rearrested after serving years of prison terms.

8. Discretion pervades the criminal justice system. Discretion is necessary for the system to survive.

Although nobody believes that all these generalizations happen all the time, everywhere, there is enough evidence to prove their support. There is also evidence to prove their negation. For example, there is some evidence that punishment does deter and rehabilitate some offenders.[9] There is evidence that plea-bargaining existed even when court calendars were not overcrowded.[10] Although discretion pervades the criminal justice system, some believe that discretion should be structured and limited.[11] The fight for determinate sentencing is a fight against too much discretion in sentencing and a fight against prior record as a determinant in sentencing. In other words, determinate sentencing is an attempt to limit disparity and inequality in the criminal justice system.

Discrimination is so subtle that it is difficult to detect. Some believe and have proven that minority groups have received preferential treatment in criminal justice. Some say that the increased educational, political, and legal rights of minority groups in the last decade and the influx of black judges in the courts have reduced discrimination against minority groups. Corporate crime is being investigated more today than in the past.

Some defendants in remand do manage to escape prison. Should those in remand suffer more than those who are not? What is the policy toward bail? Generally, defendants with more serious crimes suffer more serious bail requirements. However, some rich defendants are able to raise the bail necessary to leave prison. Is it logical for defendants with more serious crimes to suffer more than others?

Are these generalizations a mark of science? Even though they are based on empirical evidence, and even though they don't hold everywhere all the time, and even though they are challenged and are being revived, are they a sign of maturity of criminal justice? Do they make the system logical? These generalizations act as pivot points in the system which criminal justice personnel use to emphasize their arguments and to logically justify their decisions.

For example, prosecutors can always argue that a long, severe record is an indication that a particular offender is dangerous and should be remanded before sentencing. The argument seems logical to them and to the public even though dangerousness is difficult to predict. The prosecutor can argue with the same reasons that a defendant with a long, serious record should receive a maximum jail sentence for the crime of gambling, which generally is not dangerous to other members of society. The judge can accept the prosecutor's recommendations, using the same logical argument—i.e., a long, serious record poses a potential threat to society, therefore the defendant should be incarcerated for the maximum term.

Lawyers defending a case can use the fact that although a defendant has a long, prior record, he is trying to obtain a job, which is a sign that he is trying to rehabilitate himself. After all, some defendants are rehabilitated. The evidence is not all negative. The same defendant might show remorse for the crime, which is a first step in rehabilitation.

A probation officer might find that a defendant has a serious alcohol problem for which he wants to seek therapy. This argument might be used to justify that a defendant is trying to rehabilitate himself and should stay out of prison. A prosecutor might argue that the defendant injured the complainant so badly that he is dangerous and should be incarcerated for the maximum, even though the complainant provoked the defendant.

A judge might argue that although a defendant is famous, and although he embezzled money from the company to pay for his wife's cancer operation, white-collar crime must be detected and punished to serve as a deterrent to others.

There are many other examples of how criminal justice personnel can use certain generalizations in criminal justice either negatively or positively to enforce their arguments for a favorable or unfavorable disposition of the case. The defendant himself can argue favorably for his case. Of course, many other factors enter into the decisions. The point is that these factors very often are based on generalizations that have been accumulated from empirical evidence.

What Is Justice?

Although many books have been written in criminal justice, many authors do not define what is meant by criminal justice or even by justice itself. Generally, in books of criminal justice, three main areas are discussed, namely, the police, the courts, and corrections. These areas are subdivided into other areas, e.g., the police are subdivided into the arrest process, police bureaucracy and organization, police corruption, police discretion, victimology, etc. The courts are divided into arraignment, bail, jury selection, pretrial status, prosecution, sentencing, etc. Corrections is divided into jails and prisons, probation and parole, halfway houses, prison release programs, etc. Although not all authors emphasize all aspects of the criminal justice system in one book, there is general agreement on what areas to include.

But what is justice? Very few authors attempt to describe it. Edward Cahn is one who has made the attempt. He states:

> Justice, as many attempted definitions have already demonstrated, is unwilling to be captured in a formula.... Justice is, of course, an ideal value of highest ranks, but its positive embodiments are so thoroughly alloyed with other values and interests that it can never be completely refined out ... For this reason, the name "sense of injustice" seems much to be preferred.[12]

He finally defines justice:

> "Justice," as we shall use the term, means the *active process* of remedying or preventing what would arouse the sense of injustice.[13]

He gives examples of injustice found not only in criminal justice, but in all areas of life:

> ... the sense of injustice protests all the more rapidly against abuse of legal procedures to serve oppressive or vindictive ends ... The sense

of injustice may find as much offense in a regularity that is slavish as in an inconsiderate charge . . . Among its facets are the demands for equality, desert, human dignity, conscientious adjudication, confinement of government to its proper function, and fulfillment of common expectations.[14]

There is an implication in Cahn that justice calls for retribution or for punishment of the guilty. Punishment must be fair; either lack of punishment or the wrong type of punishment may arouse our sense of injustice. This retributive argument is implied by many authors in their discussion of the criminal justice system. They imply that there must be some punishment that is based on a fair assessment of the case.

While other writers make only a passing reference to the definition of criminal justice, Alfred Cohn devotes a whole book to it. For example, Cohn and Udolf state:

> . . . The idea that ours is an adversary system is fundamental to an understanding of the operation of our legal system. . . . All the rules of evidence and procedure that will be discussed later have one purpose, to make this fight even and fair enough so that the truth will emerge from it. . . . The reader who understands this has gone a long way toward understanding the real nature of the criminal justice system.[15]

Here the authors stress the adversary system as fundamental to our criminal justice system. The fight between the accused and accuser must be fair and conducted according to due process standards. Many authors believe that our criminal justice system is based upon the adversary system. This is the essence of criminal justice. If this breaks down, then justice is not distributed to the defendants.

Many have argued that plea-bargaining vitiates the adversary system, because the defendant doesn't have a chance to present his side of the story fairly. Through plea-bargaining, they argue, cases are processed mechanically, in an assembly-line fashion, which undermines the whole adversary system. Defendants plea-bargain to reduce the severity of their sentences; perhaps some innocent defendants are forced to plead guilty to a crime they didn't commit.

Cohn and Udolf capture another important element in criminal justice. They say:

> . . . we seek to treat everyone alike in the courts (which is just the opposite of what true justice would require, for by its very nature, it would mean treating people as individuals.[16]

The fact that offenders receive individual attention in the processing of their cases is one indication that justice is being done. This is implied in many discussions of criminal justice. There is a basic conflict here. If justice and law demand equality, treating everyone alike, how can there be individual attention in the processing of each case? Some critics resolve this issue by insisting that there must be the right proportions of equality and individual justice. This is a difficult objective and involves a complex of decisions in criminal justice.

Packer summarizes the argument between the two sides of the adversary system. He proposes a crime control model and a due process model. Both models are in existence in any criminal justice system. They are not mutually exclusive. The crime control model emphasizes guilt, informality, illegal evidence, lack of counsel in every stage of the process, and lack of appeals. It emphasizes a flow of cases in a mechanical, routine way, and reduction of crime through any means that are efficient, (e.g. secrecy). The crime control model emphasizes the guilty plea-bargain to process cases quickly.

In contrast, the due process model emphasizes formal rules, counsel at all stages of the process, appeals, and presumption of innocence until proven guilty. It emphasizes error and errant police and prosecutorial decision-making. Packer believes that we are pushing toward a due process model.[17]

There are some who believe that justice is tied up with our capitalist society. They believe that injustice permeates our class system by perpetuating the norms, values, and institutions of the power-elite. Justice cannot be distributed because the poor may succumb to the capitalist power-elite. Justice in effect is a class phenomenon. In this view, there must be elimination of the capitalistic society in order to have a real sense of justice.[18]

In spite of the conflict between equality and individual processing of cases, and in spite of the conflict between the mass production of cases and due process accorded to each case, there are some who do not believe that criminal justice is a system at all. For example, Cohn and Udolf state that criminal justice

> . . . . is not a system, and it has little to do with justice as that term is ordinarily understood.[19]

There are many others who don't believe that our system is a system. For example, Wright and Fox state that

> The criminal justice system . . . is frequently criticized because it is not a coordinated structure—not really a system. In many ways this is true.[20]

The argument against criminal justice as a system is that the parts of the system are disunified. For example, the police and the prosecutors very often work independently of each other. The police can arrest a defendant for serious charges, but the prosecutors can dismiss the case. Criminal justice varies by jurisdiction and by time periods. This doesn't mean that there is no cooperation among components of the system. For example, judges and lawyers are very often obliged to accept the recommendations of the prosecutors in order to process a case. Some have argued that formal cooperation and normative constraints are the crux of the criminal justice system.

In spite of this disunity, some believe that criminal justice *is* a system. Dawson states that

> Administration of justice can be regarded as a system by most standards. It may be a poorly functioning system, but it does meet the criteria nonetheless. The systems approach is still in its infancy.[21]

La Patra says:

> . . . I do believe that a criminal justice system does exist, but that it functions very poorly. The CJS is a loosely connected, nonharmonious, group of social entities.[22]

Both sides of the argument have been presented in the literature.

What Others Say About Science and Criminology

The Italian school made an early attempt to apply scientific methods to criminology.[23] Beccaria demanded equal justice for all.[24] He believed in particular penalties for particular crimes. All offenders should receive identical sentences for the same offense. The insane, however, should be tried separately.[25] He believed that torture in prison should be stopped. Prison sentences should be short and less severe. Punishment should be imposed to the point in which it inflicted the least possible harm to the criminal, and had the greatest effect on others. Punishment should be certain and swift. He questioned the death penalty.[26]

Jeremy Bentham believed that penalties should not be greater or smaller than necessary to deter crime.[27] This was the philosophy of the Utilitarian school.

It is debatable whether either Beccaria or Bentham approached the scientific point of view. Even if they offered specific penalties for particular offenses, they haven't proven that the penalties involved were functional for the criminal justice system. That is, they haven't proven that specific penalties deter or rehabilitate criminals.

Henry M. Boies wrote a whole book describing the science of penology. He defines penology as an exact science. Penology consists of a series of laws:

> . . . . This knowledge is now sufficiently extensive and exact, and the consensus of intelligence concerning these laws and principles ample enough to warrant the presentation of a distinct system which will constitute a complete and independent science.

Boies divides penology into three departments: diagnostics, therapeutics, and hygienics. Under diagnostics, science is explained, crime defined, the criminal class identified, classes of criminals specified, and classification and early treatment of criminals designated. Therapeutics is the division which regulates the repression of the criminal class, and formulates laws for the punishment and treatment of criminals. Hygienics is the branch of penology which deals with the causes of crime and criminals, and the measures used to eradicate the criminal from society.

Boies believes that crime is a disease analogous to disease in medicine, and like any other disease, can be cured. The criminal class cannot always be distinguished from the other classes, and it consists of individuals from every rank of society. However, in practice, there are certain characteristics of the criminal class in physique, appearance, and moral turpitude which distinguish them readily from others.

He divides criminals into three classes: the instinctive , the habitual, and the simple offender. He also defines a fourth type, the presumptive criminal. The instinctive criminal is a born criminal. The habitual offender is one who is a criminal by reason of his environment. The single offender is a one-time offender. The presumptive criminal is the undetected or young offender. These classes are not mutually exclusive.

The fundamental principle of the science of penology, according to Boies, is that all violations of law are crimes. He states that although laws have changed, the proportion of criminals has remained constant, namely 2 percent. This is a constant proportion in society.

He believes that some of the causes of crime are unfavorable environment, moral depravity, dense concentration of people into communities which invade privacy, and the propagation of criminal children from criminal parents. He believes that penology can reduce crime by reducing moral turpitude and other causes of crime.

He specifies certain axioms and laws in penology. For example, it is a law that every person convicted of a crime must be confined. It is a law that the fear of punishment doesn't restrain crime. It is an axiom that county jails are hotbeds of crime. It's a law that punishment must be certain, immediate, and uniform. It's part of the science of penology that each criminal requires individual attention and individual punishment. Boies believes in the indeterminate sentence as a basis for individual attention. The reformation of criminals is a definite science. Criminals can be cured, except, perhaps, the instinctive criminal.

Prison terms, Boies says, should vary according to the needs of the criminal. He believes there is a law which requires all prisoners to be engaged in productive labor.

There are certain preventives which can keep the criminal classes from spreading. First, there should be an intelligent, reliable, and efficient state police force. Second, all children, including institutionalized children, should have proper family training. Third, the certainty and celerity of punishment must be used to prevent crime. Fourth, punishment must fit the criminal, not the crime. Fifth, emphasis should be placed on wholesome training and education of our children. Sixth, the incorrigible should be restrained, and the curable criminal reformed.[28]

Some of Boies' ideas have been presented previously by other criminologists (for example, Beccaria and the classical school), and some are still prevalent today. But although Boies gives a theoretical presentation of crime, he doesn't offer any empirical evidence to support his axioms, theories, or laws. He doesn't introduce all dimensions of the problem. For example, he doesn't discuss who formulates laws and how they are enacted, what kind of rehabilitation is needed, how reformation cures criminality, why the proportion of criminality in the population is constant, what kind of education and training are needed for children, etc. (The field of statistics was not then as well developed as today.) It is debatable whether Boies really contributed anything new to either penology or criminal justice.

It seems that many authors of today simply pass lightly by the question of whether criminal justice is a science. Either they don't mention the question, or they give superficial answers. Either they state that criminal justice is a science because it employs the scientific method, or they maintain that it is not a science because of lack of definite laws or because it hasn't developed any cure for recidivism. The following are some examples:

Carney simply states that corrections is not an exact science. However, he believes that corrections is a science to the extent that it employs the scientific method.[29] Cohn and Udolf believe that a science of jury selection is yet to come, because of the uniqueness of each case.[30] Roscoe Pound states that a balance between rules of law and magisterial decisions is one of the most difficult tasks for the science of law.[31] La Patra states that sociology is not a science because it has no theories appropriately related to empirical facts, and offers no scientific explanations. He believes that it is more magic than science. Although he mentions sociology, his book is about criminal justice.[32] Niederhoffer doesn't believe that police science is a true science because it has borrowed heavily from the well-established disciplines.[33]

Although all the literature hasn't been reviewed, it can be seen that very little has been said about criminal justice as a science. It is really a complicated issue which needs a great deal of attention and analysis. Although no empirical evidence has been collected by this author relating to this issue, this author believes that many people in the field still believe that criminal justice is an art, not a true science. This book is an analysis of the problem.

Chapter II
What Is Science?

Generally, attempts to define and fully explain science have been restricted to the discipline of philosophy, or particularly, to the division of that discipline known as the philosophy of science. There is little effort to define or explain science in books on criminal justice. When criminologists do explain science, they usually define it tersely and concisely; they are satisfied with only defining it and not expanding on the implications of it. For example, Fuller, a sociologist, defines science as "an arrangement of propositions about natural phenomena in an ascending order of generality."[1]

Science Defined

Gareis, talking about the science of law, states:

> Like every other science, the science of law is systematic knowledge. The possibility of collateral and subordinate classification and the generalization of all ideas under higher notions, are also realized. Systematic knowledge of related facts is what constitutes a science.[2]

Gareis goes on:

> The scientist proceeds from single phenomena which he gathers through experiment and observation, and summing up, and arises to a generic notion, that is, the highest conception, law, or law of nature — which is nothing more than the generalization of a phenomena under higher conceptions (the inductive method). On the other hand, he may proceed unitrifugally, as it were, and draw, or deduce from the general, from the law, or from the principle, inference of the particular.[3]

On the other hand, Ernest Nagel, a philosopher, gives an expanded and critical definition of science. His whole book is about science. He writes many pages on the definition of science alone. He states:

11

It is undoubtedly the case that the sciences are organized bodies of knowledge and that in all of them classification of their materials into significant types or kinds (as in biology, the classification of living things into species) is an indispensable task. It is clear, nonetheless, that the proposed formula does not adequately express the characteristic difference between science and common sense. . . .

It is the desire for explanations which are at once systematic and controllable by factual evidence that generates science, and it is the organization and classification of knowledge on the basis of explanatory principles that is the distinctive goal of the sciences. More specifically, the sciences seek to discover and to formulate in general terms the conditions under which events of various sorts occur, the statements of such determining conditions being the explanation of the corresponding happenings. Patterns of relations may be discovered that are pervasive in vast ranges of facts, so that with the help of a small number of explanatory principles an infinitely large number of propositions about these facts can be shown to institute a logically unified body of knowledge.[4]

Nagel sums up his definition of science:

To explain, to establish some relation of dependence between propositions superficially unrelated, to exhibit systematic connections between apparently miscellaneous items of information, are distinctive marks of scientific inquiry.[5]

Carl Hempel, a philosopher, devotes a whole book to the subject of science. Although he doesn't explicitly define science, he talks about its function:

Broadly speaking, the vocabulary of science has two basic functions: first, to permit an adequate *description* of the things and events that are the objects of scientific investigation; second, to permit the establishment of general laws and theories by means of which particular events may be *explained* and *predicted* and thus *scientifically understood*, for to understand a phenomenon scientifically is to show that it occurs in accordance with general laws or theoretical principles.[6]

He talks about the aims of scientific explanation:

. . . The understanding it conveys lies rather in the insight that the explanation fits into, or can be subsumed under, a system of uniformities represented by empirical laws or theoretical principles.[7]

The point is that the philosophers seem to expand on all facets of the subject of science. They can hardly separate a definition of science from its other aspects. The criminologists, on the other hand, are satisfied with a terse definition which they believe satisfies their audiences. Criminologists don't believe that a definition of science is essential to their argument. This criticism doesn't necessarily apply to sociologists, because there has been literature on the sociology of science.

Max Weber

One of the earliest sociologists to discuss science in relation to the social sciences was Max Weber. Weber's thesis is that social scientists can have value judgments if they recognize them and do not allow their value judgments to interfere with the measurement of their science.[8] Weber distinguishes between value judgments and science. He states:

> What we most vigorously oppose is the view that one may be "scientifically" contented with the conventional self-evidentness of very widely accepted value judgments. The specific function of science, it seems to me, is first the opposite, namely, to ask questions about those things which convention makes self-evident.[9]

Weber believes that empirical science can never tell a person what he should or ought to do, only what he *could* do. He states that the construction of "ideal types" is necessary for empirical reality to be discovered. These "ideal types" are abstractions by which we compare and measure social reality. Weber believes that causal laws, although a function of science, are infinite and only a means, not an end in themselves. There are no finalities in science, although science aims at regularities. The knowledge of the general is never valuable in itself. It is only a means to another end. Weber writes that science can progress only by solving problems that require empirical measurements. He theorizes that social sciences advance the most when cultural problems are posed with a critical attitude toward concept construction.[10]

Weber stresses the separation of value judgment from scientific methodology. Although he is talking about the social sciences, his emphasis has implications for criminal justice. Many believe that criminal justice is permeated with value judgments. Critics of the system agree that certain types of punishment reflect the political value judgments of certain groups in our society.

The history of criminal justice innovation reveals that political movements of certain groups in our society represent the value judgments of those who have a direct or indirect interest in crime control. The emphasis on longer prison sentences may be the consensus of the white, middle-class power-elite who want to punish offenders who infringe on their neighborhoods or places of business. The movement for determinate sentencing may reflect the interests of prison officials who are interested in putting a stop to prison riots. The movement for psychotherapy in criminal justice may reflect the wishes of psychiatrists, psychologists, and social workers who wish to expand their power in their profession. The movement to reinstate the death penalty may reflect the wishes of political figures who want to satisfy public opinion so that they can be reelected. Many of these "reforms" are based on political considerations and value judgments, not on scientific evidence — so say the critics. It is doubtful that there is unanimity in all criminal justice policies.

Karl Popper

Karl Popper has written extensively on the philosophy of science. He generally repeats his themes throughout his many works, and he is generally clear and consistent in what he says. Let us discuss and analyze some of his main theses.

Popper doesn't believe that science starts from scratch. There are always predetermined theories which guide the scientist. The scientist doesn't start from observation, but from these predetermined theories. Observation, however, can initiate a problem. Scientists must get involved with a problem, not a theory. The scientific method is initiated with a problem which cuts across many disciplines.

Popper criticizes the inductive method, which he says is invalid because it leads to an infinite regress — that is, it leads back to where one started. The deductive method in science is the only true method, because all scientists start with problems in which there is a body of predetermined theory.

Popper believes that no theory is irrefutable; all are subject to criticism and are temporary. Science never stops. Only theories which are refutable are scientific. Knowledge, he states, progresses through conjecture and criticisms, which lead to refutations. The aim of science, however, is regularity and predictability. The "open society" is the critical society in which individuals make decisions compared to the "closed" or "tribal society" in which decisions are based on magical forces.[11]

Popper's central ideas in science can be summed up in the following statement:

> I think that we shall have to get accustomed to the idea that we must not look upon science as a "body of knowledge," but rather as a system of hypotheses; that is to say, as a system of guesses and anticipations which on principle, cannot be justified, but with which we work as long as they stand up to tests, and of which we are never justified in saying that we know that they are "true," or "more or less certain" or even "provable."[12]

The implication for criminal justice here is that criminal justice has many theories and empirical studies which are constantly criticized and reevaluated. For example, the critics say that rehabilitation doesn't help, but research in rehabilitation continues. Even generalizations which are believed to be true most of the time are reevaluated with new research, e.g. research in punishment.

There are some philosophers who agree with Popper that induction is not a scientific method. For example, Blatt states that "Induction is an art, not a science or a system of mechanical routines."[13]

Carl Hempel believes that both the inductive and deductive methods are used in science.[14] The philosopher Braithwaite believes that a scientific theory is a "deductive system."[15]

Thomas S. Kuhn

The philosopher Thomas Kuhn believes that all science starts with definite paradigms, which involve predetermined methods and rules for solving complex problems in a discipline. He believes that all problems can be solved with the use of a paradigm. Paradigms can change, but a new paradigm is the result of a revolution in science — a rejection of the old scientific ways. When an old paradigm is rejected, failure to accept a new paradigm is tantamount to a rejection of science itself.[16]

Criminal justice does have paradigms in Kuhn's sense. The theories and methods act as a guide to research. For example, the criminal justice system assumes a capitalistic society, and any suggestions to change parts of the system revolve around the continuation of the existing capitalistic society. For another example, research in criminal justice revolves around showing relationships among familiar variables, e.g. pretrial status, seriousness of charge, prior record, sentence length, etc. For a third example, research in deterrence assumes that our typical forms of punishment can have an effect on offenders.

Lewis Feuer

Lewis Feuer gives a psychological orientation to science. Science to him results from generational conflict. There must be a certain intellectual climate for science to develop. However, a revolution in science proceeds peacefully, without tension, with relative calmness compared to political revolutions, which involve class conflict and upheaval. A revolution in science doesn't negate classical theories.[17]

It is difficult to find new theories in criminal justice, which originated by a generational revolution between classical theorists and new theorists. Most of the old theories in criminal justice are still prevalent. However, an exception might be the conflict between the criminologist who believes in the existing capitalistic system and the Marxist criminologist who believes that our capitalist system should be superseded by another system because equality in criminal justice and solutions in crime cannot be achieved in any other way.[18]

Ernest Nagel

Nagel believes classification is indispensable to science. He also believes that science is abstract. Compared to everyday beliefs, which sometimes last for centuries, scientific explanations have a short life. Science conforms to standards, as compared to "common-sense" beliefs, which are usually accepted without critical evaluation. Nagel disagrees that truth is valid in universal statements.

Theory is not simply a generalization. Nagel defines a theory as a system of several related statements. There is no difference between theories and law. The purpose of a theory is to serve as a guide or rule to analyze experience. A theory cannot be simply true or false, but must be tested for truth or falsity. No theory contains *a priori* truth. Theory must have boundary conditions.

Nagel states that every positive science contains singular statements which are based on observation. Every science must have codified rules. Most sciences have statements which are certified as true. Many sciences take over everyday expressions. There is an overlap of meaning in many expressions among different sciences.

It seems that Nagel's ideas have implications for criminal justice. There are many ideas in criminal justice which many relegate to everyday common beliefs. There is disagreement about what is relegated to belief and what is relegated to scientific achievement. For example, many believe that prison deters offenders from committing crimes, and they present empirical evidence to prove this. Others believe that criminals are not deterred by prison, and although they cite no empirical evidence except to state generally that offenders with long prison records commit crimes, they propagate their beliefs as if they were accepted as fact.

Carl G. Hempel

Hempel doesn't believe that science can be reduced to rules of induction. Science uses both the inductive and deductive methods. There is no theory of induction. Science contains hypotheses which must be tested. No hypothesis is completely proven. He claims that there is no systematic theory of confirmation. Theories involve concepts, and science describes theories and general laws. Hempel states that the greatest advances of science are on the abstract level. He believes that all sciences must overlap. He believes that science aims at regularities. Science, he states, doesn't include all the facts.

It is probably true that criminal justice researchers use both deductive and inductive methods. Criminal justice research, in this author's opinion, has been mainly on the concrete rather than on the abstract level. It seems that criminal justice does overlap with other fields. For example, criminal justice research involves both statistical and sociological concepts. Criminal justice research aims at regularities.

Other Philosophers

Shils believes that science depends on predecessors, that is, it depends on what went on before the present.[19] Benisin believes that science doesn't progress linearly. That is, progress in science cannot be measured evenly. More research doesn't necessarily mean more progress.[20] Campbell defines a theory as a connected set of propositions.[21] Tweney and others believe that scientific thinking is often illogical.[22]

It is probably true that criminal justice research doesn't progress linearly. Much research is just reported ideas which have already been proven. Of course, as in other sciences, criminal justice research depends on ideas of earlier theorists. It is also true that many statements in criminal justice are not logical. They don't logically follow from stated premises. Who can say that ten years in prison is more logical than three years in prison for the same crime?

Criminal Justice, Natural Sciences, Social Sciences

Popper noted that judges can make mistakes; there is no such thing as absolute justice. This view is congruent with his definition of science, in which he consistently believes that science is not absolute:

> The belief of a liberal — the belief in the possibility of a rule of law, of equal justice, fundamental rights and a free society — can easily survive the recognition that judges are not omniscient and may make mistakes about facts and that, in practice, absolute justice is hardly ever realized in any particular case . . . and that the judge cannot have made a factual mistake because he can no more be wrong about the facts than he can be right.[23]

Popper believes that the social sciences are in a state of backwardness because they use essentialist methods, that is, methods which try to seek essences in science. However, he believes that sociology still has a few natural laws or sociological laws, for example, the economic theory of international trade. He believes that the natural sciences are very similar to the social sciences.[24]

Chomsky states that the natural and social sciences are not very different. He also believes that an interdisciplinary approach to science is needed. He states:

> The differences between the natural and the social sciences have been both exaggerated and minimized. . . . My main point is that concrete events in history, particular cases in the real world, are rarely, if ever, explained with the aid of a single discipline, but require application of several fields of knowledge.[25]

Edil believes that a successful theory in one discipline finds its way into other disciplines. He cites the fact that Euclidian models in geometry were used in ethics, Newtonian models in physics were used in economics and ethics, and evolutionary models were used in all disciplines.[26]

Nagel doesn't believe that the social sciences are advanced as much as the natural sciences. He states:

> But in any event, in no area of social inquiry has a body of general laws been established comparable with understanding theories in the natural sciences in scope of explanatory power or in capacity to yield precise, reliable predictions.[27]

He also believes that social laws are possible:

> In short, if the knowledge men possess of social processes is a variable that enters into the determination of social phenomena, there are no a priori grounds for maintaining that changes in that variable and the effects they may produce cannot be the subject of social laws.[28]

Hempel believes that most explanations in history or sociology fail to include an explanation of the general regularities they presuppose. He also believes that no discipline in science is autonomous; there must be overlap among the disciplines.[29]

Bernal believes that sociology is not a real science. He states that "sociology is even more of a pseudo-science; the units with which it deals are indeterminate and shifting."[30]

Edward Shils doesn't believe that sociology is scientific. He states:

> There are differences, of course, among the various substantive fields of sociology, some being more scientific than others, but on the whole the standard of scientific accomplishment is low . . . It only means that much of contemporary social science is not very scientific in the sense in which the term has come to be understood.[31]

He goes on to say that sociology is discontinuous, that is, sociologists take up a subject and drop it before the subject has been brought to intellectual fruition. He also says that sociology really only has at its disposal a few variables, and that categories are vague. The data vary too much from observer to observer.[32] He states:

It might be said that the unifying classes of sociology are important to its contemporary practitioner because sociology is not at present a real science. If sociology were a science, its master-works would have become so assimilated into the flow of sociological work that their accomplishments would have been taken for granted.[33]

Characteristics of Science

A review of the literature reveals certain characteristics of science. First, science involves a classification of some kind. Second, science consists of guidelines, rules, generalizations, and even laws. This may be the result of inductive or deductive methods. These methods are important to give science a life of its own. Third, science consists of concepts, propositions, and theories which are related in some systematic way. Fourth, science is concerned with real-life problems, based on curiosity and observation. Fifth, science is not final; any conclusion is only temporary. Science must always be subject to scrutiny because conclusions are only tentative. They can be modified or refuted partly or wholly. Scientific theories and generalizations can be very complex, however. Sixth, the natural and social sciences are not mutually exclusive. Social scientists adopt many ways of the natural scientists. As a final characteristic — although the literature does not specifically emphasize it — science consists of assumptions.

The fact that criminal justice meets the above-mentioned criteria doesn't answer the question of whether or not criminal justice is a science. It is incumbent to state what the science is all about. It has been shown that many critics doubt that sociology is a science, and although criminal justice is not specifically mentioned, it can be part of sociology or the social sciences. It has also been stated that generalizations in criminal justice, as in any science, are constantly subject to criticism and open to contradictions. Even if criminal justice meets the above-mentioned criteria for a science, it is necessary to locate and present the scientific aspects of the system.

At this point it is necessary to delineate some of the important theories in the three main aspects of criminal justice, namely, the police, the courts, and punishment and corrections.

Chapter III
Theories of the Police

The police are seen as a very important institution in our society, and in many societies throughout the world. After all, the police are the ones who initiate an arrest.[1] Whether or not the police apprehend and arrest a suspect has implications for the criminal justice system. The suspects who are arrested and booked are processed through the criminal justice system from arraignment and pretrial status to sentencing and punishment,[2] and along with this processing through the criminal justice system go much activity, much energy, much money, many personnel, and much time. The suspect who manages to avoid arrest avoids all this processing through the system.

There has been a great deal of literature on the police in the last fifteen years. The police have traditionally been considered an isolated, secretive institution, with their activities and policies closed to the public and outsiders. To a certain extent this is still true today. However, the police have gradually opened their doors to the public. Researchers, psychologists, and sociologists have gained access to police. There have been several empirical studies of the police in the last twenty years, with administration of questionnaires, analysis of police records, interviewing, and participant observation as the methodologies employed in research. We now know more about the police than we did twenty years ago because of this research.

Perspectives on the Police — the Police Role

The police can be studied from many different perspectives, and hypotheses, propositions, and generalizations can be systematically related to form theories about police activity, administration, and behavior. For example, the police can be studied from the role aspects of their job. What is the proper role of the police? Is there an ideal role for the police, or are there many roles representing different expectations of the public? The evidence seems to indicate that the policeman's role is ambiguous and vaguely defined, and that conflict exists among the police themselves and various sectors of the public about the proper role of the police.[3]

20

Since the concept of role is considered a sociological concept, an appropriate question raised in the literature is whether the personality of the police is the determining factor in the police role, or whether the police role is constrained by organizational, institutional, or societal structures. Do the police act according to expectations of their supervisors and the community, or do they act according to certain personality factors which they bring into their role from the days before they began their careers as policemen? Although it is difficult to disentangle the concept of personality from that of role, there has been some empirical evidence on this question. There is evidence that the police learn their role from the organizational constraints under which they work and from other situations inherent in their role performance rather than from their personality.[4]

The police role can be divided into two main aspects, namely, crime control and service work. Police are expected to prevent crime and catch criminals, but they are also expected to give directions, take old people across streets, take people to hospitals, return runaways, and prevent suicides, etc. A study revealed that the police regard the service aspects of their role as demeaning.[5]

Some believe that the police role today is more complicated and requires many more thought-provoking decisions than formerly.[6] After all, the police were seen as a very important force in the 1960s during the disturbances in the colleges and universities throughout the nation and the racial riots in the cities. An incident between a citizen and a policeman was seen as the cause of a riot.[7] Although the college incidents and racial disturbances have abated, there is a possibility that they can recur. How the police act and how the citizen perceives the action of the police in such incidents have serious implications for our nation. Even if the incidents of the 1960s were atypical, many citizens who remember them and have been involved in them may view police action more critically than formerly. In addition, the police are a scapegoat for the problems of society, e.g. the Vietnam war, military and racial crises, etc. Occasionally, one hears of a police officer killed by hostile citizens, either on- or off-duty.

One can perceive the question of police role from a structural-functional approach. Our society is becoming more complex, and the police role is changing according to the complexity of our society. The police today must know more things and know how to handle more diverse groups than formerly. This is one reason why a college education is recommended for a police officer.

In certain respects, the police role pervades all theories of the police. The use of discretion, force, the bureaucratic rules under which the police work, the personality of the police, their attitudes and behavior, their prejudices, their deviant behavior, etc., can all be directly or indirectly caused by the role aspects of their job. There can be two-way causation. It is possible for these variables to affect their role performance. The point is that the role is a crucial aspect of police analysis and pervades many different perspectives of police work.

The Public

The police can be studied from the viewpoint of the public. How much respect do the police have from the public? A North-Hatt survey ranked the status of the police just below the midpoint of ninety occupations, in fifty-fifth place.[8] There is disagreement on the issue. Allen Silver believes that the public regards the police as low in status and prestige.[9] Niederhoffer states that some college students rank police higher in status than does the general public, and that other college students rank police lower than does the public.[10] A study revealed that ex-convicts accepted the police.[11] National opinion polls show that the public has a high regard for the police.[12] It is known in the literature that minorities have a negative opinion of the police.[13]

Surveys show that the police believe that the public doesn't respect them.[14] The police can't find a public that is favorable to them or an identifiable constituency that enjoys their services and will provide political support for them.[15] McNamara cited a study which showed that the police believed that respect for themselves was low.[16] Confidence in the police is declining.[17]

Bureaucracy

If one has a sociological perspective on the police, then the police can be studied from the bureaucratic structure under which they serve. The police organization has many characteristics of other organizations. There are formal and informal sets of rules and norms which influence the police and shape their activities.[18] The hierarchical authority structure under which they work also influences them. Are police under close surveillance by their supervisors? The consensus of opinion seems to be that police have a great deal of discretion, particularly at the arresting stage, at lower police ranks, and that police officers receive only very cursory supervision.[19] Brown believes that there are limits to police administrators' supervising their men. He also believes that conflict between the values of professionalism and police culture is the root of the contradiction in police bureaucracies.[20] In addition, since sergeants and lieutenants were police officers themselves, promoted from the ranks, they condone many police practices, both legal and illegal.

Conflict also exists between officers. There is conflict between college-educated and non–college-educated officers, for example, since the former may view the police role from a professional standpoint and the latter from a nonprofessional standpoint.[21] There may be conflict between black and white officers.[22] There may be conflict among policemen and between policemen and administrators.[23] Yet the police are said to form a very consolidated, tightly-knit group.[24]

The police can also be influenced by outside constraints, such as the community in which they work or political pressure from certain groups. The police can get involved in police-community relations, for example, or be influenced directly or indirectly by political appointees who promise to fight for their requests.

Corruption

The police can be studied from the perspective of corruption. There has been a lot of rumors about police corruption, and the evidence seems to indicate that police corruption exists throughout our society. How much corruption exists? What do police authorities do about corruption? How does police corruption affect the police role? More fundamentally, what causes police corruption? These and other questions have been posed in the literature.

The Courts

The police can be studied from their relation to other parts of the criminal justice system. How do police perceive their role in the system? The police perception of their influence in the criminal justice system can directly or indirectly be responsible for some of their actions.

Littrell, for example, states that the police have a great deal of authority which the prosecutor and the courts accept as part of the presumption of the guilt of the offender.[25] Reiss and Bordua believe that the police perceive themselves dishonored by the courts' decisions.[26] There are several million illegal arrests each year, and how prosecutors and the courts accept police evidence is important in criminal justice.[27] The police believe that the courts are lenient to defendants and believe that they themselves are treated as defendants.[28]

The police believe that the courts don't understand them, probably because it is true. Moreover, the police don't understand the operations of the courts. There is a lack of cooperation between police and courts in many jurisdictions.[29] Very rarely will a prosecutor investigate the police.[30]

Use of Force

The police can be studied in relation to their use of force.[31] Some believe that the police use too much force in making an arrest. The police have to be careful of public opinion and legal redress against too much brutality. The police are empowered to shoot, but very often the amount of force used to restrain a suspect is a matter of discretion.

Minorities

Police policies in regard to minorities are important. Do police show disparity in arresting minorities? Minorities are not only defined as ethnic minorities (e.g. blacks, Puerto Ricans, Chicanos, etc.) but also drunkards, hippies, homosexuals, juveniles, youth, etc. How the police perceive these minorities reflects in their arrest policies.

Police Training

The police can be studied from the perspective of training. Do police receive the right kind of training in relation to their role? Is a college education necessary for the police? What should be the length of training and what areas should be included in the training?

Change

Can the police change? Neither psychology nor sociology states that change is impossible. Perhaps both a psychological and a sociological perspective are needed to outline a theory of police change. Many believe that the police are essentially conservative, not prone to change, and that police have historically displayed qualities of authoritarianism, prejudice and discrimination, and toughness. However, there is some evidence that police have changed. For example, Burnham states that the police of New York are less violent today than they were twenty or thirty years ago.[32] Broderick believes that the quality of the police has changed over the years, for the better.[33]

There are many other perspectives from which the police can be studied. It must be remembered that police vary by jurisdiction. Our criminal justice system is fragmented, and it may be impossible to generalize about police. However, we will propose a few generalizations, such as theories to suggest how the police act in arresting an offender. These theories are the ones proposed in the literature. The author does not pretend that all theories are included. Remembering that theorizing on criminal justice is still on a relatively low level,[34] the author will now present some of the most important theories of the police.

Theories on the Function of the Police

Some literature exists on the functions of the police. Skolnick sees their function as maintaining law and order in society. However, he sees this as a duality of functions that presents a conflict for the police. Police are obliged to enforce the law, but sometimes this must be forfeited in order to maintain order. This conflict places a strain upon the police. Therefore, the police must compromise between conflicting ideas. Skolnick calls our justice system a system of "justice without trial" because police assume a presumption of guilt — a negation of innocence — when they arrest.[35]

Manning believes that the function of the police is to maintain the status quo and to enforce social control. This is a structural-functional argument. He believes that the entire range of police activities is a rationalization for a show to the public. He calls this the "police myth." The police are really the servants of the state.[36]

Beckman believes that the blacks in the ghetto see the police as an army of occupation, rather than someone who serves them.[37] This, of course, is not a new finding, but whether the view is widespread is an empirical question. It is conceivable that oppressed minorities, e.g. blacks, Chicanos, Puerto Ricans, etc., may perceive the police as an oppressor who can do more harm than good.

Whether one sees the police as preservers of social control, maintainers of order and enforcers of the law, or an army of occupation — whether one sees them serving a combination of these functions, or some other functions — the reasons for the police establishment can be viewed on a theoretical level. A structural-functional argument, for example, would suggest a theory for maintaining the police establishment because it contributes to the maintenance of society. If one believes that police do more harm than good, one can propose a radical solution and theorize that the police should be eliminated and replaced with something more beneficial to society, perhaps a private citizen watch group.

Theories of Discretion

It is well known that police use discretion in performing their duties. It is also true that our criminal justice system is pervaded with discretion in many respects. One can interpolate the reasons why police use discretion on their job. The police daily face criminals who are dangerous not only to themselves but also to the public. They must constantly face various types of individuals, suspects and others, whose behavior they can never exactly predict. This uncertainty of human behavior and the complications of their role performance, some argue, give them a license to use discretion, negatively or positively, to perform their role duties.

Kenneth Culp Davis conducted a study of the Chicago police based on 300 interviews with the police. He concluded that police at the lower levels of the hierarchy, at the level of patrolmen, are the ones who make policy. Many studies seem to confirm that the police on the street have the greatest discretion in performing their role. Davis claims that the Chicago police have no written statement of policy procedures. As a result, the police make their own law. One of his most important conclusions is that there is an open, selective enforcement of police policies toward arrest which, Davis claims, is legal. The police pretend to enforce all laws, but they don't.

Davis believes that the police should announce a selective enforcement of the laws. He believes that the Chicago police need rules to guide them; however, he states that these rules should be informal and act as a guide to police activity. If this occurs, says Davis, police activity will be under judicial review. He believes that discretion is absolutely necessary and that only a minority of police officers abuse their discretion. He believes that the American legislative bodies know that police enforcement is selective. He emphasizes that excessive and unnecessary discretion should be eliminated and necessary discretion should be controlled.[38]

Certainly this is not a new finding. A review of the literature reveals that many have seen a need to limit police discretion. Nor is it a new finding that police are selective in law enforcement; many have indicated that the police don't have either the time or the resources to enforce all the laws on the books. Open-selective enforcement is necessary in order for the system to function.

Skolnick and Woodworth state that if all criminal offenses were brought to the attention of the police, this might place a burden on the criminal justice system.[39] Kinnane states that if an officer arrested everyone who was rude to him, he would spend all his free time in court.[40]

Lundman reported on a study of drunkenness encounters with the police in 1970. He found that out of 195 police-citizen encounters, only 31 percent ended in arrest. He found certain variables were associated with the probability of arrest. For example, if the police, rather than the citizen, initiated an arrest, the probability of arrest for the offender was significantly greater. Drunkenness offenders encountered in downtown locations were arrested more than in other places. Native American and declassified drunkenness offenders, that is, Americans of any ethnic origin born here and members of the lower classes, were arrested more than others. Offenders in conspicuous places were arrested more.[41]

Black conducted studies based on observations of police-citizen encounters in four cities and on an analysis of case records. The four cities were Boston, Chicago, Detroit, and Washington. One study consisted of analyzing 550 cases in which victim and offender were intimate in some way. Black concluded that police behavior varied by setting and by the interaction of the complainant, offender, and police. He found that the preferences of the complainant were very important in an arrest. For example, he found that the police wrote reports only when the complainant preferred them. Police gave greater recognition to a case when victim and offenders were strangers rather than intimates. Offenders who were disrespectful were subject to arrest more than offenders who were not disrespectful.

An arrest was made in 58 percent of the felonies and 44 percent of the misdemeanors. An arrest occurred in about one-fourth of the violent felony cases and in almost one-half of the violent misdemeanor cases. Black found that class made a difference regardless of race; police were more attentive to the middle class than to the lower class in disputes between intimates. The business class received more attention than others.[42]

Brown, based on a study of three police departments in California, concluded that patrolmen were selective as to which victims they believed. The police believed victims' stories on the basis of the victims' social and personal characteristics, their evidence, their race, their sex, and whether or not the victims were using drugs and alcohol. They also considered victims who were businessmen more seriously than others. Police also took more action in a public than a private place because their authority was at stake. In stopping someone, police usually used three indicators, namely, incongruity (that is, someone or something out of place, e.g. an older man hanging around a school), prior information on the offender, and appearance of an offender.[43]

Wilson names three styles of police behavior in his study of various police departments. One style is the "watchman style." In this style, the police act as if maintenance of order is their prime function (although they admit that order has never been defined). In this style of police activity, no serious crime has taken place. The police act according to the immediate and personal consequences of the situation rather than according to what the law says. The police follow the path of least resistance in this type of activity.

In a "legalistic style" of policing, the police will act according to the spirit and letter of the law, with a single standard rather than as if there were different standards for different groups. The police will look for offenders who break the law. The policeman looks at attributes of behavior rather than attributes of the person.

In a "service style" of policing, the police act as if there were a market for police service. There will be more informal activities of the police, such as lectures, warnings issued to motorists, etc. The police emphasize courtesy. They emphasize prompt appearance and visibility. Here, the service function of the police is emphasized, e.g. giving directions, taking people to hospitals, etc.

Wilson states that community pressures and politics indirectly influence the three styles of police activity. He also states that the three styles are not mutually exclusive and they are not the only styles that the police use.[44]

La Fave, in his study of arrest practices, states that the police don't make an immediate arrest in some cases. The reason is that it would interfere with some law enforcement objective or cause harm to an offender.[45]

It is believed that police use force from time to time. There is discretion in the use of this force. Chevigny talks about police brutality and abuses in New York City. He shows that police brutality is the result of defiance of authority.[46] In fact, disrespect for the police and defiance of authority are important causes for police arresting a suspect. Black reports that offenders who are disrespectful are arrested more than others.[47] Westley found that disrespect for the police was the most common reason for the use of force.[48] Lundman found that drunken offenders who were disrespectful to the police were arrested more than others.[49] Reiss notes the same thing in his study of police encounters.[50] Blacks who show defiance toward authority are given more serious dispositions than others.[51] Black and Reiss in their study of juveniles noted that juveniles who were both unusually respectful and unusually disrespectful were arrested more than others.[52] Pilliavin and Briar, in their study of police encounters with juveniles, showed that race, prior record, grooming, and demeanor were key factors in arrest. Negroes were arrested more because of their demeanor than because of their race.[53]

Police sometimes arrest on flimsy evidence. La Fave admits that there is a great deal of discretion which the police wish to hide. He says that all states have laws pertaining to police discretion, but they neither affirm nor deny police discretion; they only identify certain enforcement practices as unconstitutional. La Fave states that police act only to prevent further police action, and they don't want to write a report all the time because they don't want to admit their discretion.[54]

Littrell, based on empirical evidence in New Jersey, states that the police, in charging an offender after arrest, will sometimes judge the moral character of the offender who is arrested and decide appropriate punishment for the offender before officially charging him with a crime.[55]

The review of the literature reveals that discretion is prevalent among all the police. Police do not arrest everyone. However, discretion is not completely unguided. Police do have certain guidelines they employ in arresting an offender. Very often, these guidelines depend on the situation, as the examples above have demonstrated. The point is that discretion is very often structured.

The theory of discretion holds that police discretion is necessary in order to catch criminals and prevent crime from spreading. The police are given formal and informal license to use discretion in order to maximize their role performance satisfactorily. Uncertainty in police work causes uncertainty in police activity. Guidelines do not explain all police action. Very often discretion is optional with the police department and personality of the individual policeman. Although one may not agree with the reasons for police discretion, and may believe it should be guided, regulated, structured, and legalized to a great extent, the arguments documenting police discretion should be considered among the theories of police action.

Theories of Police Personality

One of the most comprehensive studies of police personality was undertaken by Niederhoffer in New York City. Although he particularly studied cynicism and anomie, he proposed a theoretical analysis for the relation between police personality and police work. He stated that the desire for security was the most frequent reason for becoming a policeman, and that during the depression of the 1930s many college graduates entered the police force. The typical policeman is a high school graduate with less than average intelligence, a curious personality, and above average physical endowment. Many police from lower-class backgrounds consider the job of policeman as a stepping-stone to success; however, the police must display middle-class values because they enforce the law.

Niederhoffer states that cynicism affects men at the start of their career. It's the police system, he says, that turns a policeman into an authoritarian personality; this is the result of the police role. This authoritarian personality causes police to emphasize sexuality, condemn homosexuals and sexual offenders, and show ambivalence towards women; the ambivalence towards women, he states, might be the result of their experience with them on the job. Niederhoffer believes that police officers are by nature no more authoritarian than the rest of the population; they are not self-selected in authoritarianism. The most authoritarian policemen are at the bottom of the occupational pyramid, on the street.

Niederhoffer developed eleven hypotheses which he analyzed in the light of empirical data. He administered a questionnaire to 220 members of the New York City police force. One hundred eighty-six were the experimental group and thirty-four were the control group. The control group had no police experience at all. The eleven hypotheses were:

1. Cynicism will increase up to the first five years of service and will tend to level off after five to ten years of service.

2. Men newly appointed will show less cynicism than recruits who have been in the police academy for some time. Men in the lower ranks have more reason to feel frustrated than their superiors.

3. Superior officers will be less cynical than patrolmen.

4. Among the lower ranks, college-educated patrolmen will show more cynicism than noneducated patrolmen because their expectations for promotion are greater.

5. Patrolmen with preferred assignments will be less cynical than other patrolmen.

6. Foot patrolmen will feel more cynical than other men because of their low status on the job.

7. Patrolmen who receive awards for meritorious service will be less cynical than others, and policemen who have departmental charges lodged against them will be more cynical.

8. Jewish patrolmen will be more cynical than non–Jewish patrolmen, possibly because Jewish expectations for occupational mobility preclude police work.

9. When members of the force have seventeen or eighteen years of experience, they will become less cynical.

10. Members of the vice squad will become more cynical than members of the youth division.

11. Patrolmen from middle-class backgrounds will be less cynical than patrolmen from lower-class backgrounds.

Niederhoffer concluded that the first four hypotheses were confirmed. Evidence for hypothesis number five was inconclusive. Hypotheses six through nine were corroborated. However, hypotheses ten and eleven were not tested due to insufficient data. Niederhoffer stated that age was unimportant as a factor in the results.

Niederhoffer found in interviews that the police believed that academy training was a waste of time. Two-thirds of the police force had a cynical attitude toward education. (Education and professionalism can lead to cynicism.) The majority of the police believed that they would be found guilty of departmental charges even when they had a good defense. Less than ten percent believed that the rules were fair and sensible. (The superior officers seemed to denigrate the police system more than the men.) Seventy-five percent of the sample believed they couldn't trust the public to cooperate with the police. They had a cynical attitude toward the press and the courts.

Niederhoffer believes that the typical police recruit starts his career without a trace of cynicism. Soon he realizes that the professional atmosphere around him is a sham. A high arrest record reinforces his cynicism, but also makes him feel superior to other men because of his constant dealing with crime.

Niederhoffer introduces the concept of anomie, the symptoms of which are loss of faith in people, lack of enthusiasm for the high ideals of police work, and loss of pride and integrity. Anomie occurs when old values are replaced by new values, which is what occurs in police work. Anomie can develop from cynicism, the feelings of which are hate, envy, hostility, and a sour-grapes attitude. Police cynicism consists of two kinds — one aimed at the world, life, people, and the other at the police system itself.

Niederhoffer believes that the police have a higher suicide rate than the general population, possibly due to anomie and cynicism.[56] Cynicism may lead to anomie, but it doesn't have to. Some police may manage to overcome cynicism and dedicate and commit themselves to the ideal of a decent and honorable career in the police force. However, a policeman can be absorbed into the delinquent occupational subculture of cynicism, dedicated to a philosophy of cynicism, alienated from a former group and absorbed into the new reference group. The stages leading from cynicism to anomie may be viewed as a continuum with commitment on one end, anomie on the other, and cynicism in-between. Cynicism is prevalent during the last stages of a policeman's career. Niederhoffer believes that corruption can result from cynicism. However, cynicism is the mechanism which enables the police to support the system. Cynicism can be viewed as a rationalization for adjusting to the police subculture.[57]

Niederhoffer offers a sociological explanation for police behavior. Although he confines his study to New York City, he believes that his findings apply throughout the police world. He gives us some insight into the relation between police personality, the police role, and the police subculture. Although he admits that the relation between personality and occupational choice is an open question, his theoretical and empirical perspectives lead him to conclude that the police personality is virtually entirely due to the constraints of the police role.

Others have also noted the relation between personality and the role of the policeman. Skolnick, for example, has noted that the variables of danger and authority in police work have interacted with a constant pressure to identify a distinctive "working personality" of the policeman. The police regard themselves as "craftsmen" or "workers" and demand a lack of constraint upon their initiative. Skolnick also believes that the police are more prejudiced today than their fellow citizens who are not policemen.[58]

George Kirkham notes that the police are humanitarian as a group. He bases this conclusion on a participant-observation study of the police, in which he actually assumed the role of a policeman.[59]

Basing his findings on a questionnaire administered to the Chicago police and on interviews, James Q. Wilson found the Chicago police suspicious and demoralized, due mainly to citizen hostility. The police were very low in morale. After five years of reform in the department, the police thought the department was better run but not fairly run; they were still low in morale.[60]

McNamara, basing his findings on questionnaires, interviews, and tests in New York City, indicates that scores for the F test for measuring authoritarianism were surprisingly low. However, although the recruits' scores were within the expected range for their socio-economic origins, the scores still exceeded those of a cross-section of the public presented by Adorno in the original study. McNamara believes than men are attracted to police work mainly for civil service security and the economic benefits attributed to the job. He also reports that the recruits' scores on a punitiveness scale indicated that recruits were nonpunitive.

The recruits in McNamara's sample believed that police work was prestigious, but believed that the public didn't perceive the work as prestigious. After years of field experience, police believed that there was not enough legal authority attached to their job; this was in evidence by an increase in the F scores. Police recruits at the end of their training believed that more force was necessary. Some police believed that they must instill fear into the citizens as part of their work. McNamara believes that uncertainty is responsible for the difficulties police fear in their role, and that police are unaware of different citizen values.[61]

Kinnane reports that a researcher found that the police ranked "equality" lower on a list of values than did a national sample of white males, and much lower than did a national sample of black males. Kinnane, however, doesn't suggest whether the values assigned to equality are the result of personality traits that police bring to the job, or the result of constraints on the job. She also believes that police officers are more competent and responsible than their superiors assume.[62]

Muir, Jr., reports on a study based on interviews with 28 young policemen in a sizeable American city. He claims that police arrest irrational persons every day. Police work is full of ambiguity. Muir believes that there are many ways of doing acceptable police work. He believes that the police are no more inclined than the rest of us to hurt others. Police do change. His most important conclusion is that there is great diversity among police styles and police departments, although the police depend on similar concepts for judgmental purposes.[63]

Albert J. Reiss reports, based on his own participant observation of police behavior and on other studies, that police do not use force as frequently as they use other forms of misconduct toward citizens. About one in four officers was observed to seriously violate the rules.[64]

Michael Banton reports that some police in America and Scotland resign after a short spell of duty because they feel guilty about arresting someone; he reports that even after 20 years of experience, some men feel guilty about charging someone with a crime. He also states that Westley found that many police condemned violence and got desk jobs to avoid using it. Banton believes that there is a conflict between the policeman's private life and occupational role.[65]

Broderick tells about a study based on a questionnaire administered to police officers. Results suggested that the officers didn't believe that police work necessarily led to authoritarianism. Broderick doubts that there is one typical police type.[66]

Bayley and Mendelsohn found no evidence of particular personality types in their study of the Denver police. Denver police actually scored lower in the anomie scale than the general public. They concluded that there is evidence that Denver police are less authoritarian than the general public.[67]

Brown, based on his study of the police, concludes that police are adventurous, seeking the unpredictable. Police react differently to similar situations. He names four types of police which correspond to actions that he calls "operational style." The Old Style Crime Fighter is interested in using aggressive methods to fight crime. The Clean Beat policeman believes in rigid enforcement of the laws. The Professional Style policeman is active but not overly aggressive. He is cautious and legalistic, however. The Service Style policeman believes that crime suppression is less important than assisting people in solving their problems. Brown believes that the occupational role of the officer, and not the personality background, is primarily responsible for the operational style of the individual policeman. He also believes that the police become less aggressive with more experience.[68]

The results of these few studies seem to conclude that the police role, the police organization, and police relations in the community are responsible for whatever characteristics and personality traits police have. There is no evidence, according to research, that police come to their jobs possessing certain personality traits. After all, the police role is so complicated that the man must be fitted to the job and acquire whatever personality traits the job requires. If toughness and authoritarianism are required, the policeman must adjust to the situation, or he will not survive on the job.

It is possible that the police come to the job with certain personality traits that the job emphasizes, but this conclusion is speculative. Such variables as danger, citizen hostility, encounters with various segments of the public, and pressure from superiors, courts, and the public are some of the factors affecting the police directly or indirectly.

The consensus seems to be that there are various police types. Police departments vary and so do policemen. Police also change; there is evidence that they must change because of the changing aspects of their role. For example, some believe that police are more humane now than previously. Some have reported examples of police humanity. It would be interesting and important to show the mechanism involved in changing police personality.

Theories of Police Corruption

First, as Kinnane suggests, police corruption is not a unitary concept.[69] Second, as Muir, Jr., observed in his study of the police, there are many graft-free police departments in the United States.[70] Third, Goldstein points out that some of the most corrupt departments did an excellent job of handling the riots of the 1960s. He also points out that some cities which were once known for police corruption are now relatively free of it. Corruption, he says, is heavily influenced by the community surrounding the police. He observes that police corruption thrives best in organizations which are poorly run, where lines of authority are vague, and where supervision is minimal. He also states that there is disagreement about what constitutes corruption, and that corruption is difficult to measure. The important conclusion is that corruption by a single police officer brings the entire department under suspicion.[71]

Stoddard believes that police corruption is socially determined through the informal code of the police organization rather than as a result of personal inadequacies of the individual policemen. Stoddard finds that police must violate the very laws they are trying to enforce because of the requirements of their role. However, Stoddard says, this doesn't mean that police corruption is universal or that it should be condoned where it exists.[72]

Roebuck, too, believes that police corruption is best understood as group behavior guided by contradictory sets of norms linked to the police organization. Those police who report corruption, says Roebuck, are rarely able to supply evidence to support their accusations of police corruption. Some police, he says, kill professional criminals because they will "sing" and expose the corrupt police to buy their freedom. Roebuck believes that police corruption comes and goes over time.[73]

Rubinstein, in his study of the Philadelphia police, believes that the constant demand for vice arrests and the violations of the law that police must engage in to make good arrests force policemen to engage in criminal acts. Police will illegally search suspects for evidence or manufacture evidence to make an arrest. Many drug arrests are illegal, and the courts know this.[74]

Leonard Savitz notes that police officers revealed that they had felt it was appropriate for them to inform a supervisor about a partner who was a grafter, an agitator, or an alcoholic, or was incompetent or unnecessarily violent. He concludes that secrecy and mutual confidence among police officers are not part of a policeman's occupational code.[75] This is contrary to the generalization often stated that police are secretive and will not "rat" on a fellow police officer.[76]

One of the most comprehensive and theoretical studies on police corruption was undertaken by Laurence W. Sherman. Sherman claims that police corruption *is* universal and has occurred historically since the beginning of the police. Paraphrasing William Chambliss, he states that corruption means different things to different people. Paraphrasing Gardner, he states that laws defining corrupt behavior are ambiguous. He also believes that the problem of police corruption is a part of the general problem of corruption in our society. One of his main conclusions is that police corruptors become deviant through a gradual process involving confrontation, contingencies, and moral decisions.

Sherman lists fourteen propositions concerning police corruption. He strongly bases these propositions on the belief that police corruption is related to the community which the police officer serves, and that there is a minimal amount of corruption in every police department; however, beyond the minimum, police corruption varies greatly.

The fourteen propositions are:

1. There will be less police corruption in a community with little anomie, in terms of both corruptors and corruptees.

2. There will be less police corruption in communities with a more public-regarding ethos.

3. There will be less police corruption in a community with less culture conflict.

4. A punishment-centered police bureaucracy will have the least corruption, a representative pattern will have more, and a mock pattern will have the most.

5. There will be less corruption in a police agency having leadership highly reputed for integrity.

6. There will be less organized police corruption when there is less work-group solidarity.

7. The less gradual the probable steps in a corrupt policeman's moral career, the less the ultimate seriousness (self-defined) of the grafting.

8. The greater the policeman's perception of legitimate advancement opportunities, the less likelihood there will be of his accepting corruption opportunities.

9. A decrease in either the scope of morals laws or the demand for the services they proscribe, while holding the other constant, will reduce police corruption opportunities (or the converse).

10. An increase in either the scope of the regulative laws or the economic

incentive to violate them, while holding the other constant, will increase corruption opportunities (also the converse).

11. There will be a greater risk of apprehension for corruption in police agencies that have an internal investigation unit.

12. There will be proportionately less undiscovered corruption in police agencies that have an internal investigation unit using proactive methods.

13. Controls will decrease corruption only when they can avoid amplifying the corruptor's extent or method.

14. Less corruption will go undiscovered in a police agency watched by a vigorous and uncensored news media.

One can see that Sherman believes that when communities are permeated with conflict and anomie, the police will increase their corruption because of more opportunities for corruption. He also believes that the police organization and police bureaucracy are related to police corruption. When organizations punish deviant behavior, there will be less corruption. When police are not entirely united, when they are not entirely immersed in their work-groups, there will be less corruption. When police organizations extol leadership, this will serve as an example to prevent police corruption.

Sherman also believes that police corruption is related to the perception of the policeman's steps to advancement in his career. When policemen perceive legitimate advancement opportunities, and when corrupt policemen advance rapidly in their moral careers, they will be prone to less corruption. He also believes that there will be less corruption in police agencies having an internal investigation unit or in agencies having an internal investigating unit using proactive methods, that is, when police investigate the corruption themselves rather than from some other source, e.g. other policemen.

Sherman also believes that corruption is related to the law. An increase in the scope of the law, e.g. morals law or regulative law, and in the economic gains accruable by violating it, or the demand for the services they proscribe, while holding either demand for services or economic gains constant, will increase corruption among policemen.

Sherman believes that measures introduced to control corruption can amplify the extent of corruption. Therefore, remedial measures must be enacted which will avoid the extent of the corruption. He believes that the news media can be very instrumental in exposing and preventing police corruption.[77]

Sherman also studied the police files of four criminally corrupt police departments. He chose these departments because they allowed him access to files, records, and documents. He supplemented his investigation with interviews. He defined police corruption as "a misuse of organizational power for personal gain." He also concludes that an entire department is not involved in corruption or in the same type of corruption. He notes that specialized units in police departments are a relatively new phenomenon for investigating police corruption.

Sherman states that police departments do dismiss policemen for corrupt activities. Sometimes a corrupt policeman about to be exposed will resign under pressure, before the case comes to an administrative trial. He found a positive association between the dismissal rate and internal policing for a twenty-year time period. However, he admits that dismissals may be related to easy-to-win cases. He also notes that if a corrupt policeman is not dismissed when his corruption is proven, the department uses many informal sanctions against him.

Sherman concludes that a little scandal will not produce a decrease in police corruption. A big scandal against corrupt police departments produces a bigger effect, but it has only a short-term effect. What is really needed to produce a major decrease in corruption is big scandal coupled with premonitory controls. Premonitory controls are those policies which are enacted by police departments to prevent corruption from spreading or beginning.[78]

The Knapp Commission in New York City was created to investigate police corruption. The majority of policemen, it was discovered, deal only in small graft. Corruption is not confined to the police, but is found to some extent among prosecutors, lawyers, judges, and in other agencies. The Commission believes that corruption is partially caused by laws which are on the books officially, but are very rarely ever enforced. Such laws include Sabbath laws and proscriptions against gambling, prostitution, and drugs. The Commission recommends that policemen be taken out of bars, restaurants, and building sites, because these are places where opportunities for corruption are abundant.

The Commission recommends that penalties for corruption be increased. Light penalties do not deter corruption. The Commission recommends that a record be made of all police activities to prevent corruption. The Knapp Commission empowered policemen to investigate and to provide evidence for police corruption in New York City.

The Commission discovered that police manufactured evidence to make an arrest they needed in order to meet informal quotas. For example, when police needed a gambling arrest, they would pick up a known gambler and plant phony chips on him and arrest him; they would plant phony gambling slips on people and demand money not to arrest them. The Commission also found evidence that defense attorneys in narcotics cases would pay policemen for lying and procuring confidential police and judicial records in their clients' cases. The Commission also discovered that the laws in the building industry and drinking establishments are so conflicting and numerous that virtually everyone is guilty of a violation; hence, there are abundant opportunities for corruption.

The Commission discovered that it was common for police to offer money to other police for special favors or for choice assignments. Some policemen have bribed police surgeons to certify that they were permanently disabled so that they could retire early with pay.

The Knapp Commission has revealed that 26 police officers and 14 civilians have been indicted by various federal and state prosecutors in cases originated by the Commission. Although it is difficult to evaluate policy implementation for police corruption, there is indication that there has been some reduction in corruption as a result of the Commission's activities. The Commission believes that the fight against corruption is very important because the average citizen's most frequent contact with the government is through the police, and the manner in which the police perform their duties is what makes most people decide how our government is functioning.[79]

It seems that corruption is seen as an organizational phenomenon and not as the result of individual aberrations. It can also be rationalized by the desire to compensate for the rather low salary relative to the dangers inherent in the work. It can be caused by the nature of the police job, which involves contact with deviant members of society.

Corruption generally involves small amounts of money and some very minor violations, but it can also involve serious consequences, like manufacturing evidence to make illegal arrests. Although there is some evidence that police corruption has been reduced, the question arises whether corruption can be eradicated within the police structure or whether it has to be eradicated in other areas because it permeates various sectors of society.

Theories of Discrimination

It has been stated that the police discriminate against minority groups, especially blacks, Puerto Ricans, and Mexicans, in the ghetto or outside of the ghetto. However, this discrimination can also extend to other minorities, such as ex-felons, hippies, homosexuals, lower social classes, the retarded, the poor, etc.

One reason suggested for this discrimination is that the police are intolerant of diverse value systems, and since they are embodied to enforce the laws of the white, middle-class, dominant society, they look with intolerance at subcultures. This reason would follow logically, since the police are said to be conservative. This intolerance might be due to ignorance or to lack of education. Another reason suggested for discrimination is that police are supposed to be tough and "manly" and must show their authority and power. Since minority groups might be considered deviant, they are the logical targets for the police. Another reason is that some minority groups are more visible than other groups and thus their activities are scrutinized more than others.

Discrimination can take two forms. The police can discriminate directly on the basis of class, race, life-styles, etc., by making arrests among certain groups. The other form discrimination can take is when the police do nothing; that is, if crime is rampant in the ghetto, the police can discriminate by looking the other way, by not responding to a call, or by doing nothing when answering an alarm. The reasoning behind doing nothing is that deviant behavior is common in ghetto areas, and the best thing to do is to take crime lightly there because minorities will work it out themselves. This outrages certain segments of the minorities, and because of political pressures from these communities and from police departments, the police are forced to change. For years, minorities have accused police of enacting a double standard of justice.

A comprehensive study was undertaken by Bayley and Mendelsohn in Denver. They conducted four surveys, two among ethnic groups — Negroes and Spanish-named — and dominants, one survey of Denver policemen, and one survey of community leaders. They found that two to three times more minorities than dominants said the reputation of the police was low. They found that since the proportion of people who called the police was the same for each ethnic group, minority people are less willing to call the police since their need to call the police exceeds the need of the dominants. They found greater alienation between Spanish-speaking people and the police than between Negroes and the police. Prejudicial policemen are constrained to use force more in minority areas than elsewhere. Minorities are much less likely to talk over a problem with the police, but they are two to three times more inclined than the dominants to call the police for help in regard to illness. The police are aware of the lower opinion minorities have of them.

The authors note that there are less rigid patterns of discrimination in Denver than elsewhere. Also, the standard of living for minority groups is higher and the pattern of residential exclusion and physical deterioration much less prevalent. Nevertheless, the authors believe that our culture is sufficiently homogeneous to generalize the findings of Denver to other cities.[80]

Edward Green studied the Negro-white differential arrest rate in a small industrial city in Michigan for the years 1942 through 1965. He found that migrants to the city were arrested more than natives. However, controlling occupation and nativity, he found that the higher arrest rate for Negroes was the result of lower social class characteristics associated with crime. When occupation and nativity were controlled, the arrest rate for whites was sometimes higher than for blacks. The effect of socioeconomic status works independently of race.[81]

Black, in his study, found that there was no discrimination against blacks. The higher arrest rate for blacks was a result of the higher disrespect that blacks showed when they were apprehended by the police. The poor and blacks were least likely to be helped in a dispute, but this was because they were at the bottom of society, not because of race *per se*. The police complied in 61 percent of the disputes involving whites but in only about 47 percent of the disputes involving blacks. The police seemed to be more interested in white disputes than in black disputes. The blacks were more likely to be threatened and arrested than whites in disputes. The police were more helpful when the parties were middle-class, regardless of race. Since blacks in the study were mainly from the lower classes, they received less help.[82]

Black also cites evidence which shows that black officers were more concerned about black victims than white officers, a pattern which might result in a higher arrest rate. He also concludes that blacks call police more because authority between blacks is more equal than authority between whites; the lower-class black woman is self-supporting, but the white woman is more dependent on her husband for support. Therefore, since people call police more when authority is equal between disputants, blacks call police more than whites, because authority is more unequal among whites.[83]

James Alexander cites evidence that blacks on the force in New York City were discriminated against by white police officers. There is evidence that although there was a black officer on the force in 1865, blacks as a group entered the New York City police department in the 1890s under great economic, social, and political stress. There is evidence that there was discrimination against blacks by white officers from the start; black officers were given the least desirable assignments, assigned to black neighborhoods, made the object of racial slurs by white officers, excluded from special assignments (e.g. detective division), rarely promoted to higher-level jobs (e.g. sergeant, lieutenant, and commander), and were wounded or killed more often than whites.

Alexander cites evidence that the blacks on the force were aware of this discriminatory treatment as early as the 1940s. He states that the Guardians, an organization of black policemen, was formed in direct response to the discriminatory treatment accorded blacks; however, the Guardians were not recognized by the department from 1943 to 1949. By 1969 there were approximately 2,000 black and Hispanic police officers on the New York City force. Alexander states that layoffs affect the minority police first because they are the last to be hired. He believes that prejudice and discrimination against black police officers still exist on the police force.[84]

The study by Lundman already cited indicated that in drunkenness arrests, police discriminate against native Americans and declassified people, that is, on the basis of race and class; however, they do not single out the blacks in particular, although native Americans include blacks and others.[85]

Piliavin and Briar's study of juveniles revealed that race was a factor associated with juvenile arrest. Negroes were arrested more because they exhibited the aspects of demeanor associated with delinquency.[86]

Ferdinand and Luchterhand studied a random sample of 1,525 teenagers in six neighborhoods in 1964. Interviews and questionnaires were employed in the study to assess attitudes and behavior. Black first offenders who possessed less antisocial attitudes and behavior than whites received more severe dispositions from the police than whites. Female delinquents were also dealt with more harshly by the police. The authors question Werthman's and Piliavin's belief that the police are influenced by assumptions regarding the antisocial nature of offenders' attitudes and by disorganization in offenders' homes. Black offenders against property who displayed defiant attitudes toward authority were given more severe disposition than others.

There was a double standard of justice; black youngsters were given dispositions based largely in terms of their superficial attitudes and demeanor toward the police, and white youngsters were judged by different criteria. However, as the crime became more serious, e.g. offenses against persons rather than offenses against property, the police treated white and black youth more equally in arrest.[87]

Wintersmith states that police practices against blacks originated in slavery. In his study, he concludes that blacks believe that police make a distinction between policing poor white communities and middle-class white communities. However, the blacks strongly believe that the police should stay in their communities regardless of their prejudices and behavioral practices.[88]

Black and Reiss, in their study of police encounters in three cities in 1966, believe that police don't discriminate in arresting black juveniles. Black juveniles are arrested more than white juveniles because black complainants in cases involving black juveniles express a preference for police arrest, compared to white complainants in cases involving white juveniles, who express a preference for leniency. The arrest rate for police-black encounters is 21 percent, compared to the 8 percent arrest rate for police-white encounters.[89]

La Fave, in his study of police practices in three states, notes that the police arrest transvestites on flimsy evidence. Although transvestites do commit crimes such as theft and soliciting and accosting, there is no evidence that the transvestites arrested have actually committed these crimes.[90]

W. Eugene Groves and Peter Rossi, in their study of three ghettos in Detroit, Newark, and Plainfield, New Jersey, conclude that black police perceive the black community differently than white police. Black police perceive the black community as less hostile than do white police. However, black police with prejudices similar to whites' react similarly to residents in the communities they police.[91]

Goldstein reports that fights have broken out between black and white officers in several cities. Whether this is still true is open to empirical investigation.[92]

It has already been mentioned earlier in this chapter that police arrest both white and black suspects who are defiant to them.

Thus, there is evidence that police do discriminate on the basis of race, although it is very difficult to isolate this factor. Sometimes race is disguised by class, complaint, defiance, demeanor, nativity, occupation, preference, etc. It is also possible that black and white policemen perceive minorities differently. Whether police still discriminate against minorities, and to what extent, is open to empirical study. With the influx of black judges in courts, the greater influx of black and minority policemen, the political and racial upheavals of the 1960s, the greater educational benefits to minorities, and the greater legal and political benefits to blacks, it may be that police discriminate less today than even fifteen years ago.

Conclusions

This analysis doesn't exhaust all theories on the police. Some empirical evidence has been presented either in support of or in negation of a particular theory. Certainly there is much more empirical evidence than has been reported here. Rather than considering the police as acting according to their own free will or their individual personalities, one should regard the police activity as the result of sociological variables interacting with organizational, institutional, and societal structures. Therefore, police can be studied from a micro- or macro-sociological perspective.

This is not to say that personality is unimportant. It simply means that personality is not the principal answer to the problem of the police.

How is police theory connected to the science of criminal justice? First, police theory constrains the police to act in certain ways. If the police, for example, are prejudiced against the lower-class suspects regardless of race, they will display a double standard of justice, acting one way toward the lower class and another way toward the middle and upper classes.

Second, police theory can predict how police will act. That is, theory tells us that police behavior is not entirely random. The behavior of the police can be predicted to a certain extent, provided one knows the theory behind the action. For example, if theory states that police action depends on the interaction of the police, suspects, and victim, then one can predict that complainants' preferences will very often be a key to police decisions to arrest.

Third, police theory defining police behavior can be related to other aspects of the criminal justice system. If police perceive the court in a hostile way, they may be constrained to enhance the seriousness of the crime. In addition, if courts perceive the police seriously, then police testimony has great influence for the offender. The police figure very much in the fate of the offender.

It is now time to discuss the other aspects of the criminal justice system. Theories of the court have very important outcomes for the fate of the offender. The court can be analyzed from different perspectives, and there are many different theories on the different aspects of the court. Some theories of the court will now be analyzed and discussed.

Chapter IV
Theories of the Court

The court is a very important part of the criminal justice system. In fact, the President's Commission on Law Enforcement and the Administration of Justice believes that the criminal court is the system's most crucial part.[1] One reason for the importance of the court is the complexity of its functions. In court, an offender is told of the charges, allowed to plead guilty or not guilty, remanded or given bail or released on his own recognizance, confronted by his lawyer, allowed to speak on his own behalf, told of his sentence. The court is a place where juries try cases, where defendants are supposed to be given justice according to an adversary system, where victim or complainant tells his story, where prosecutors and defense lawyers present their arguments either for the state or for the defendants. The list of functions can be multiplied.

The court consists of many different parts. There is arraignment, grand jury, regular jury, prosecution, public and private defenders, bail-setting, sentencing, etc. These parts are both separated and connected; the various parts of the court are related to each other, but each part can be analyzed separately.[2] How and to what extent they are related will be discussed in this chapter and in subsequent chapters.

Important theories of the various parts of the court will be discussed and analyzed. However, some general theories of the court will be discussed in the following section.

General Theories of the Court

Eisenstein and Jacob do not see the courts as bureaucracies. Courts lack the hierarchy of a bureaucratic organization. However, they believe the courts are organizations. They introduce the term "workgroups" as the focus of interaction among principal legal actors, namely, prosecutors, defense attorneys, and judges. The principal actors in these workgroups develop norms which make behavior predictable in criminal justice. Eisenstein and Jacob do not believe, however, that courtroom depositions are an assembly-line process.[3]

Laurence Mohr doesn't believe that organizational theory applies to the courts. He considers courts to be like "decision-making systems" rather than like organizations. In certain respects, however, courts are considered like organizations — for example, in details of case assignment, and in the management of personnel such as clerks and stenographers. Paraphrasing theorists like Max Weber, Mohr states that organizational effectiveness depends upon the correct manipulation of a hierarchy, rules, specialization, spans of control, qualifications for office, and other bureaucratic characteristics. Courts do not have what organizational theorists mean by "management."

Mohr also believes that certain other aspects of organizations apply to the courts. Courts have goals and structure. Structure is defined as "the forms taken by interaction among personnel on the process of getting the work accomplished." Organizational goals and structure depend upon technology and environment. Courts have the same technology, which accounts for the little variation in goals and structure, but their environments differ widely by court and geographical area. Mohr concludes that although the fit between courts and organizations is not perfect, many themes of organizational theory can apply to the courts.[4]

Joseph Hoane doubts that courts can be called organizations or even bureaucracies. Following Weber's analysis, courts cannot be called bureaucracies because they lack a hierarchy of offices, strict and systematic discipline, and a contractual method of employment. Although the court is not an organization, it is a system of interrelated parts, which is somewhat centralized. He calls it a "partially centralized segmentary system." Following Durkheim, a segmentary system is one composed of similar and similarly functioning parts. A system of division of labor is one in which each part is different and makes a different contribution to the whole. The court is never a true system of divided labor because courtrooms are autonomous and each performs a ritual task of clarifying statuses.

The task of the court is to conduct rituals which publicly clarify the status of the accused person. The ritual role of courtrooms prevents them from being defined as a bureaucracy or an organization. However, courts do use bureaucratic power, as in plea bargaining.[5]

Roberta Rovner-Pieczenik believes that courts can be viewed as large-scale organizations in which there is interaction among various subgroups concerning their interests and a meeting of these interests. However, she states that most court analysts view the court as a "Rational Actor." In this view, the court is understood as a unified entity and personified as a Rational Actor. The Rational Actor Model looks at the organization's objectives and demonstrates how its actions are reasonable, given its objectives. The Rational Actor makes the optimum choices, and the most efficient alternatives, the ones that maximize output for a given input.

Rovner-Pieczenik believes that the Rational Actor Model is helpful in explaining the court's screening behavior, but is not helpful in explaining convictions, pleas, and actual sentences. These can best be explained by conflicting internal organizational processes among the principal legal actors, namely, prosecutors, defense attorneys, and judges. The Rational Actor Model overlooks these internal dynamics by reducing these complexities to the behavior of a single actor with a single motive for choice of action. It overlooks the fact that organizations, including the court, define alternatives and estimate consequences on the basis of the different interests, needs, and perceptions of different subgroups. The Organizational Model, however, assumes that no internal consensus necessarily exists at the level of operational goals. Rovner-Pieczenik introduces a third model, the Bureaucratic Politics Model, which looks more closely at different individuals within each subgroup in terms of power in reference to their decision-making.[6]

Feeley states that although there are elements of bureaucratic organization within the courts, discretion has more in common with decentralized, nonhierarchical forms of bargain and decisions than with bureaucracies. Although there is a superficial resemblance to bureaucratic control in the adversary process, the criminal justice system is more like a market than a bureaucracy. Efficient solutions are arrived at because of shared goals, not because of conflicting interests.[7]

There are other facts about courts which are interesting by themselves, and for which a theoretical orientation can be implied. For example, two researchers studying a lower criminal court in New York City note that disruption in the court occurs infrequently, usually involving highly emotional defendants facing serious charges, who are dissatisfied with their lawyers and with the way proceedings are going. Disorder usually occurs when a defendant represents himself, or when a relative learns of the sentencing.[8]

Felix Frankfurter and Roscoe Pound note that the federal criminal courts proceed in an orderly way because there is nothing inherent in criminal trials that make disorder inevitable.[9]

One can only guess that disorder occurs infrequently because citizens respect the institution of the courts, or because they fear retaliation by the court security force, or both, or for some other reason. This is in spite of the fact that a survey shows that only a small percentage of the public approves of the way the courts are operating.[10]

Courts are overloaded with cases. More and more people turn to the courts to solve their problems.[11] The overloading causes a very real problem of court delay. However, many conflicts are not taken to court because courts offer no appropriate remedy.[12] As Jerome Frank points out, if every potential lawsuit became an actual lawsuit, this would be disastrous for the court system and society.[13]

Some researchers have studied and analyzed court delay. Hans Zeisel and others have suggested that increasing judge time without actually increasing the number of judges is one way to reduce delay. They also suggest that a centralized administration of the court system to shift judicial manpower from court to court can reduce delay. They suggest using auditors and referees in place of judges where appropriate. They also suggest a system of substitute judges to reduce delay.[14]

Some cases do proceed rapidly. Maureen Mileski, in her observation of a lower criminal court, noted that misdemeanors against the public were processed rapidly.[15] Nor are causes of delay easy to discern. Martin Levin, in his study of five courts, observed that the size of the caseload had no relation to court delay.[16]

It is known that courts keep inadequate statistics. Several sources have confirmed this.[17] One reason perhaps is that personnel doing the statistics are not trained properly or motivated for this type of work. This has implications for evaluation, policy, and research. Researchers, for example, will have to look at primary sources, e.g. court papers, court documents, docket books, etc., rather than court statistics.

Courts are increasingly employing administrators to supervise the operations of the courts. In addition, many schools of criminal justice have instituted courses and conferences on court administration.[18] This is perhaps because courts are becoming more complex than in the past, and a centralized authority is needed to make the court function properly.

Theories of Arraignment and Preliminary Hearing

Arraignment is the part of the criminal justice system where hearings are held, pleas entered, and bail set. Some have noted the function of the preliminary hearing. Rovner-Pieczenik states that the preliminary hearing determines whether a case will go any further or not.[19] Raymond Moley believes that the preliminary hearing is very important because it has links to the final decisions in the criminal justice system.[20]

Yet in spite of this belief in its importance, the preliminary hearing has either virtually disappeared or fallen into disuse in a number of states. Its purpose today is chiefly to set bail or appoint counsel.[21] Preliminary hearings have disappeared in misdemeanors.[22] Statistics indicate that a preliminary hearing is only heard in one out of six of all cases.[23] Arraignments are brief and stereotyped.[24]

In Manhattan in 1977, 63 percent of all cases were disposed of at arraignment. This didn't include a certain percentage of cases that had been thrown out before they had come to court, such as kids smoking marijuana or teenagers trespassing in abandoned buildings.[25] It is known that only a small percentage of cases which come to court finally reach sentencing; the rest are either dismissed at arraignment or dismissed by the grand jury or prosecutor.[26]

One can speculate that preliminary hearings have virtually disappeared in some states or have become less important and are shorter because courts are overburdened with cases and must process cases speedily. However, this is only speculation. One can also speculate that a large percentage of cases is dismissed at arraignment because the evidence or the charges are not substantiated by either the prosecutor or the judge. Perhaps lawyers are important in dismissing some cases. Perhaps prosecutors believe that the crime is not worth pursuing, even though guilt is verified. Perhaps court overload is another reason for dismissals. These and many more reasons seem logical, but this is open to empirical investigation.

Theories of Bail

Theoretically bail is set to assure the court that the defendant will return to court.[27] However, bail is used for other purposes. Bail is often used as punishment.[28] Very often, judges set bail according to expectations of sentencing.[29] That is, defendants who will be sentenced to prison are given higher bail than defendants who will be sentenced to probation because judges or other legal actors don't want certain defendants released to the streets.

The problem of bail is important for several reasons. The United States is one of the few countries that has a bail system.[30] The Constitution of the United States prohibits excessive bail. Silverstein states that bail practices in the United States are not uniform.[31] Very often judges don't give reasons for their decisions, including bail practices. In setting bail, a presumption of guilt operates before a suspect becomes a defendant.[32] Rosett and Cressey point out that defendants who are detained in jail are more likely to plead guilty than those released before sentencing.[33] Pretrial detention is costly, and very often offenders who are placed in pretrial detention lose their jobs, if employed. Studies show that the poor are released on bail less than the affluent offenders, possibly because of lack of resources to fight their cases.[34] Some bail bondsmen are of undesirable character, and are former felons themselves.[35]

The study of bail is important for its position in the criminal justice system. If bail is excessive, a defendant who can't meet bail is detained before sentencing. A defendant who is detained before sentencing very often doesn't have the time or money to fight his case, because of his remand status. Many studies have shown that defendants who are in remand before sentencing receive more negative sanctions at the time of sentencing than others — for example, they receive prison instead of probation. Bing and Rosenfeld found that poor people in the courts are more likely to be charged with serious crimes, more likely to be committed to jail for failure to make money bail, more likely to be found guilty, and more likely to be sentenced to jail than the nonpoor.[36] Although empirical evidence must ascertain the crucial variables, bail certainly figures in the outcome, directly or indirectly. It makes no difference whether bail is a direct or indirect contributor; studies emphatically demonstrate its importance.

Many studies have indicated that several factors are important in setting bail. The type of crime (severity of charge) is important. The prior record and community ties of the accused seem very important. Age, sex, employment, family connections, and record of reporting to court are important. Marital status is a factor. Behavioral disorders are important. Whether a defendant is on probation and parole, whether he resists arrest, whether there are cash alternatives, and whether there are detainers on him figure in bail. The prosecutor's recommendation is important.

It seems that these variables are important in other areas of criminal justice. However, not all of these variables are important all the time; sometimes the results are even contradictory. For example, Packer claims that bail is set mechanically on the basis of the offense charged.[37] Ebbeson and Konečni agree and also state that community ties are only weakly related to bail, if at all;[38] however, Silverstein found in his study that community ties were important.[39] Katz and others believe that judges rarely look into the defendants' characters in setting bail,[40] although Beeley found that personality was sometimes important; however, Beeley also found that bail was often set arbitrarily, with little or no regard to personality, social history, or financial background.[41]

Examples of our contradictory bail system may be found in recent history. During the riots in our cities, sometimes the normal criteria for bail-setting were not employed. In Detroit, for example, during the riots, authorities were inclined to incarcerate everyone during the duration of the riot. At first, bail was much higher than normal, and only about 2 percent of the defendants were able to meet the exuberant amounts of bail. Bail bore no relation to offense, prior record, or employment. Later, however, bail was reduced, and virtually all the offenders were released from prison.[42]

Colista and Domonkos also reveal that during the civil disorders bail bore no relation to employment, marital status, or severity of crime.[43]

Does our bail system work? Is it logical? Several studies give contradictory reports on the operations of our bail system. Ebbesen and Konečni reveal in their study that prior record, severity of crime, community ties, and other defendant characteristics were unable to predict to any reasonable degree whether or not defendants would appear in court.[44] Beeley found that defendants with good character and less severe crimes were more apt to appear voluntarily in court than others; however, this study was done in the 1920s.[45] Goldfarb states that studies indicate that carefully screened defendants who are treated with dignity and released pending trial will appear in court.[46]

Wice, in his study, concludes that the seriousness of the offense is not a valid criterion of whether the defendant will appear in court. He believes that a program of efficient pretrial supervision is a more valid predictor of appearance in court.[47] Goldfarb, referring to the Vera Project in Manhattan in which certain criteria for release pending sentence were employed in lieu of bail, found that more people on bail failed to return to court than those who were released on their own recognizance.[48] Landes revealed that probation and parole status and severity of the bond are not accurate predictors of whether or not defendants will appear in court; however, resisting arrest and active detainers are predictors of returning to court.[49]

Thus, some of the criteria for bail seem to be illogical and contradictory, and will not predict appearance in court. Nevertheless, bail is a critical variable in the criminal justice system. Its meaning and implications are complicated, and there is a complex formal and informal social system in reference to it because of the consequences for the defendant.

Theories of the Jury

One type of jury to be discussed is the grand jury. This is composed of between sixteen and twenty-three men and women selected, in many cases, in the same way as regular jurors. At least sixteen members must be present to conduct business.[50] However, as Rosett and Cressey point out, the requirement of grand jury action has virtually disappeared in felony cases, and in routine cases, e.g. misdemeanors, the prosecutor acting alone draws up evidence.[51] Many have noted the dominance of the prosecutor in grand jury action. Cohn and Udolf, for example, note how grand juries often act as rubber stamps for prosecutors.[52]

One purpose of the grand jury is to determine evidence of guilt to justify carrying the case to other stages of the criminal justice system.[53] Rovner-Pieczenik states that the function of the grand jury is to indict the accused felons, advise the prosecutor to return the case to a lower court as a misdemeanor, or to dismiss the case entirely. She also states that the grand jury reviews legal evidence against the accused in a closed, secret session; only the prosecutor is present. The defendant and judge are both absent from the grand jury, although the defendant can be asked to appear to give evidence on his own behalf.[54] Remington and others have noted that one of the defects of the grand jury is its secrecy.[55]

Hewitt, in a discussion of the New York City grand jury, mentions that the grand jury must inquire into every person incarcerated in jail who has not been indicted, and must inquire into every willful and corrupt misconduct in office of public officials of every description. The grand jury may inquire into the conditions and management of prisoners.

Grand juries serve indictments, an accusation in writing charging a person with a crime. At least twelve grand jurors must be present to indict. If a grand jury dismisses a charge, the charge can be resubmitted to the grand jury with proper evidence by the prosecutor.[56]

How important the grand jury is or whether it is functional is a matter of speculation. Whether it should be eliminated or taken over by other structures is open to speculation.

We turn now to a discussion of the regular jury. Although the jury is not strong everywhere, it is still important in many jurisdictions. The jury system is also in decline in many countries outside of the United States.[57] Juries are supposed to weigh evidence, determine guilt or innocence, and sometimes determine sentencing. Juries represent laymen in criminal justice.[58] They are selected from telephone directories, city directories, and census lists.[59]

There is evidence that although juries are supposed to be impartial, they can be influenced by other legal actors in the system. Littrell believes that juries serve the interests of other prosecutors.[60] Kerr believes that the moods of both prosecutors and defense attorneys influence juries and hence the outcomes of trials.[61] There is evidence that defense attorneys can sway juries and judges.[62] Bryan talks about how physical cues and gestures can be very important in influencing juries, and that the ability to pick the right jury is important for trial outcomes.[63] Jackson indicates that about 50 percent of the messages in a trial are non-verbal.[64]

It is believed that jurors are supposed to be equal. There is a widespread norm that group members should act towards one another as equals. The reinforcement of the norm of equality is supported by the requirement that the verdict be unanimous.[65]

The various factors associated with jury decisions are revealed in several empirical studies. Kerr, for example, collected data on 1,296 separate trial forms in San Diego in 1974–1976. The trials all involved felonies. They represented a broad range of charges. A one-way analysis of variance and multiple regression was performed. The results showed that none of the characteristics of the behavior of the defendants was associated with jury outcomes. Victims' age and sex were not important. The demographic and behavioral characteristics of the victim were not important, except that isolated sexual offenses against a female victim resulted in a low conviction rate. Kerr concludes that evidence and the moods and gestures of the principal legal actors are decisive for jury outcomes.[66]

Kalven, Jr., and Zeisel provide us with an extensive study of jury decisions. A questionnaire was mailed to 600 judges throughout the country representing 3,576 mock jury trials to see how they would analyze and decide on these cases. The judges were to decide how they would settle the case before the jury gave its verdict. However, the authors of the questionnaire point out that there may be shortcomings in studies such as this in which the data are hypothetical.

The authors list several factors associated or not associated with jury outcomes. Marital status is not important. Age, sex, and race enter into the decision. Defendants under 21, female defendants, older defendants, and Negro defendants rank from favorable to unfavorable in the eyes of the jurors. Individual differences among defendants don't enter significantly into jury decisions. The circumstances of the case are important. For example, in cases of excessive brutality by the police, the jury will acquit even when a defendant kills a policeman. The jury will also acquit in cases of an improper police or prosecutorial action. Intraracial crime (blacks against blacks, Indians against Indians) is considered more leniently by the jury because jurors believe that these groups lack the self-control of the whites.

The agreement-disagreement rate between judge and jury was analyzed. The results showed that judges are critical of the jury's performance in only 9 percent of the cases. The judge is not critical of the jury's performance in two-thirds of the cases in which he disagrees; he is critical of the jury's performance in only one-third of the cases in which he disagrees. These are usually cases in which the jury has been too lenient. Although the judge is not critical of the jury's performance in over two-thirds of the cases in which he disagrees, he is critical of the jury's values in 78 percent of these cases.

The results of the study showed that judge and jury agree 75 percent of the time. This rate of agreement is uniform in both civil and criminal cases. Judge and jury agree in very serious cases. About 80 percent of the disagreement involved evidentiary problems. There was also disagreement about the law and the defendant. The authors conclude that most cases are routine and understood by the jury; the juries largely understand the facts and get the case straight. The authors also conclude that the extensive agreement between judge and jury indicates the widespread consensus on values embodied in the law.[67]

Kalven, Jr., and Zeisel have been analyzed by other critics. For example, George McCall states that in the study reported by Kalven, Jr., and Zeisel, judges reported that the defendant seemed to have prejudiced the jury because of some unattractive behavior associated with the crime. Judges also reported that defendants with good work records, high prestige occupations, members of the armed forces, students, and public officials impressed the jury favorably. Defendants who were ill, handicapped, or showed strong emotions gained the jury's sympathy.[68] Perhaps this again shows the agreement over values in our society.

Other researchers report judge-jury agreement. Bloomstein notes that the University of Chicago Law School completed a survey in which 500 judges were questioned about the jurors over which they presided. These were live trials. The results showed that judge and jury agreed in 80 percent of the cases.[69]

A study in California examined 238 cases for the years 1958 through 1966 in which the death penalty could have been given. A total of 78 measurement variables was employed in the study. A cluster analysis was employed on the data.

The results showed that race had no effect on outcomes. Prior record was decisive, but differences in seriousness of prior offenses were not important. Employment history was very important. Unstable psychiatric histories were not important. Unstable home backgrounds of defendants did influence the jury. The military background of the defendant did not influence the juries in itself. Sex was not important. The physical characteristics of the defendants did not influence the jury. Age, race, and economic background of the victim were not independently associated with jury decisions.

The jury did show more severe treatment in cases involving kidnap-murders. There was a rape-kidnap syndrome, and when all factors were controlled, the defendants who committed this type of crime were more apt to receive the death penalty than others. Juries were negatively influenced when defendants resisted arrest. However, defendants who were under the influence of alcohol at the time of the murder were less likely to receive the death penalty. Defendants who attempted to invoke the insanity defense received the death penalty more than others. The adverse testimony of the co-defendant influenced the jury independently of all aspects of the case.

Other relationships were also noted. The type of attorney had no effect on jury decisions. Blacks who killed whites did not receive harsher treatment than others. Juries were, however, lenient toward white collar defendants. The death penalty was high among professional criminals, the unemployed, and those with poor job stability. The death penalty was higher among those with poor or no military records as compared to those with good military records.[70]

The authors conclude that juries show a definite pattern in decision-making. A blue collar background was negative for the jury, while a white collar background was a mitigating factor. The fact that the defendant himself actually killed at least one person was looked at negatively by the jury. The authors conclude that although a smaller number of variables could have been sufficient to analyze the data, the results did distinguish between important and unimportant factors.[71]

It seems that there is evidence of judge-jury agreement. There is evidence that many different factors are associated with jury decisions, e.g., circumstances of crime, seriousness of case, prior record, economic factors, prosecutors' decisions, physical cues and gestures, etc. Some factors show contradictory results in different studies.

There are many critics of the jury system. In some jurisdictions, the jury system is declining. Some believe that since the jury system is composed of lay persons, it is not capable of making rational, unbiased decisions. Some believe that the jury system is influenced by the principal legal actors in both the selection of jurors and their decisions.

There are others who believe that the jury system is not invoked enough. They claim that since the majority of defendants plead guilty, the adversary system no longer operates in our society. That is, innocent defendants may be punished because they don't possess the resources to fight their cases by trial. They plead guilty automatically to guarantee the certainty of a shorter sentence rather than a longer sentence as a result of a trial.

The jury system theoretically is supposed to decide guilt or innocence and punishment in cases in which the defendant maintains his innocence and the judge and prosecutor maintain his guilt. Although the majority of defendants plead guilty, the jury system exists for anyone who really wishes to use it. It can be seen as another structure in the criminal justice system that is functional to certain defendants. The jury system represents the idea that the common man is rational and is capable of deciding whether his fellow citizen is guilty of committing a crime which, as Cahn suggests, outrages his "sense of injustice."[72]

Theories of Prosecution

Although there have been numerous case studies of prosecutors' offices, there has been little systematic or comparative research regarding the reasons for plea-bargaining or the relation of these reasons to actual practice.[73] The guilty-plea process is becoming more elaborate, and more focused on evidence of the defendants' guilt than in the past; in addition, guilty pleas are receiving more attention by the appellate courts.[74]

It is common knowledge that charging is not done solely by the prosecutor. Judges and legal representatives enter into the charging process. The importance of the legal actor's position in charging and plea-bargaining varies by jurisdiction. In Prairie City, for example, Neubauer found that prosecutors dominate the charging process.[75] White found that judges in New York City play a more dominant role in plea-bargaining than do judges in Philadelphia.[76] The principal legal actors apparently confer in charging.

Several critics of the criminal justice system have noted the importance of the prosecutors' discretion and power. In addition, prosecutors don't have to give reasons for their decisions. Some note that prosecutorial discretion is never reviewed by the judiciary or any other administrative body.[77] New York, for example, has a statute requiring judges to file a statement giving reasons for plea-bargaining, but this statute is vague, general, and virtually never enforced.[78]

There are several examples in the literature emphasizing the prosecutors' power. A study was analyzed in which 100 questionnaires were returned from district attorneys' offices in 41 states. The results showed that the vast majority of prosecutors do participate in sentencing, independent of whether or not a probation officer makes a recommendation. A plurality of the offices believed that their recommendations were followed all the time.[79] In support of this, there is evidence that judges very often follow the recommendations of the prosecutors.[80]

Casper gives another example of prosecutorial power. The defendants he interviewed believed that the prosecutor was the man who set the time. They also believed that he was the central figure in the criminal justice system.[81]

Another national study of trial judges revealed that in both felony and misdemeanor courts, the majority of trial judges, about two-thirds, restrict their role to ratifying in court bargains struck between prosecutors and defense counsel.[82]

There are other reasons for the importance of plea-bargaining. Plea-bargaining can be prolonged and delayed, or a hurried exchange in a corridor of a courtroom.[83] Prosecutors may institute civil procedures.[84] Innocent defendants may plead guilty. Some argue that a high rate of guilty pleas undermines our adversary system.[85] The prosecutor makes important decisions, but yet rarely does he fully investigate the case and the offender's background.[86]

Public opinion polls show strong opposition to plea-bargaining.[87] There is evidence that charge reduction has no relation to sentencing.[88] The charging process can also be part of the labeling process, with all of its negative consequences.

What are some of the reasons for plea-bargaining? Why do defendants plead guilty? What is the actual theory behind plea-bargaining? One reason already mentioned is the excessive caseloads that pervade the courts. This is the strongest reason mentioned for plea-bargaining. Defendants are allowed to plead guilty to a lesser charge and hence a lesser sentence in exchange for not going to trial. If all offenders refused to plead guilty, the majority would have to go to trial, and the system would be overloaded due to lack of resources and time; the overload would lead to a breakdown in the criminal justice system.

This conclusion has been disputed. There is some evidence that plea-bargaining existed a hundred years ago, when caseloads were normal, not excessive. Heumann analyzed case records from Connecticut that were about 100 years old and found that plea-bargaining was in effect then, in spite of the normal caseloads at that time in that state.[89] Eisenstein and Jacob, in their study of three courts in three cities, reveal that plea-bargaining is not the result of heavy caseloads. There was no relation between guilty pleas and courtroom overload.[90] Hoane states in his anthropological study of a New York City court that examination of lawyers' and judges' motivations made doubtful the notion that case overload was the sole cause of plea-bargaining. Rather, he states, plea-bargaining was the outgrowth of values in American society. Plea-bargaining was not a mechanical process.[91]

Rosett and Cressey have another theory. They believe that since guilt is difficult to determine with certainty, it is best to plead guilty. Guilty pleas also have important social control functions. They also claim that guilty pleas are made to mitigate the harsh punishment of the law. American law is too harsh to be enforced rigorously. Guilty pleas have the function of making the accused accept some punishment, but not the full punishment prescribed by law.[92]

Others have noted that plea-bargaining serves to reduce punishment. Miller states that plea-bargaining serves to reduce punishment which administrators believe is too harsh.[93] Alschuler claims that one of the goals of plea-bargaining is to mitigate harsh punishment.[94] Neubauer believes that guilty pleas serve to mitigate harsh punishment on one hand, and acquittal on the other.[95]

Littrell believes that plea-bargaining is a myth. The defendants are labeled according to their prior record and to their most sinister characteristics in order to charge them with an appropriate crime. He differentiates between "bureaucratic justice" and "individualized justice." In the former, the offender is assumed guilty early in the charging process, not only by the prosecutor, but by the police and juries.

The prosecutor in conjunction with the police tailor charges they deem appropriate to specific cases. The organization of prosecution aims at conviction and punishment. No one person is responsible for charging; the decision is made all the way through the criminal justice system. Defendants do little to influence their fate or to undermine the legal theory of authority. Littrell claims that some bargaining does occur. The "bureaucratic justice" is contradictory of "individualized justice" for each case.[96]

Newman claims that the strongest motive for plea-bargaining is to individualize punishment.[97] Rosett and Cressey believe that in addition to mitigating punishment, plea-bargaining individualizes punishment in the interests of justice. They also believe that although there are many reasons for an offender to plead guilty, the basic motivation is fear of punishment.[98] Some believe that plea-bargaining is a market transaction, in which prosecutors buy guilty pleas in exchange for a sentence of leniency.[99] Forer points out that crimes are technically committed against the state, not against the victim. The victim is only a witness.[100]

There are many factors associated with plea-bargaining. Empirical research has proven some of these factors to be important. For example, Cohn and Udolf assert that charge reduction depends on how uncertain the prosecutor is of a conviction, the seriousness of the offense, and the defendant's prior record. Some prosecutors establish rules for charge reduction. For example, if an individual is indicted for a class A drug felony, he must plead guilty to at least a class C felony.[101]

Knudten reports that Kress cites three factors commonly involved in the charging process. One is whether there is sufficient evidence to charge a certain crime; a second is whether prosecution for a particular crime is in the public interest, including resources, costs, and cooperation of the subject; and the third is alternatives to plea-bargaining. Knudten reports on a survey of county prosecutors in Wisconsin and Michigan. The prosecutors were asked to respond to a Likert-type scale to rate the importance of reasons for entering into negotiations with defendants. The most important conclusion was that prosecutors vary in reasons for negotiations, according to the particular decision involved. However, legal problems were cited as the most important reason for negotiations with a defendant.[102]

La Patra states that cases are more likely to be accepted for prosecution when the victim is a business firm, controlling other factors.[103] Apparently, the social status of the victim is a factor in prosecution.

Gross claims that criminal justice administrators, including prosecutors, often allow themselves to be guided by a person's moral worth in deciding what charges to make, what pleas to accept, and even deciding whether to prosecute at all.[104] Newman says in his study of the states that prosecutors use a great deal of discretion in charging; however, a great many decisions are routine.[105]

Carter mentions that because prosecutors often don't have the complete story of an offender's case, they don't adhere to rules in deciding on a case. They don't process cases in an assembly-line manner because they don't know all the facts in advance. They don't agree, for example, on the importance of the prior record; convictions seem to have more weight than the number of arrests.[106]

It is well known that the victim or complainant plays a major part in plea-bargaining. Newman, for example, found that the reluctance of the victim or complainant to testify is one of the strongest reasons for dismissal of cases.[107]

Packer states that prosecutors somehow must make probabilities about past events, ranging from temperament, the importance of the case, and pressure from the public.[108]

Miller, in his study, states that in Detroit very few family complaints resulted in prosecution. In his study of three states, he found that relatively minor offenses, the expense involved in prosecution, and the harm to the suspects' reputation were all factors considered important in not charging an offense. He found that the distance the prosecutor must travel to obtain a suspect for prosecution was important. Prosecutors in Detroit will not charge well-to-do persons who commit certain crimes such as homosexuality or exhibitionism. However, prosecutors will enforce full charges when public opinion favors it. Sometimes prosecutors will charge when ordinarily they wouldn't charge, in order to perform some badly needed social service function. Miller concludes that prosecutors do not charge suspects they believe are innocent.[109]

Alschuler believes that the strength of the evidence is the primary factor in plea-bargaining.[110] Reed concludes that prosecutors assess the chances of going to trial as an important factor in charging. For example, he hypothesizes that guilty pleas and dismissals both increase as the threat of trial increases. Delay time is also related to the threat of trial and indirectly related to pleas and dismissals.[111]

Newman, in his study, cites several factors in charging. He claims that the circumstances of the offense are confusing, and, therefore, prosecutors don't always have the full facts. Sometimes the charges are reduced or dismissed when a defendant is really emotionally disturbed or when the motive for the crime is understandable. Reduction in charges is sometimes made when a vicim would be subjected to trauma by going to trial. Charge reduction is sometimes made to obtain restitution. Sometimes prosecutors acquit because the police practice illegal enforcement methods.[112]

Neubauer, in his study of Prairie City, states that the prosecutor dismissed few cases once charges were filed. Since sex and battery cases were difficult to prove, many of these cases were reduced to misdemeanors. The seriousness of the offense, the prior record of the defendant, and the legal strength of the case involving evidence were the most important factors in plea-bargaining.[113]

Sudnow states that prosecutors in his study take certain factors into account in reducing crimes to "typical features" which induce guilty pleas. The manner in which the crime was committed, the setting in which it occurred, the types of victims involved, the biography of the offender and the manner in which he committed the crime, criminal history, and psychological and social background are the "typical features" which help prosecutors to reduce all crimes to "typical reduced charges." The reduced charge may bear no relation to the original charge. Prosecutors assume guilt. The reduced charge must not be so great as to induce a punishment similar to the original charge or so lenient as to make the defendant believe he isn't punished at all.[114]

Sudnow has been criticized. For example, Hoane states that Sudnow has studied only minor types of crimes, and therefore his findings are not generalizable to all crimes.[115]

Mather found that the more serious charges were the ones likely to go to trial.[116] White discovered in his study of Philadelphia plea-bargaining practices that prosecutors did not adhere solely to such factors as type of crime and prior record, etc. Very often the personal characteristics of the defendant were very important in prosecution.[117] Rhodes in his study found that defendants went to trial when the sentence they received for a guilty plea was severe.[118]

A study was done in Indiana on a sample of 980 cases for January 1974 through June 1976. The strength of the evidence was important in outcomes. Early decisions by prosecutors differed from later decisions. Prosecutors looked for "study case typifications," factors that allowed for certain convictions and sentences. A strong case involved a credible and blameless victim and a discreditable and culpable defendant. Cases involving white victims were prosecuted more fully than others. A legally serious offense enhanced the probability of full conviction. Cases in which defendant and victim were familiar or intimate were not necessarily dismissed. Legally serious cases proceeded to trial more than others. Employed defendants proceeded to trial more than others. Evidence of the defendant's guilt, a credible witness, and a dangerous defendant also increased the chances of proceeding to trial.[119]

Hoane found in his study of a New York City court that charges pleaded to usually had no relation to the original charge. He found that crimes were not reduced to a "normal crime stereotype," as Sudnow claimed. Rather, they were reduced to their worth in terms of legal seriousness and sentence. Burglarizing a dwelling, for example, was considered more serious than burglarizing a commercial establishment. Crimes committed against strangers were considered more serious than others. The prosecutors accommodated the police and the witnesses. The prosecutors individualized each case.

Hoane found that the defendant's prior record was the strongest factor in plea-bargaining. Employment worked in favor of the defendant. Older defendants and the young were sometimes given special consideration. Defendants' attitudes were important in defining the fate of the defendants. Defendants with stable family ties were regarded favorably. A college education was an important factor. Race and ethnicity might have a part in decisions.

Prosecution, according to Hoane, involves values rooted in everyday

American values. Prosecutors don't use rules but form a picture of the defendant himself. Hoane contends that defendants receive individual processing of their cases by both prosecutors and judges.[120]

McCall states that prosecutors very often divert drug addicts, alcoholics, and youthful offenders to treatment. He states that prosecutors are more concerned with obtaining convictions rather than sentences, as long as sentences don't depart too far from the worth of the case.[121]

Rovner-Pieczenik found in her study that many reductions in charges were the result of insufficient evidence to proceed further. She also states that overcharging by the police is a tactic to induce guilty pleas.[122]

Meyers did a study of prosecution in Indiana. There were different factors associated with different stages of prosecution, e.g. charging, conviction, and trial. For charging, prior record was important. Seriousness of charge was important. Victims' characteristics or legal record had no effect. However, defendants who committed crimes against female victims were charged with more serious offenses. Crimes committed against strangers were looked at more seriously. Property loss and injury to the victim had no relation to charging. The nature of the weapon used in a crime was important. The nature of the crime and the type of weapon were the most important factors in charging. Males were convicted of more serious charges, the young of less serious charges. If a victim engaged in deviant behavior, charging was less serious.

Pretrial status and type of counsel had no effect on case dismissal. The victims' willingness to prosecute was very important. More cases were dismissed if victims were considered careless than if they were considered noncareless. If a victim was willing to prosecute, was nonnegligent, and was employed in a low-status job, full prosecution was likely. The low-status job of the victim was indirectly related to prosecution, since these victims were involved in serious crimes.

If the victim was employed in a high-status job, or if the victim was young, defendants were more likely to be convicted. If a victim had no prior record, defendants were more likely to be prosecuted. If defendants stole large sums of money, conviction was likely. The type of crime, record of defendant, and weapon used had no effect on conviction; however, these factors were important in charging. Males were convicted more than others.

There was a different set of factors for trial. Victims' status and amount of harm were important. Helplessness had no effect. Defendants who had codefendants proceeded to trial. Prior record was important. Defendants with extensive records were more likely to proceed to trial. Defendants with high bail went to trial. Cases with weak evidence proceeded to trial.[123]

Littrell in his study found that the crime itself was not a factor in charging. He found that 70.5 percent of the cases were accepted by the prosecutor's office without change.[124] Hoffman, in his study of a Manhattan court, indicated that prosecutors must follow certain rules of procedure.[125] Thus, there are legal and social criteria in charging.

During the riots of the 1960s, out of 3,400 arrested, over 3,000 were prosecuted for either felonies or misdemeanors. In Detroit, through adversary proceedings, many charges were dismissed or reduced to much lower crimes; most offenders were charged with one or two types of offenses, thus indicating that there was little or no individual attention to cases; 930 of 3,154 defendants had their cases dismissed, which was four times the normal rate; and there was an absence of the usual police-prosecutorial screening found in normal times.

In Chicago, multiple charges and high bail were set at first to induce defendants to plead guilty.[126] Chambliss and Seidman point out that during the Chicago riots of 1968, the prosecutors were either unwilling or unable to bring charges against the police.[127]

These examples emphasize that during the riots of the 1960s, even though prosecutors deviated from the norm in many cases, the criminal justice system managed to survive and to function. However, as seen, there are many instances in normal times when prosecutors use discretion in carrying out their duties.

A national study revealed that although prosecutors set different priorities for different cases, prosecutors in the United States act consistently and uniformly in decision-making. The three most important factors all prosecutors employ are the seriousness of the offense, prior record of the defendant, and the evidentiary strength of the case.[128]

It can be seen that prosecutors use many of the same factors in charging that are found important in criminal justice at every stage of the system. The prior record of the defendant, seriousness of the offense, victim preferences, social characteristics of the defendant, degree of injury or property loss, strength of the evidence, mental state of the defendant, and the tactics of the police, are just some of the factors which enter into charging. Some of these factors are important in some jurisdictions, and unimportant in others.

There are many critics of the plea-bargaining system. Some even advocate the abolition of plea-bargaining as practiced in our society.[129] On the other hand, others believe that our plea-bargaining system is necessary and functional to the maintenance of the criminal justice system.

Some believe that the plea-bargaining system should remain but offer some suggestions for its improvement. Miller suggests that license revocation is an alternative to prosecution in violation of infractions of state or local liquor laws.[130] Friesen believes that prosecutors in the future will need to know about computers to process their cases.[131] Campbell believes that prosecutors should not ordinarily make sentencing recommendations.[132]

Smith and Pollack provide us with a good example of how a prosecutor can make the office exemplary. They mention Hogan as an example of an excellent prosecutor in New York City. During a lengthy incumbency, he depoliticized the process of choosing the assistant district attorneys. He continuously fought to upgrade salaries and appoint lawyers on merit rather than on political considerations. He offered full-time service to the job. His office was considered a model for the whole country.[133]

How important prosecution is to the criminal justice system is open to speculation.

Theories of Legal Representation

In the spring of 1972, the Supreme Court held that any defendant charged with a crime which might result in imprisonment had a constitutional right to a lawyer. This decision was embodied in the case of *Argersinger* v. *Hamlin* and was extended to the ruling in the landmark case of *Gideon* v. *Wainwright* to include misdemeanors.[134] Now virtually every defendant has a legal right to representation, even if he is indigent; it is up to the court to provide him with free legal services.

As mentioned in Chapter I, Cohn and Udolf believe that the adversary system is basic to the operation of our legal system and hence our criminal justice system. Many critics believe this also. Cohn and Udolf say that the fact that due process of law is not exactly defined is one of its strengths. Due process of law protects the individual from the abusive, enormous power of the law. Cohn and Udolf say that *stare decisis* is the basic principle in American law today, both civil and criminal. This means that once a decision has been made, it becomes binding upon the court to decide all future cases in the same way. The principle of *stare decisis* is not designed to take account of individual justice in each case; it is designed for uniformity and predictability in the laws.[135]

This principle certainly has implications for the criminal justice system. Uniformity of law must be balanced against due process and individual justice.

Our adversary system provides for a prosecutor to represent the state and a lawyer to represent the defendant. Lawyers are not only functional for defending offenders, but they are also functional for obtaining guilty pleas to allow the system to continue in the usual way. Blumberg, for example, asserts that lawyers influence relatives to convince defendants to plead guilty. Blumberg calls this "cooling out" the accused.[136] Rosett and Cressey say the same thing. They say the public defender's job is more a matter of obtaining guilty pleas than of defending clients.[137]

Since many defendants are poor and are provided free legal service, there have been some empirical studies comparing the results of cases defended by private versus public defenders. The results are mixed and contradictory.

Arafat and McCatherty report on a questionnaire administered to respondents in New York City. The results showed that females were more satisfied than males with their cases and with the efforts made by public defenders on their behalf. Those represented by public defenders were more likely than others to blame their lawyers for the outcome of their cases. The results showed that the young, blacks, and the lower-income groups were the ones primarily dissatisfied with the present legal system. Almost 87 percent of the sample could not tell whether they would process a complaint or initiate action against a lawyer. The blacks showed more negative attitudes toward legal aid than did the whites and Hispanics.[138]

Bing and Rosenfeld in their study in Boston concluded that defendants with assigned counsel receive fewer continuances, have higher bail set, and are found guilty more often than defendants with private counsel. Defendants with assigned counsel do little better, or sometimes worse, than defendants who have no lawyer.[139]

Silverstein in his study revealed that the public defender was as able as the retained counsel, and sometimes he was more experienced. No firm conclusion was drawn about whether the public defender or the assigned counsel was better.[140]

Oaks and Lehman report that in 1964, public defenders obtained probation for 28 percent of their clients, compared to 14 percent for clients represented by other types of counsel. However, they report that Silverstein found that public defenders obtained probation 18 percent, compared to 39 percent for retained counsel.[141]

Alschuler states that studies controlling other variables indicate that there are only minor differences in sentencing outcomes between cases settled by public defenders and cases settled by private attorneys.[142]

Wice and Suwak discovered in their survey of nine cities that public defenders who had the lowest caseloads and the most money to spend per case were the ones who achieved the highest success scores in terms of sentencing dispositions.[143]

Hermann and others interviewed legal actors and defendants in three cities, namely, New York, Los Angeles, and Washington, D.C.; all except 7 out of 166 interviewed believed that they would rather have a lawyer than no lawyer at all. However, about 45 percent believed that lawyers in general did a good job, and only 31 percent said the lawyers in their last case did a good job. Using advanced statistical techniques, they found that the type of lawyer had very little effect on the likelihood of being convicted or imprisoned. They concluded that lawyers' performances might not be influential in the criminal justice system.[144]

Casper, in his study of defendants in Connecticut, found that defendants believed that lawyers were not on their side. The defendants believed that public defenders had not adequately represented them. They believed that legal aid lawyers were somewhat better than public defenders because they were able to spend more time with them and make visits to jail. However, the private attorneys were seen as the best type of attorney. The defendants believed that since public defenders and legal aid lawyers were free, they couldn't be as good as what one must pay for.[145]

Rovner-Pieczenik, in her study of the criminal court, concludes that private attorneys and public defenders manage their cases differently. Public defenders close their cases more quickly than private attorneys, possibly due to the heavy caseloads. Defendants represented by public defenders are more likely to be in jail pending the outcome of their case. Public defenders offer more pleas, and private attorneys go to trial more often in the lower court. Her findings show that the relation between favorableness of case disposition, operationalized as either a dismissal, or a finding of a felony or misdemeanor, and the type of attorney, was not statistically significant in either the lower court or the superior court.

The type of attorney made no difference in pretrial status. Rovner-Pieczenik found that in sentencing, the results showed that defendants who had one or no prior convictions, were nonwhite, were charged with assault, and were heard in the superior court had more favorable dispositions in sentencing if they were represented by private attorneys rather than by public defenders. Private attorneys in the lower court who closed quickly did better than those who didn't close quickly.[146]

Meyers, in her study in Indiana, found that defendants with more extensive prior criminal records were more likely to secure the services of private attorneys than were others. She states that this supports the findings of other research.[147]

Nagel found that in federal offenses, court-appointed lawyers were less apt to ask for delays. Court-appointed lawyers might not be inclined to put in the time and trouble necessary for a case compared to private lawyers, or they might want to get their clients out of jail if the defendant were in remand.[148]

Chambliss found that men experienced in the ways of the criminal justice system, recidivists, for example, could arrange their own fate better than the inexperienced.[149] Lizotte also found in his study in Chicago that men who had no counsel did better than those who did have counsel.[150] Bing and Rosenfeld found that defendants with assigned counsel did no better, and sometimes did worse, than defendants who had no lawyers.[151] Balbus found that in Detroit, during the riots of the 1960s, the executive judge at first refused to allow lawyers into the courtroom, and in nearly every courtroom where they were permitted to enter, their arguments for lower bail were simply rejected or ignored.[152]

Lawyers have been criticized by criminal justice analysts. Cohn and Udolf, for example, believe that lawyers know the legal aspects of the system, but know little about the psychology of changing human behavior. They also state that in law school the emphasis is on civil law, and, as a result, the average law school graduate might have no training in criminal law beyond a three-credit course. Therefore, attorneys wishing to specialize in criminal justice must depend on elective or graduate courses or experience in legal aid offices, in prosecutors' offices, or in law firms.

They believe that legal aid society lawyers are more experienced in the operation of criminal courts than any other lawyers except assistant district attorneys. They also state that there are no certifying boards to certify specialties in law as in other professions (e.g. medicine).[153]

The accusation of lack of training in criminal law has been confirmed by a number of critics. For example, Whitney North Seymour, Jr., states that only a small proportion of lawyers make a career out of practicing criminal law, and, as a result, most have no knowledge of how the criminal court works or what its problems are. Criminal law is a strange and an unknown world for most lawyers.[154] As a result, a defendant can choose among only a small proportion of all lawyers to settle his or her case.

The President's Commission states that criminal lawyers have no real grasp of the correctional aspects of criminal justice.[155] This is important, because all areas of the criminal justice systems are interrelated.

How important legal representation is in criminal justice is open to empirical investigation. Does legal representation serve the primary function of obtaining guilty pleas? Is its function to defend offenders? Does it make only a slight difference in outcomes? Is its job to put on a show before the judge? Does it serve to label a defendant "deviant"?

Whatever the duties and outcomes of legal representation, its importance is seen as functional, relatively speaking, to the operation of the criminal justice system.

Theories of Sentencing

Sentencing perhaps is the most crucial aspect of the criminal justice system. This is when the defendants learn of the fate they must suffer for their crime — when justice may be emphasized.

Since all parts of the criminal justice system are interrelated, it is difficult to study one aspect independently of other aspects. For example, since sentencing depends on the arrest process, sentencing is related to both the police and prosecution. However, sentencing will be discussed here in the light of the most relevant theories found in the literature.

Disparity

One of the most important theories of sentencing involves disparity. "Disparity" can be defined as unequal sentences for similar crimes or cases. For example, if one defendant has five prior arrests, with two felony convictions resulting in prison, and three misdemeanor convictions resulting in fines, and another defendant has one prior misdemeanor conviction resulting in a conditional discharge, and both defendants are presently charged with possession of drugs, the two cases are dissimilar. One defendant has a heavy record and the other has a light record, relatively speaking. Both defendants, however, have similar final charges. How is the judge to sentence these defendants? If no disparity exists, obviously the one with the heavier prior record should receive a more severe sentence.

However, other factors intervene. Perhaps the defendant with a heavier prior record is younger than the one with the lighter prior record. Perhaps the one with the heavier record is trying to rehabilitate himself, and a severe sentence would prohibit rehabilitation. Perhaps the one with a heavier record is steadily employed, and a prison sentence would interfere with his or her employment. These and other circumstances could cause the judge to consider extralegal factors or mitigating circumstances in order to impose a light sentence.

Smith and Pollack believe that both disparity in sentencing and a lack of a consistent policy of punishment stem, in large part, from the absence of an acceptable theory of the causation of criminal behavior.[156] As Pamuela Samuelson states, there is little agreement about what sentencing disparity really is.[157] Even when empirical studies control many variables, it is difficult to determine the precise degree of sentence disparity.[158] Rubin points out that disparity is unconstitutional.[159] Disparity in sentencing can be related to other areas of the criminal justice system, e.g. plea-bargaining.[160]

The literature is full of examples of disparity in sentencing. Only a couple of examples will be given here.

Balbus gives examples which show that sentences were lighter in minor revolts during the riots of the 1960s than in normal times. He believes that this was caused by the conflict between law and order. The sentences were less severe in spite of the demand of the prosecution for full penalties under the law. Over 4,000 cases were disposed of within four months. In Chicago, only a minority of the defendants were sentenced to jail in addition to the remand time already imposed. Ninety-one percent of the convicted defendants in Chicago received no penalties other than small fines.[161]

There is some evidence that defendants who go to trial are sentenced more harshly than others.[162]

Determinate sentencing is an attempt to remedy some of the disparity in sentencing. Under determinate sentencing, defendants would be given identical sentences for identical crimes and identical arrest records. There would be some area for discretion because it is difficult to find two cases which are equal in all respects. Some mitigating circumstances would be taken into consideration.

Although a determinate sentencing statute has been passed in California, critics believe that in a number of important ways the sentencing in California remains just as indeterminate as before the statute was passed. First, prison sentences for the very few crimes for which the law imposes life penalties are left to the discretion of a governing board. Second, the problem of imposing probation or a suspended sentence, and of imposing a fine or prison of a year or less, is still subject to discretion and has not been structured properly. Third, judges seem to impose greater penalties under the determinate sentencing law. Fourth, defendants will not know the penalty until the time of sentencing. Fifth, future recidivism from an assessment of the defendant's personal characteristics remains important.[163]

Another critique of determinate sentencing in California involves dissatisfaction with the law. For example, neither misdemeanor sentences nor alternative dispositions for felonies, e.g. probation, are affected. The law doesn't offer dispositions for first-degree murder. Under the new law, concurrent terms may not be shorter than consecutive terms. The new law doesn't provide answers for prisoners who have completed their determinate sentences but still impose a danger to society. However, the new law requests that judges state reasons for imposing a sentence.[164]

There are other criticisms of determinate sentencing. One of the purposes of the indeterminate sentence is rehabilitation.[165] This may be removed in determinate sentencing. Determinate sentencing removes the power of selecting sentences from judges to prosecutors.[166]

Some of the advantages of indeterminate sentencing have been listed. First, it provides a chance to achieve uniformity in sentencing. Second, it places the decision of release time from prisons in the hands of parole boards, where some believe it should be.[167] These advantages may be eliminated under determinate sentencing.

Maine has a "flat sentencing law." This eliminates indeterminate sentencing only if doing so seems appropriate for the individual offender. However, these mandatory sentences are often as individualized as other sentences.[168]

It seems difficult to eliminate disparity in sentencing. There are problems of recognition and measurement. During the riots of the 1960s, normal sentences had to be suspended in order to preserve order. There are value considerations. Even the new laws on determinate sentencing don't eliminate disparity in sentencing. This is because too many factors are involved.

Conflict Theory

Conflict theory asserts that defendants are sentenced on the basis of occupation, race, and social class.[169] These are extralegal factors and show that sentencing is biased and partial. This is related to disparity in sentencing because it shows inconsistency and inequality in sentencing; however, conflict theory concentrates specifically on social class, occupation, and race.

Discrimination in sentencing, which can be defined as preferential treatment for defendants based on race, class, and occupation, can work in two ways. It can work directly on the basis of race, class, and occupation, or it can work indirectly because defendants can be denied access to bail, private attorneys, etc. — resources which have been found important in gaining a favorable sentencing disposition. For example, poor defendants may not be able to afford bail and therefore have to be incarcerated before sentencing. Incarceration before sentencing can mean a jail sentence instead of probation. This is an example of indirect discrimination.

One study by Clinard and Yeager shows the punishment imposed for white-collar and corporate crime. They point out that administratively imposed warnings are often the first step in enforcing punishment against a corporation. In this study, 582 corporations were analyzed. The authors note that corporate crime represents far more significant personal, social, and monetary damage than does ordinary crime.

The authors discovered that 40 percent of the corporations were not charged with any crime. Some simply were not caught or policed or might have been familiar enough with the law to prevent such action. However, 90 percent of all prosecutions resulted in plea-bargaining of one type or another. Fines were imposed in many cases, and corporations were allowed to claim fines as deductible expenses. The fines exposed were often substantially lower than the maximum allowed. Congress has now increased fines dramatically, but the maximum is rarely imposed.

Probation very often is used as a sanction. In the event of kickbacks, private individuals are generally punished more than corporations because corporations manage to hide kickbacks. Generally, judges don't impose a minimum sentence of jail on corporate offenders as they do on individual criminals.

Total government enforcement of corporate crime is not possible; laws rely upon voluntary compliance. Publicity through the mass media represents the most fearful consequences for corporations, but this is not used often; very little publicity is given to corporate crimes. It is difficult to pinpoint responsibility in corporate crimes because, for example, there are multiple corporations with multiple brand-names and subsidies. In addition, academics have not been interested in corporate crime; they have been mainly interested in ordinary crimes. Victims of corporate crimes, with the exception of such crimes as fraud, don't know that they have been cheated. In addition, corporate crime and white-collar crime don't generate extreme fear among the public. Corporations are seldom referred to as "lawbreakers" or "criminals" in enforcement proceedings, thus obviating the criminal label.[170]

This example shows how sanctions are based on social class and occupation and, perhaps, even on race. Many corporations are million-dollar enterprises, and many corporate executives tend to be in the upper strata of society. Sentences are generally relatively light, and corporations can afford the monetary sanctions imposed on them. Very often, corporations are allowed to hide their crimes, and the public doesn't seem to be concerned about imposing sanctions, perhaps because it is a part of our capitalist society.

Swigert and Farrell studied 444 cases of murder for the years 1955 through 1975. They concluded that the label "normal primitive" worked to indirectly deny defendants so designated access to bail, trial by jury, and access to private legal counsel. These resources were associated with favorable sentencing outcomes. The concept "normal primitive" was based on a popular stereotype or a popular image of defendants who were less educated, older, and less intelligent than other defendants. They were generally from lower-class backgrounds and black, but they also included whites.[171]

Lizotte studied 816 cases in Chicago for the years 1971–1972. He found that both black and white laborers in the lower SES classes were twice as likely as high SES white proprietors to remain incarcerated before sentencing, and were thus more likely to receive longer prison sentences compared to white proprietors. He also found that white laborers were given longer prison sentences compared to black laborers, indicating that judges believed that crimes against blacks were less serious and more normative to black culture than crimes against whites.[172]

Nagel conducted a study on 846 assault cases and 1,103 larceny cases on the state level, and 196 assault and 785 larceny cases on the federal level, for the year 1962. This was a national study involving 50 states. After controlling many variables, he found that the indigent were found guilty more often than the nonindigent. The indigent were less likely to be granted probation and suspended sentences compared to the nonindigent. He found that blacks were discriminated against more in the South than in the North.[173]

These are just a few examples of sentencing based on the conflict theory. There are probably other studies. Sometimes researchers have analyzed studies and concluded that there was no evidence of the conflict theory involved in their samples. For example, Ciricos and Waldo tested the conflict theory by examining 10,458 cases in three states for 17 offenses. They concluded that since the correlation between sentence length and social class was very low, even when controlling many variables, there was no evidence for the conflict theory in sentencing.[174] They have been criticized by several researchers, however, especially by Charles Reasons for including mainly lower SES defendants in their sample.[175]

Organizational Theory

Part of organizational theory involves who is influential in sentencing. For example, La Patra states that there is a significant connection between the thoroughness of a police investigation and the final disposition of a case.[176] Therefore, the police are indirectly influential in sentencing.

Probation officers very often figure in the sentence because they often make sentencing recommendations.[177] However, these recommendations are not always influential.[178] Very often, probation officers have other functions. For example, Newman found that in Michigan the function of the presentence report was to gather evidence in support of, or in contradiction to, the plea of guilty.[179] Sometimes the presentence report by probation officers is scanty, and these reports reflect scarce resources for alternative dispositions.[180]

Dawson, in his study of Milwaukee, found that a presentence report prepared by the probation department was discussed with the prosecutor, defense attorney, probation officer, and the judge.[181] There are some states that don't have a probation service for misdemeanants.[182] However, a presentence report is required in most states.[183]

Defendants themselves have certain perceptions of where the power and influence lie. Casper found in his study in Connecticut that defendants believed that judges were figureheads in decision-making. They believed that judges possessed power but delegated it to the prosecutor.[184]

Thus, it can be seen that power and influence in sentencing is shared among judges, prosecutors, defense attorneys, and probation officers. How much each influences the sentencing process varies by jurisdiction and time. Sentencing is not exclusively a judicial function.

Empirical Evidence

There are many studies on sentencing, dating back to the early part of this century. The list is too long to mention here.[185] Many factors go into sentencing — legal, extralegal, or a combination of legal and extralegal factors.[186] These factors or variables vary by jurisdiction and time, as in other criminal justice analyses.

For example, Silberman states that 85 percent of sentences can be predicted on the basis of the nature of the offense and on the offender's prior record. He also believes that offenses between strangers are given more punitive sanctions than offenses between acquaintances. Therefore, says Silberman, sentencing could be predicted on the basis of a small amount of information.[187] Konečni and Ebbesen believe that very few factors influence the sentencing decision.[188]

The study in Indiana by Meyers revealed that defendants' cases in which the complainant exhibited deviant behavior had less chance of receiving a harsh sentence. The victim's social status had no effect on sentencing. The more serious the conviction charge, the greater the likelihood of an executed sentence; however, the type of sentence was not related to the charge directly or indirectly. The status of the defendant, indirectly, through the charge convicted, had an effect on sentencing; higher-status defendants received more lenient sanctions.[189]

Other factors influence sentencing. Smith and Pollack believe that little has been done to assess the background factors of judges in decision-making.[190] However, Hogarth found that judges' backgrounds were crucial.[191] Nagel also found that judges' backgrounds were very important.[192] The judges' demeanors were also found to be very important.[193] Austin and Williams in their study of judges' responses to five hypothetical cases concluded that there was a high rate of agreement on the verdict of guilt or innocence, but substantial variance on the type of sentence imposed.[194] Campbell found in his study that judges gave a lot of weight to psychiatric evaluations.[195] Neubauer found in Prairie City that rules were important in sentencing.[196] Rosett and Cressey believe that judges sentence mechanically,[197] but Eisenstein and Jacob believe that each case is given a lot of individual attention.[198]

Fines are the most frequent sentence.[199] Most persons are rarely given the maximum sentence.[200]

There are many factors that go into sentencing. Some of these are contradictory, that is, they are important sometimes and unimportant other times. Some have large effects on sentencing, and some have small effects. Judges don't always state reasons for imposing a particular sentence. Frankel believes that judges receive absolutely no instruction in sentencing.[201] Appellate review has little impact on sentencing.[202] Most states don't provide for appellate review.[203]

Some believe that perhaps judges will have to understand management techniques in the future. There will have to be specialists in sentencing.[204]

An Overview

This analysis has included many aspects of the courts. There are probably many other aspects that have not been analyzed. The important points emphasized in this analysis of the courts are that, first, many structures and functions and criminal justice personnel go into the operation of the court. Second, decisions are made all along the way. Third, various factors have various effects and outcomes. Sometimes these factors are similar and sometimes these factors are dissimilar in various aspects of the court system. Fourth, sometimes decisions can be predicted and sometimes they can't. Fifth, in a system such as ours it may be wrong and illogical to solely blame the judge for outcomes. Sixth, the average layman doesn't analyze the criminal justice system in depth.

We now turn to an analysis of the punishment aspects of criminal justice. This is related to corrections. The analysis of punishment and corrections will complete the analysis of the main aspects of the criminal justice system, namely, police, courts, and corrections.

Chapter V
Theories of Punishment

Although punishment is discussed in this chapter and corrections in the following chapter, this division is only for analytical purposes. Also, the subject matter of punishment and corrections is too vast to discuss in one chapter. However, this chapter and the following should be thought of as a whole; punishment and corrections should really be discussed together, because they are related. When a defendant receives a punishment for his crime, whether it is a prison sentence, probation, a conditional discharge, a fine, a drug-treatment program, etc., he or she is not only being punished, but is also expected to reform and to be deterred from future criminal activity.

This chapter will discuss theories of punishment, history of punishment, and reforms of punishment; some empirical examples will be analyzed.

Functions of Punishment

Generally, punishment is divided into four classifications, or functions: incapacitation, deterrence, retribution, and reformation.[1] This author believes, after reviewing the literature, that all four functions of punishment existed from the earliest history of mankind to the present. This author also believes, based on a review of the literature, that all four functions of punishment exist in any form or disposition of punishment imposed on an offender. For example, if an offender is given a prison sentence, the explicit or implicit functions of this sentence are incapacitation, deterrence, retribution, and reformation. The same is true of parole and probation; although the offender is not incapacitated here (i.e., not incarcerated), the threat of incarceration exists if an offender violates the rules of probation or parole. Also, the rules may be an impingement on an offender's freedom, and thus may be perceived as a form of incapacitation.

In other words, the four functions of punishment are not mutually exclusive. It is true that one or two functions are emphasized to the exclusion or diminution of the other functions, but the other functions exist, at least implicitly. There is both agreement and disagreement on this. For example,

Frances A. Allen believes that incapacitation is the real function of the rehabilitation ideal.[2] Honderich doesn't believe that punishment is either treatment or revenge.[3] The government of Canada believes that deterrence and rehabilitation are difficult to reconcile.[4] Lonford believes that the deterrent, reformative, and protective functions of punishment may conflict.[5]

The debate goes on. Reviewing the literature, one finds that some believe that the functions of punishment are separated, are mutually exclusive. Some, on the other hand, believe that all functions are intermixed and difficult to separate, even for analytical purposes.[6] There is really no right or wrong answer. It is possible to emphasize one function of punishment to the exclusion of the other functions, perhaps because the other functions are hidden. Incarceration, for example, is thought of mainly as incapacitation, because the reformative aspects of prison are hidden and not explicitly stated. The purpose of fines, for example, is mainly perceived as deterrence, because offenders must pay money to gain their freedom; the other functions are not emphasized. Further examples abound.

It is also revealed in the literature that the debate on punishment is both universal and quite old, dating back to antiquity. Punishment is universal, found on every level of society, from the primitive to the most highly advanced.[7] Corrections, defined as the means by which society punishes those who break the rules, predates written history.[8]

It is also the author's belief that the four functions of punishment existed from very early times of recorded history. The origin of any form of punishment is debatable. Allen believes that reformation and rehabilitation have their origin in the thought of the medieval churchmen.[9] Plato believed that punishment and education were intermixed.[10] Bentham, probably the most influential of the Utilitarian school, believed that punishment served the threefold functions of incapacitation, deterrence, and reformation.[11] Treatment of offenders dates to at least the introduction of the medical model, which is at least several hundred years old.[12] In the nineteenth century, in England, deterrence was the sole aim of the penal law.[13]

Most critics believe that the modern prison as we know it is the product of recent times, the last two hundred years or so. However, Newman believes that prisons as a punishment device existed for centuries. Newman also believes that punishment as a reforming device was rarely considered in the past.[14] Socrates believed that punishment should both deter and reform the criminal.[15] These examples are evidence, in this author's opinion, that the four functions of punishment had their origin in very early times of recorded history, and that the functions are intermixed.

What Is Punishment?

There is no agreement on the definition of punishment or on what constitutes treatment. There is no agreement on the severity of punishment.

Punishment means different things to different people. However, punishment involves values of some kind which are imbedded in our society. Punishment must be administered by a legal authority or institution. One purpose of punishment is to reinforce the social order, to preserve the status quo. Fear is implicit in punishment.

Two men who receive the same punishment may benefit very differently from it. A sentence of five years in prison is not necessarily five times greater than one year in prison; this relationship may not be linear. Individual factors interact to produce different effects for identical or similar punishments. However, if punishment is to be individualized, there must exist unequal punishments for similar offenses. In fact, our legal system doesn't recognize individualization of punishment.

It is believed that dangerousness of offenders cannot be predicted.[16] Dangerousness is not the only criterion in punishment. Other factors are important. Punishment itself may have long-term effects which cannot be evaluated for a long time after it is administered. The argument against punishment is that no one is responsible for his actions and perhaps society is to blame. This is the old and famous debate between free will and determinism in criminal justice.

There have been many critics of our punishment system, and many philosophical questions have been posed. Herbert Morris asks whether it is just to punish.[17] D.J.B. Hawkins asserts that a scale of penalties would not necessarily correspond to the moral guilt involved in an offense.[18] Gordon Hawkins compares a sentence an offender receives after trial and conviction to a public degradation ceremony in which the public identity of the offender is lowered in the eyes of the social scale. He believes that the public degradation ceremonies are universal, with the exception that the conditions of degradation ceremonies are lacking in societies where anomie exists.[19]

Wilson asks the question: Do judges know what amount of suffering they are inflicting when they sentence an offender according to the law? She states that Americans didn't realize how cruel imprisonment was when they substituted imprisonment for floggings and hence made their sentences long. She believes that America is 50 years behind England in penal matters.[20]

Moberly believes that an exact mathematical equality between crime and punishment is impractical, meaningless, and misconceived. He believes that punishment cannot make a conscience where none exists; the offender must regard punishment as just for him. Cases that look alike, says Moberly, may differ widely beneath the surface. Moberly believes that it is delusive to think that a set of rules can be applied universally in punishment. He emphasizes that punishment need not be intensely painful to obtain its purpose.[21]

Esselstyn does not believe that we have a well-articulated theory of justice as yet. Therefore, we don't have a well-articulated theory of punishment.[22] Newman believes that punishment must involve some kind of pain, deprivation or suffering to be considered punishment.[23] This is somewhat contradictory to Moberly's assertion that punishment need not be intensely painful to be effective.[24]

We do not know how informed the public is about criminal penalties.[25] Freeman asks under what circumstances it is ethical to compel an offender to be treated under the concept of corrections.[26] Forer remarks that judges rarely know what therapy is or what effect it has on offenders.[27]

These and similar assertions and questions have been raised by various critics of our punishment and correctional system throughout history. This is why a single definition of punishment will not suffice. One definition of punishment often given is the imposition of penal sanctions by a legal authority against offenders who commit crimes against the people. However, this hardly does justice to the concept.

Historical Theoretical Schools of Punishment

The Classical and Neoclassical schools were prominent several hundred years ago. Abadinsky states that free will is basic to the Classical school,[28] but it is difficult to determine if he was talking about the old Classical school or the new Classical school. However, according to Saleilles, in the Classical school, all criminals were placed on the same footing. They were regarded as equally responsible. The punishment imposed was the same for all. Saleilles also distinguishes between the Italian school, which reduces everything to natural factors, to the environment, and Neoclassicism, which reduces everything to responsibility and free will. The Neoclassical position takes account of the individual, state of the will, and degree of culpability, while the Italian school leaves no room for these factors.[29]

One of the strongest figures in the Neoclassical school was Beccaria, an Italian. Beccaria defined penalties for different crimes. He believed that punishment should correspond to the severity of the crime, although punishment might not deter crime. He believed that there should be particular penalties for particular crimes, and that judges should give equal sanctions; he knew of unequal sentences for the rich and the poor. He believed in a system of fines, prison, and banishment, but he opposed confiscation of property. He favored humane conditions in prison. He believed that certain persons, the insane for example, should be treated in a certain manner and be excluded from regular punishment.

Beccaria believed that capital punishment didn't deter crime, and should only be used in unusual cases. He believed that prison was a good alternative to execution and torture, which were prevalent in his day. He believed that the rate of crime varied inversely with the certainty, celerity, and severity of punishment. However, he believed that the certainty of punishment was more important than the severity of punishment. He was not concerned with rehabilitation.[30]

Gibbs believes that Beccaria failed to formulate a specific theory of punishment. He applies the same criticism to Bentham.[31] Neier states that Beccaria was far ahead of his time, and even our time. He states that Beccaria had a major influence on the American colonies. He states that Jefferson was influenced by Beccaria; like Beccaria, Jefferson believed that punishment should not be too severe.[32] Newman believes that Beccaria didn't know the law.[33]

Another prominent school of punishment was Utilitarianism, with Jeremy Bentham as one of the principal adherents. Some critics classify Bentham as a Neoclassicist. However, Newman believes that the Utilitarian principle is probably the oldest form of punishment, and that it is the most dominant in Western civilization. According to Newman, the basic Utilitarian punisher saw nothing wrong with pain and would inflict it when necessary. According to the Utilitarians, the state is essential for the administration of punishment.[34]

Bentham worked out a complex system of pain and pleasure for various acts. He also worked out a comprehensive system of social reform which included criminal law, government, penology, suffrage, welfare, etc. He believed that the penalties for crime should not be any greater than the distress caused by the crime. Like Beccaria, he believed that punishment should be certain, severe, and swift, but that certainty was the most important. Bentham had lofty aims of public and social welfare, not just of crime and punishment. He was the first to relate prison to crime. He considered banishment bad because it had an unequal effect on different offenders. He advocated individualization of punishment based on age, sex, fortune, etc. He showed sentiment for the welfare of the offender.[35]

The Positivist school of punishment was another major theme in the history of punishment. The Positivists emphasized law and prediction. Their theme was that punishment should fit the criminal, not the crime. Therefore, under Positivism, all criminals would not receive the same punishment for identical crimes. Under the Positivist school, emphasis was on treatment, reformation, and rehabilitation.

There were many critics of punishment who historically were outspoken in the development of punishment. It is difficult to place some of these critics into particular schools. Kant, for example, a prominent philosopher, believed that offenders should be punished because they deserved it. He believed that severity of punishment depended upon the seriousness of the crime. He believed that the offender should suffer as much injury as he inflicted upon the victim, and that punishment should be analogous to the injury suffered by the victim.[36] He believed in retribution and believed in treating persons as an end.[37] Voltaire and Montesquieu deplored punishment. In fact, Beccaria was influenced by them.[38]

Enrico Ferri was a proponent of social defense and a critic of the Classical school. He was not considered a Utilitarian. Ferri was considered a Marxist, and although he recognized reformation as a worthwhile goal of punishment, he relegated it to secondary importance. He believed that the victims of crime should be compensated by the state.[39]

Ferri believed that crime would diminish by an improvement in the individual and social conditions of the community, not by legal measures. He believed that prisons would not deter all criminals because some offenders were dedicated to a life of crime as an occupation and, therefore, calculated the risk of prison in committing crimes. He believed, like Beccaria and Bentham, that certainty of punishment was more potent than the severity of punishment. He argued that the modern system of punishment had failed to protect society against crime. He believed that restitution in the form of money rather than a short period of imprisonment would be more effective as punishment for minor crimes. He believed that 70 percent of all crimes discovered are unpunished. He affirmed that classification of offenders was more efficacious and practical than individualization of punishment.[40]

Durkheim really didn't talk about crime in great detail. However, he believed that a proper measure of punishment was the degree to which the public suffered indignation or resentment caused by the offense.[41] This coincides with his theory that the structure and integration of society were important in sociology.

Menninger believed that a psychiatric model was the only appropriate model for criminal offenders. This is indicated by the title of his book, *The Crime of Punishment*.[42]

Garofalo, a student of Lombroso, believed in death for offenders who were so psychologically unbalanced that they were unfit to live in society. Garofalo also devised a classification system which was in disagreement with that of Ferri.[43]

Owens believed that the structure of society should be changed so that no one should be punished. He set up a community in which the conditions of life were changed so that crime disappeared entirely. He proposed the abolition of laws, and he believed in the laws of nature.[44]

De Tocqueville believed that certainty of punishment was more important than severity of punishment as a prevention against crime. He believed that reformation and punishment were not effective.[45]

Thomas Jefferson wanted punishment to fit the crime and the criminal to suffer no more than his offense deserved.[46]

Theories on the Functions of Punishment

Deterrence is one function of punishment. Gibbs states that deterrence is nonobservable and hence immeasurable. He points out that studies on deterrence have been limited to capital punishment, and he notes the paucity of deterrence studies on fines, which are a very common sanction. Gibbs lists variables which must be taken into account when doing research on deterrence. These are public knowledge of punishments, cognition of criminal acts, perceived certainty of punishment, perceived severity of actual punishments, objective celerity of punishments, pereceived celerity of punishments, and perceived severity of prescribed punishments. In other words, deterrence is not a unitary concept.[47]

Clinand and Yeager believe that deterrence is the major goal of corporate criminal sanctions.[48] Miller and others suggest that penalties for crimes cannot act as a deterrent because penalties are unknown until after a person has committed a crime. Even when an offender is incarcerated, they point out, knowledge of penalties doesn't act as a strong deterrent against future criminal activity; about one-third of all offenders who are incarcerated at least once continue to recidivate.[49] This author believes that this statement is too simple. Whether a prison sentence appears to deter depends on empirical research. Unless deterrence is analyzed empirically, generalizations on deterrence are only speculative.

Retribution is another function of punishment. There has been relatively little written on this function, and practically no research on the topic. Newman states that the theory behind retribution assumes that offenders are punished in a way which is similar to the harm incurred by the offense. Theoretically — though rarely in reality — retribution is like a fair exchange which acts as an equilibrium. Newman says that history has documented that the taking of life was the primitive supreme satisfaction of vengeance. He also mentions that punishment incurred on various parts of the body was seen as a form of retribution.

Newman believes that retribution is complicated by the fact that the amount of harm done by a crime is accompanied by moral issues, and by the fact that we have no modern retributive system from which to make observations.[50]

Morris and Buckle believe that practically every society has abandoned the retribution theory.[51] This author finds that statement is debatable. Retribution can be unconsciously imbedded in a system of punishment.

Bittner and Platt state that in the Near East, mob violence against persons who offended some religious taboo was an example of retribution.[52] However, the authors don't state whether the punishment was similar to the harm caused by the offense.

The early Jews believed in retribution. They believed in an eye for an eye and a tooth for a tooth. They also believed in a life for a life. Some of this seems unjust and some just today.[53]

The early clans sought vengeance when one of their members was injured. This was an early form of retribution.[54]

The most extensive treatment of retribution is given by Ranulf. He believes that retribution is tied to moral indignation, which in turn was connected with the rising power of the lower middle classes. He claims that retribution is disguised in the disinterested tendency to inflict punishment.

Retribution disappears in communities in which the lower middle classes were of little significance and where they had obtained a certain wealth. Calvinism is associated with retribution. The Puritans, he states, were inclined toward punishment. The Japanese lack a tendency to inflict punishment. He claims that it is difficult to prove retributive tendencies among primitive people, although anthropologists assume that these tendencies exist. In Russia, Ranulf says, offenders were once rehabilitated into society;

there was no attempt to stigmatize them. However, he states , things have changed in Russia. Ranulf states that retribution will be suppressed during wars and revolutions.[55]

Treatment is another function of punishment. Toby states that the fact that industrialized societies are calling methods of dealing with offenders "treatment" rather than "punishment" means that perhaps increasing proportions of people are willing to accept the "sick" label of nonconformity. Toby states that it is erroneous to believe that treatment is always considered pleasant.[56]

The indeterminate sentence was introduced into American society in the late nineteenth century. The purpose, according to Berkson, was to individualize the needs of the offender.[57] The use of the indeterminate sentence can certainly be considered a form of treatment. Generally, treatment and rehabilitation are associated with the Positivist school of criminology and the Medical Model, but it is certainly possible that treatment originated much earlier in history.

Newman talks about the Obedience Model, which is now known as deterrence. The Obedience Model was based on inequality, and it dominated in the early periods of the history of punishment. In the Obedience Model, punisher and offender were unequal in status. A later model of punishment was the Receprocity Model, which is really retribution. The Reciprocity Model is based on punishment between equals. Newman believes that the Reciprocity Model never fully materialized because punishment is not really between equals. The state is involved in punishment. Nor does he believe that the two models are opposed to each other. He believes that physical pain is an equalizer of punishment, because it cuts across status differentials.[58]

Another function of punishment is incapacitation. This will be discussed in the next chapter in reference to prison. Other forms of incapacitation are halfway houses and drug programs.

The History of Punishment

A review of the literature reveals some of the most barbaric punishments devised by man against offenders. Some of the common forms of punishment were beheading, branding, breaking on the wheel, burning, burying alive, cannibalism, crank, cursing, cutting wrists off, disembowelling, drill, drowning, dunking stool, exile, flogging, forced labor, guillotine, hanging, incarceration, insolation, mutilation of corpses, placing heads and quarters of executed offenders in various parts of the country, pulling, rod, short drill, selling criminals into slavery, stoning, stockade, transportation, treadmill, whipping, etc. However, the history of punishment did not proceed in a linear fashion; it proceeded more in cyclical fashion. Although history records all forms of punishment, some of the most barbaric forms of punishment were restricted to certain countries and certain periods of time.[59]

For example, the death penalty almost never existed in Classical Rome, although it is debatable whether the slaves were subjected to death. Punishment for crime depended on the actions of private citizens, who hired other private citizens, the forerunners of our prosecutors, to intervene. The public authority intervened only when the offender refused to pay restitution in civil cases.[60]

Physical punishments were rare during the Middle Ages. The bulk of punishments up to the beginning of the sixteenth century were mainly economic sanctions, e.g., fines, restitution, or confiscation of possessions.[61] Death penalties were not often used in England during the Middle Ages, but when they were carried out, they were accompanied by quartering and disembowelling alive.[62] Carney believes that punishment was unknown in primitive societies, although this is debatable. Banishment was used instead, but this often meant death because the offender was usually killed by hostile tribes. Carney believes that punishment is still unknown in some primitive societies today.[63] In fact, in primitive societies it was common for victim and offender to be reconciled.[64]

Torture was not permitted among ancient Jews, but they held seven classes of offenses as punishable by death.[65] In colonial America, restitution and exile were used as forms of punishment, although whipping and branding were also used. Offenders who would not pay their fines were whipped, branded, or even subjected to capital punishment.[66] Newman believes that corporal punishment was more prevalent in colonial America than in England.[67]

Religion was also associated with punishment at various times in history. Placing of heads and distribution of quarters of bodies of executed offenders were common forms of punishment in England. Beheading in Greek and Roman times was restricted to war. Exile was prevalent as a form of punishment in Roman times. The Inquisition, in which alleged heretics were sometimes burned, lasted for six centuries, but never developed in England. Physical punishment, corporal punishment, and capital punishment began in England in the seventeenth century with the use of parliamentary power and the weakening of the monarchy. This coincided with the beginning of the Industrial Revolution. Hanging was a public spectacle in England. Bentham was influential in eliminating the worst barbaric punishments in England.[68]

The ticket-of-leave and transportation systems were prevalent in England during the eighteenth and nineteenth centuries. Prisoners and their families were sent to Australia and America, where some were given free land. Many did well, but some, especially in Australia, died of starvation and maltreatment.[69]

The barbaric forms of punishment, although cruel, had a logic to them. For example, the theory behind disembowelling was based on the fact that certain organs were thought to be the seat of crime.[70] The Greeks and the Romans believed that water from the spring or sea washed away guilt.[71] Burning of witches during the Middle Ages was based on the theory that body and soul were exterminated or sent far away, and that fire drives out demons.[72]

Rusche and Kirchheimer believed that the struggle for existence influenced the penal system in such a way that it prevented too great an increase in population.[73] Punishment has taken on the cruel forms it has because of the fear of what the criminal would do after the death. There was also some correlation between the severity of the crime and the type of penalty prescribed.[74] However, Saleilles believed that punishment didn't vary according to the crime.[75]

Inequality in Administration of Punishment

There was evidence of inequality in administering punishment throughout history. Women were treated better than men in the Middle Ages. Women in England in the fourteenth century were treated lightly and slaves more harshly.[76] The death penalty was very rarely used on women in the United States because women committed fewer murders than men.[77] During the eighteenth century burning at the stake was reserved for women. This was considered a mitigative punishment compared to the disembowelling and quartering imposed on men.[78]

The guillotine was introduced because of the practice of class distinctions on death. The aristocrats were executed by sword.[79] Hanging was reserved for commoners, beheading for kings, and the guillotine for important people.[80] The upper classes were treated preferentially compared to the lower classes during the Middle Ages.[81] The Utilitarian Period was marked by discrimination with regard to minorities, e.g. women, children, slaves, criminals, etc.[82]

Ancient Greeks had a double standard of justice, one for citizens and one for noncitizens (e.g. slaves, freemen, métis, foreigners, etc.). In German society, beheading was reserved for the rich and hanging for the poor, and in Frankish society, punishment depended on one's caste.[83] England exempted the insane from execution, and there is evidence that juveniles were treated more leniently in biblical times and from the twelfth century on.[84]

There is evidence that many offenders either escaped punishment altogether or managed to get away with light punishment even in the most punishment-oriented societies. For example, outlaws could purchase a pardon in England. During the Industrial Revolution in England, many cases were dismissed for insignificant reasons. Crime was prevalent among the young, and many cases were dismissed because of the youthfulness of the offender. During the eighteenth century in England there were many alternatives to the death penalty.[85]

In England, many prisoners were sent to the English colonies as indentured servants.[86] In some states in America — South Carolina, for example — benefit of clergy was practiced, in which the clergy were able to mitigate punishment for some offenders.[87] Benefit of clergy, which exempted anyone who could read from punishment was practiced for hundreds of years. This exempted the better-educated from punishment.[88] Benefit of clergy was practiced in England during early times. The church courts were known to be much more lenient than ordinary civil courts.[89]

There were many instances in which offenders in England were exempted from punishment. For example, if a rope broke in a hanging, a pardon was granted immediately. In England in Basle, every woman who was sentenced to drown was set free if she reached a certain place downstream. What was difficult to explain was the pardoning of every tenth man in mass executions at the will of the executioner. However, most ancient cultures had no place for pardons.[90] During the eighteenth century, death and transportation were the most prevalent forms of punishment. Courts frequently withheld punishment because of its harshness.[91]

As mentioned previously, in colonial America, punishment usually consisted of fines and exile, and offenders who couldn't pay their fines were forced to labor, were whipped, placed in stocks, and branded. However, juries realized that convictions meant harsh sentences, and they often returned a verdict of not guilty or imposed a light sentence on first offenders.[92]

In England, during the eighteenth century, juries would not convict and witnesses would not testify because they knew that the criminal code was much harsher than public opinion would tolerate. Offenders did what they could to gain a reprieve.[93]

Newman declares that up to the fifteenth century an elaborate system of pardons existed.[94] There was a rise in pardons in England in capital cases after 1750 because judges believed that the death penalty was too severe for minor infractions. There was evidence at this time that victims chose not to prosecute for fear of sending offenders to the gallows, indicating disapproval of harsh penal codes. Some prosecutors also abandoned the prosecution of minor offenses because they believed that death was excessive punishment for minor criminals.[95]

Reforms

There were many outstanding reformers of punishment throughout history. Cruel punishment, however, has been a topic for centuries.[96] For example, the death penalty was abolished in many states in America from 1794 and on. The United States was more advanced than England and much of Europe in this respect. Benjamin Rush published a paper in 1787 denouncing public executions, and by the 1830s and 1840s many states began to conduct their executions inside prison walls, although large crowds were allowed to attend inside. The last public execution in the United States took place in Kentucky on August 14, 1936.[97] Some states reenacted the death penalty in the 1970s and 1980s.

Subsequent to the entrance of Vermont into the Union in 1791, of the 36 states which had been admitted to the Union, only two, Louisiana and Arkanas, entered without a prohibition of some kind against cruel and unusual punishment. The Supreme Court's first recorded judicial opinion in the United States against cruel and unusual punishment was recorded by the Supreme Court of Errors in Connecticut in 1811. Since 1910, there have been 1,798 opinions containing the argument of cruel and unusual punishment. Most of this litigation, however, has been confined to the southeastern part of this country.[98]

The Great Law of Pennsylvania, enacted in 1682, sought to eliminate to a considerable degree the stocks, the pillories, branding irons, and the gallows.[99]

The Quakers, or Society of Friends, were the only religious groups which in early modern times protested against corporal punishment. This is in contrast to the Christians, who not only failed to demand reforms, but also actually condoned certain forms of punishment. Some of the reformers of Europe, for example, Howard and Bentham in England, and Montesquieu of France, were directly or indirectly responsible for prison reform and reform of the penal codes in the United States.[100]

We have already seen Beccaria as a prominent figure in the Classical school. He was also considered a reformer of the penal system and punishment. He believed that the accused should be treated in a humane way before trial and should be given every right and opportunity to give evidence in his own behalf. He believed in a system of fines for offenses against property, but he believed in imprisonment if the fines weren't paid. He believed that banishment was fitting for crimes against the state (e.g. treason). Beccaria believed in imprisonment compared to the death penalty, but he believed that conditions in prison should be improved by arranging for better living quarters and classifying prisoners according to sex, age, and degree of criminality.[101]

In England, in 1812 and 1814, due to the influence of Romilly, capital punishment was reduced for very obsolete crimes, and disembowelling as punishment for treason was abolished. Reform had begun in England, and acts were initiated to improve every aspect of criminal justice. Peel was most famous in the establishment of a police force.[102] Prison chaplains tended to oppose public executions. Public opinion called for the abolition of punishment.[103] Public execution was eventually abolished in England in 1868.[104]

Sellin notes that the treadmill was attacked by English humanitarians as not only cruel, but also ineffective in working any reform in the convict. Some believed that the crane was safer than the wheel, although this was never proven.[105]

Due to reform in England, the death penalty was drastically reduced: and between 1828 and 1834, only one in 20 death penalties was carried out, and still fewer were carried out in 1836. Offenders instead were sentenced to prison and transportation to Australia. Wives and children were allowed to accompany offenders to the penal colony free. They were allowed to lease or purchase land, and many single men were allowed to marry. Many seemed to live peaceful and uneventful lives.[106]

The Italian code of 1889 allowed judges to take motives into account and to substitute one punishment for another.[107]

It seemed that a system of reform spread worldwide.

Empirical Studies

There are many empirical studies on the four functions of punishment. Some of these will now be discussed.

A study revealed that rape in Philadelphia did not decline after a marked increase in the severity of prescribed punishment for this type of crime.[108]

Robert Martinson and others analyzed 238 treatment studies. They concluded that these studies gave little evidence that any mode of correctional treatment had a decisive effect in reducing recidividism.[109]

A study of rehabilitative services on 2,860 offenders in 53 projects was undertaken in New York City. After spending enormous amounts of resources and time to maximize the accuracy of the data, and after using advanced statistical techniques (e.g. regression, analysis of variance, and cluster analysis), and after studying job training and placement, remedial education, mental health counseling, and other techniques, the author concludes that rehabilitative services outside of correctional institutions do not prevent recidivism.[110]

Reports indicate that when Massachusetts closed the juvenile centers, there was no discernible increase in juvenile crime; in fact, there was a slight decrease in the arrest rate.[111]

There have been pros and cons on the prediction of dangerousness in criminal behavior. Kozol and others believe that dangerousness in criminal offenders can be reliably diagnosed and effectively treated with a recidivism rate of 6.1 percent. They base their conclusions on a study of 592 male offenders who were mainly accused of sex crimes. The treatment staff diagnosed 304 of them as not dangerous, and they were released. Twenty-six, 8.6 percent, subsequently committed serious assaults. Two hundred and twenty-six were diagnosed as dangerous. After 43 months of intensive treatment, 82 were released. Only 5, or 6.1 percent, committed serious assault crimes. Forty-nine of the originally committed patients were released against advice of the court; seventeen, 34.7 percent, committed serious assault, including one murder.

The authors conclude that dangerousness in criminal offenders can be reliably diagnosed and effectively treated with a recidivism rate of 6.1 percent. However, they also conclude that no one can predict dangerous behavior in an individual with no history of dangerous acting-out.[112]

Weeks studied 69 offenders classified as violent and nonviolent by three independent judges who had no contact with the prisoners. The ratings of the judges were based primarily on the current offense and past criminal history of the offenders. Based on analysis of variance, Weeks concluded that there was no significant difference between violent and nonviolent offenders in their actions.[113]

Sellin is known for his doctrine that the death penalty does not deter murder. Ernest van den Haag disputed this finding. Van den Haag believed that Sellin's data were inaccurate. Isaac Erlich also disputed Sellin's findings. Using multivariate statistical techniques, he believed that the death penalty might deter as many as eight murders for every execution carried out. Erlich assembled data on the frequency of murder over a ten-year period. He controlled many variables, e.g. consistency of enforcement, likelihood of capture, etc. — variables which Sellin hadn't controlled. Even interviews with murderers and felons indicated that they had been deterred by the death penalty. Some believe, however, that Erlich has overstated the deterrent effects of capital punishment.[114]

A study was done in Chicago and Milwaukee to see if special penal sanctions would deter drunken driving. Judges in Chicago announced publicly and widely that they would imprison for seven days anyone convicted of drunken driving; they also announced that they would suspend the driver's license for one year. Milwaukee did not have such a policy. The crackdown on drunken drivers began on December 18, 1970. Analysis of time series data before and after January 1969 revealed that there was a significant statistical reduction in driving fatalities both in Chicago and Milwaukee after January 1969. The authors conclude that the crackdown on drunken drivers had no deterrent effect in Chicago. They could not, however, explain the general decrease in fatalities.[115]

Data were collected on all persons accused of violent crimes in Franklin County, Ohio, in 1972. Arrest records, court records, and F.B.I. records were also analyzed. The authors conclude that incapacitation makes a small and modest impact on violent crimes. Others believe that incapacitation does not prevent much crime.[116]

Within the past ten years more than 75 scholarly papers on the subject of deterrence have been published in leading journals. A three-state study was done in New Jersey, Iowa, and Oregon. Probability sampling was used on 1,993 respondents over 15 years old. The dependent variable was a respondent's personal estimated probability of future deviance under a hypothetical condition in which he or she might commit a crime. The object was to get data on individual perceptions of the probability of being caught and punished for a variety of deviant acts and to relate these perceptions to individual self-reports of deviant conduct.

The results showed that deterrence was a complicated process. Younger respondents were less deterred. Respondents who move geographically a great deal were less deterred. Those who live in big cities were not the least deterred. Community spirit and religious association had a positive relation to deterrence. Social class was not found important in deterrence. Seriousness of offense was important in deterrence.

The author concludes that sanction fear is most effective in deterring criminals. Contrary to popular belief, perceived severity of punishment is more important than certainty of punishment for many crimes. However, certainty of punishment is still important. Informal sanctions are sometimes more important for deterrence than formal legal sanctions.

The author concludes that researchers have not taken account of perceptual thresholds and as a result make generalizations that are erroneous. For example, there will be more deterrence from perceptions of severity of informal sanctions and certainty of legal sanctions than by severity of formal sanctions and certainty of informal sanctions, because of deterrence thresholds. The author also concludes that severity is highly subjective.[117]

There are many researchers who generalize conclusions on punishment. This author believes that these generalizations are open to empirical investigation.

For example, Barnes claims that history has proven that severe punishments have never reduced crime to any marked degree.[118] Andenaes claims that carefully planned acts are more easily deterred than those that are the result of sudden emotional impulses.[119] Rusche and Kirchheimer conclude after studying the crime rates that a more severe penal policy in Italy has had no more effect on crime than a relatively lenient penal policy.[120]

The Commission of Canada in a report stated that deterrence is low regarding crimes of passion even though punishment is certain. It also states that jail sentences do not have a strong effect on check forgers. Businessmen, on the other hand, admit that even short-term sentences produce fear. Crimes against persons are usually considered to be less responsive to the threat of punishment because they involve a minimum of rational deliberation. The Commission concludes that offenders guided by impulse rather than by premeditation, judgment, and reflection are less likely to be restrained by punishment because they are less likely to reflect on the consequences of their acts. The Commission concludes that the costs of any type of penal sanction, e.g. imprisonment, varies by social class. It concludes that recidivism is not a sign that punishment is ineffective. Some of these generalizations may be true; others, in the opinion of this author, are open to empirical analysis.[121]

Conclusions

It appears that punishment is a very complicated process. We don't know for certain if punishment deters, treats, incapacitates, or is a form of retribution, in spite of empirical evidence. It seems that punishment has been debated since antiquity. The same questions about punishment bothered philosophers for centuries. Have we progressed?

It appears that punishment has abated in cruelty. We are generally more humane now than one hundred or two hundred years ago. Even capital punishment is being debated. However, social processes go in cycles, and it is possible for older forms of punishment to prevail in certain parts of the world. For example, capital punishment is being reactivated in several states in America.

Specific forms of punishment will be discussed in the next chapter. These should be thought of in conjunction with theories of correction. Prison, probation, parole, and other alternatives will be discussed in light of theoretical and empirical issues.

Chapter VI
Theories of Corrections

In this chapter there will be a discussion of some of the most important theories of prison, parole, probation, and alternatives in corrections. There will be a discussion on the history of the types of correction. Some empirical evidence will be presented. Any type of corrections should be thought of as representing the four functions of punishment.

Prison

It is a mistake to assume that all prisons are alike. One cannot generalize about prisons because prisons vary.[1] Jacobs in his study of Stateville, noted that there was no single "type" of prison.[2] Irwin noted, in his history of prisons, that a big mistake of early students of the prison was to consider prisons as isolated, uniform, and unchanging.[3]

For example, women's prisons differ from men's prisons. Maximum-security prisons may differ from minimum-security prisons. Federal prisons have more industry than most other prisons because their market consists of all federal government agencies, including the armed forces.[4] Certain institutions, like maximum-security institutions, with poor food, house low-income inmates, while "showcase" institutions, with good food, house white-collar inmates, embezzlers, or Watergate conspirators.[5] In New York, it has been stated that blacks go to Clinton, Attica, and whites go to Walkill.[6]

The jails of New York are considered to be among the best in the country.[7] South Carolina is said to have one of the most advanced prison systems in the nation.[8] What makes one prison better than another is open to empirical investigation.

There is no "typical" inmate.[9] The effects of incarceration among inmates are not uniform.[10] For example, all guards are not brutal.[11] Some observe that some guards are "pretty nice and pretty human."[12] Some have said that the brutal and sadistic guard is so rare that he is hardly considered a problem.[13] Others have remarked that it is wrong to think that guards are the wrong type of people; if they are given the right job and proper training, they can handle their job.[14]

Jails differ from prisons. Jails are supposed to house offenders awaiting sentence or trial, or short-term sentenced offenders. Goldfarb believes that jails are worse than prisons. They have been studied little. Jails hold between three to four million people. In 1967, the majority of prisoners were misdemeanants. Jail programs for misdemeanants are rare. Inmates are not given household duties in jails. About 50 percent of jails have no medical facilities. Dental treatment in jails is limited. Addicts are not noticed in jails.[15]

Offenders who spend time in jail or prison find it difficult to report life in prison accurately.[16] There have been, however, many empirical accounts of jails and prisons.

History of the Prison

As mentioned previously, some believe that prisons are a modern invention. Yet, prisons existed in antiquity and reached their height during the Spanish Inquisition.[17] The origins of imprisonment are lost in antiquity.[18] It is difficult to know the date of the beginnings of imprisonment.[19] According to McKelvey, the true history of prisons has not been written, because no student has been able to disentangle the factional rivalries and personal ambitions that have dominated prisons.[20]

Jails were used in America from 1635, but they were small and used infrequently. Maintenance was a problem. Prisons in 1801 contained many debtors, servants, and paupers.[21] Prisons were highly profitable until 1890.[22] The early prisons didn't hinder the offender from productive work, marriage, and family.[23] The prisoners earned their keep through profitable labor, and even earned enough to make restitution of debts, to pay for costs of trial, and have enough money left for themselves.[24] Prisoners were charged for their board.[25] In England, debtors were allowed to live with wives, and relatives could purchase some rights.[26]

In America, a great battle developed between the Auburn and Pennsylvania systems. Under both systems, the prisoners worked, but silence prevailed all the time under the Pennsylvania system. In the Auburn system, prisoners were allowed to interact during the day, but remained silent at night. The idea was to repent, and this was the origin of the penitentiary system. Americans adopted the Auburn system and Europeans the Pennsylvania system.[27] The penitentiary in England was criticized for being both too severe and not severe enough. In England, all prisons, schools, refuges and factories looked alike.[28]

Prisons were more open in the past than today. People went to trade, visit, and to look at condemned prisoners. In England, wives of gaolers helped their husbands run the prisons. Prisons were often sold.[29]

In early prisons, the correctional role was precise.[30] Jeremy Bentham, John Howard, Sir James MacKintosh, and Elizabeth Fry were early reformers of the prison.[31] The treatment of prisoners in colonial times was benign compared to treatment received in the penitentiary.[32] In the nineteenth and early twentieth centuries, prisons were managed by inmates, and inmates acted as police and watched other inmates; inmates were tried by inmate courts.[33] The mortality rate in the early prisons was high.[34] Prisons were overcrowded in the past and there were riots in the prisons,[35] and there is evidence that prisoners were shot in the South.[36] There were medical experiments performed on prisoners in Mississippi in 1914, and this is also true today.[37]

There was a need for reform. In the past, all kinds of offenders were in prison together, and in England, crowds tried to free prisoners in jail.[38] In America, in the past, because of racial prejudice, prisoners were separated by race.[39] This made control in prison much easier than today.[40] After 1820, silence, bread and water, and in England, the introduction of the treadmill, all marked steps to tighten security. However, in London, people started to steal to get committed to houses of correction, because economic conditions were better in prison than on the outside.[41] Men in prison sometimes had more to eat than the starving poor outside.[42]

Weekend furloughs in prisons are at least 200 years old.[43] Conjugal visiting started in Mississippi in 1918, but it started in America in 1900.[44] The treatment of imprisoned women between 1790 and 1870 was primitive; there were overcrowded conditions with poor food and poor medical care, with little hope of employment upon discharge. There was need for a separate women's prison. During the twentieth century major improvements were made in the treatment of female offenders in New York City.[45]

De Tocqueville was a major critic of the penitentiary in the United States. Generally he believed that prisons were not successful.[46] Crofton introduced work-release programs in Ireland, and Maconochie in Norfolk, Australia, introduced indeterminate sentences and established work programs. He also introduced a system of marks for good behavior. Maconochie, as governor of the colony of Australia, opened up his prison to inmate involvement and initiated humane reforms and originated parole. Gill in America and Maconochie in Australia had inmates serving in the police force with no ill effects.[47]

Some believe that the contemporary prison is not an improvement over the whipping-post or stocks.[48] About 50,000 prisoners are still housed in maximum-security prisons which were built before 1900.[49] Some believe that prisons are no less brutal today than in the past. Psychological coercion has replaced physical coercion. Mental brutality sometimes is more severe than physical brutality.[50]

Prisoners won many legal rights recently. The decisions in prisoners' favor between 1967 and 1972 prohibited prison authorities from impeding prisoners' efforts to gain judicial relief or from discriminating against prisoners on the basis of their religion, race, or sex. They also outlawed the worst conditions and forms of punishment in prison. They required the prison officials to provide some procedural safeguards on disciplining a prisoner, and they protected some forms of political expression by prisoners.[51]

A good account of the history of prisons in America is given by Irwin. The Big House was the first type of prison. This was followed by the correctional institution. The last type is the contemporary prison.

In the Big House, which started about 1900, guards protected inmates from each other, but in the contemporary prison they withdraw from this function. Prior to the Big House, prison staff imposed physical violence against prisoners. (Some prisons still have staff who practice physical cruelties against inmates.) There was an unstable peace in the Big House. However, there were many departures from the ideal Big House type of prison.

The correctional prison, which originated after World War II, emphasized classification, indeterminate sentences, treatment, and community corrections. Emphasis was on the amelioration of personal and social problems, and on curing the criminal. This led to policy implications for money and reform for treatment. There was more freedom in the correctional institution. Rehabilitation is still emphasized in many prisons.

With the contemporary prison, white dominance in prisons ended. Racial tensions, especially prevalent during the 1960s, may have led to increased violence. Guards in contemporary prisons say that their job is dangerous, and they are organized into factions to push for salary increases, better working conditions, and other benefits. There are violent cliques and gangs in many prisons, with emphasis on self-protection by attachment to an interest or to a racial group. Public support for prisons has now dwindled.

Irwin believes that prisoners have gained few rights in prisons. However, they have gained the right to be advised of charges, to call witnesses, and to cross-examine witnesses, and they have fuller rights in parole revocation hearings. Prisoners receive more visits, correspond with fewer restrictions, receive more literature, and receive better medical attention in prison. They are not returned to prison with lack of dispatch and lack of due process. The most significant change is the conception of the prisoner as a human being and as a citizen in a temporary reduced status, instead of as a prisoner. Courts, however, reflect a hands-off policy, and allow prison administrators to run prisons.

Irwin believes that prison sentences should be short and that prisoners should be allowed to have an active role in prison administration. This will reduce the factionalism now prevalent in prisons. He suggests that prisoners be allowed to enter informally into community correctional programs. He insists that prisoners must be considered human beings.[52]

Theories of Prison-Inmate Social System

Clemmer is considered the first sociologist who studied the sociological aspects of a prison. In his study of a maximum-security prison in Illinois, he found that about one-fifth of the men belonged to primary groups, two-fifths belonged to semiprimary groups, and the other two-fifths were ungrouped. He found that the increasing length of incarceration tended to reduce not only the number but also the size of the primary groups. Those who committed serious crimes tended to become members of groups more than those who committed trivial offenses. The prison community was not made up of a number of highly integrated groups. Many of the ungrouped men had strong positive relations with outside groups.

Clemmer found that leaders gained their reputation because of admiration by their followers and because these leaders were loyal. However, he believed that leadership in the prison community was different from that in the outside world. Inmates adhered to a code which refrained from helping the government of the prison. The inmates obeyed the rules, not out of respect for the rules or for the guards, but because they wanted to gain parole. The inexperienced inmate was punished more for rule infractions than the inexperienced inmate.

Clemmer found that the diet was adequate but monotonous; the guards were offensive but also displayed moments of kindness. He found that idleness pervaded the prison community; however, whatever prison activities there were seemed mainly boring. Yearning for sex with women was the most painful problem for the men. Homosexual activities prevailed. Clemmer found that the men were of the same intellectual capacity as the general population.

Clemmer coined the term "prisonization" to indicate the adoption in greater or lesser agree of the folkways, mores, customs, and general culture of the prison. The word is analogous to the term "assimilation." He found that prisoners whose short terms of confinement kept them from becoming integrated into prison culture had an easier time adjusting to the outside world. He also concluded that consensus, solidarity, and the "we"-feeling of prisoners had been exaggerated.[53]

Clemmer has been reviewed both positively and negatively. For example, Irwin notes that Clemmer failed to consider the identity of the subcultural systems which were carried into prison from the outside, particularly that of the thief. Irwin also states that Clemmer failed to recognize the corrupt relationships of the prison merchants, politicians, and other big shots which were formed with the prison administration. Irwin adds that Clemmer did his research from a middle-class perspective. Finally, Irwin states that Clemmer began with the concept of the primary group.[54]

Clemmer observed stratification in the prison community based on class, but it was not clear-cut.[55] Clemmer believed that 80 percent of the prisoners didn't feel part of any group, and hence existed in various degrees of isolation.[56] Clemmer didn't exactly define the concept of "prisonization." He employed only three categories to designate the entire prison population, namely, the "elite," the "middle class," and "hoosier,"[57] although he offered some significance into intermediate structures in the prison community with these three divisions.[58] Kassebaum *et al.* state that Clemmer did not make an effort to account for the prison community but was concerned only with describing social life. Later examination not only found inmate types similar to Clemmer's but also processes by which inmate types developed.[59]

Clemmer found that inmates will become most prisonized if they have a relatively well-developed and mature set of criminal values and orientations upon their admission into prison.[60] Clemmer suggested that prisonization varied inversely with relationships and objectives outside of prison.[61]

Sykes offers us another theory of prison. He studied a maximum-security prison in Trenton, New Jersey. Sykes found that prison guards and administration had to resort to a system of rewards and punishments to keep peace in the prison. Guards constantly looked the other way and didn't report rule infractions. There was also an argot and an informal role structure in the prison which served as an expression of group loyalty and membership. The merchant and peddler, for example, were despised because they offered a hard bargain and denied unity. The man who fought back was considered a troublemaker. The fight of a single inmate against the power of the custodians was considered as loss of self-control, not as an act of heroism.

The prison was not characterized either by complete solidarity or as a warring aggregate. It was a mixture of both, and there were compromises. The greater the degree of inmate solidarity, the less the prisoners felt the "pains of imprisonment" or the deprivation suffered while there.[62]

The concept of prison role and prison social structure has received theoretical attention in the literature. Clemmer was the first prominent sociologist to draw attention to it. However, Goodstein doubts that many inmates consistently conform to specific roles; rather, she says, they conform to certain attitudinal perspectives and change their behavior to adapt to specific situations. Commenting on Wheeler's thesis that prisoners adapt in a U-shaped fashion in prison — that is, prisoners at first conform to prison rules, then deviate from prison rules in the middle of their confinement, and conform to prison rules again near the end of their incarceration — she notes that Wheeler's thesis has not been replicated. Garabedian concluded that inmates conformed to Wheeler's U-shaped curve according to social type. The "square johns" and "right guys," for example, conformed to Wheeler's U-shaped finding.[63]

Jacobs, in his study of Stateville, notes that during the 1930s, power and prestige in the inmate social structure were tied to the formal organization, while today they are independent of the formal organization. The inmate social structure in the past was stable due to long prison terms and low inmate turnover. Racial antagonisms have made cooperation between guards and inmates more problematic today than previously.[64]

Garabedian notes that social roles among inmates can be either collectively or individually oriented. The "square john" and "right guy" are both collectively oriented because they both want to promote group values. However, the square john is committed to legitimate norms and the right guy to illegitimate norms. Politicians and outlaws are individually oriented because they are neutral with respect to norms. Inmates conform to role types by degrees, and they conform to more than one role type. Roles among inmates make inmate behavior predictable.[65]

Thomas and Fists found in their research that adaptation to imprisonment depended on extraprison influences, such as social class, preprison criminal activities, contacts with individuals in free society, and inmates' perceptions of their postprison life. This is known as the "Importation Model."[66]

Schrag, in his research, noted that inmates tended to choose leaders who had committed crimes similar to their own, but they also chose leaders who had committed crimes of violence. Leaders did not differ from other inmates in respect to age, education, ethnicity, I.Q., marital status, and occupation. However, whites tended to choose whites and Negroes tended to choose Negroes. The inmates tended to choose leaders who were similar to themselves in criminal records, ethnicity, institutional adjustment, I.Q., offense, and sentence.[67]

Kassebaum *et al.* state that the function of the inmate social system is to restore the status of the free world.[68] Sykes and Messinger believe that sociologists have failed to explain the remarkable similarity in the inmate social systems found in various custodial institutions.[69] However, Hefferman believes that there is no single inmate social system, but many inmate social systems, which reflect various adaptations to prison life.[70]

Sykes and Messinger describe other social roles of the inmates. An inmate who betrays a fellow inmate is a "rat" or a "squealer." He is hated. Prisoners who exhibit highly aggressive behavior and fight easily are known as "toughs." A "gorilla" is an inmate who used violence to gain his ends. A "merchant" or "peddler" exploits his fellow inmates by manipulation and trickery, and sells and trades goods that are in short supply. A "weakling" or a "weak sister" is an inmate who can't withstand the pressure of prison. An inmate who can't endure the deprivation of heterosexual relations in prison is known as a "wolfe" or "fag," depending on which role he assumes in homosexual relations. An inmate who continues to plead his case is known as a "rapo" or an "innocent." A "square john" takes on the values of the prison officials and is therefore ridiculed. A "right guy" is always loyal to his fellow inmates.[71]

Manocchio and Dunn believe that prison is a caste system and that some inmates receive more status inside prison than outside.[72]

Researchers have questioned Irwin's and Cressey's finding that an inmate's behavior depended on one of the three distinct subcultures outside of prison. Researchers say that there are similarities among the three subcultures, that the indicators used to establish membership in the thief subculture are invalid, and that all prisoners must come to terms with the pains of inprisonment regardless of their prior experiences.[73]

Women's Prisons

The social status inside women's prisons is different from that in men's prisons. Giallombardo studied a women's federal reformatory, Alderson, in West Virginia. The dominant theme in the inmate social system was on homosexuality, and anyone who didn't engage in it was labelled a "square." Stealing was universal in prison. Females praised those who could get a good business enterprise going; in men's prisons, the merchant is despised. No sharp line was made between selling and giving. No inmate completely trusted other inmates. Distinctions made on the basis of violence and among different offenses so prevalent in the male prisons were absent in the women's prisons.

The emphasis was on permanent relationships in prison. Kinship ties characterized the social system. Homosexual relations were established on a voluntary basis; there was no coercion as occurred in the men's prisons. Inmates acted out various kinship roles, e.g., lover, boyfriend, girlfriend, mother, aunt, grandmother, etc. An inmate might engage in homosexual relations to solve an economic problem. Marriage among inmates tended to be unstable. Divorce between inmates could sometimes lead to new friendships between the divorced woman and man. The kinship structure preserved the inmate social system.

There were institutional means to preserve and regulate the marriage relationship; this prevented a war against all. The kinship links to others, both married and unmarried, preserved the marriage relationship. Sex and age were the principal bases of kinship ties, but kinship ties pervaded race and social class. Members of a family had a strong "we"-feeling. The stability of the kinship ties was preserved by incest restrictions. Although parents were the leaders of a family, all members joined in decision-making. Each inmate usually assumed only one sex role.

Giallombardo believes that differences between male and female roles in prison cannot be explained as a response to the deprivation in prison. She believes that the role differences found in American society which are brought into prison are responsible for these differences. For example, in men's prisons, the "wolves" who engage in temporary homosexual relations to ease the deprivation of heterosexuality are acting consistently with the male role of aggression. This role is absent in civil society, since homosexuals are labelled "feminine." She believes that one must study both the outside culture and prison culture for better understanding of the prison community. She concludes that everyone in the prison community, including visitors, must be fitted into one of the roles in the status hierarchy.[74]

Ward and Kassebaum studied the California Institute for Women at Frontera, California. Inmates weren't completely deprived of personal possessions as were male inmates in men's prisons. They noted that a "regular" was analogous to the "good guy" or "right guy" in male prisons, and these roles indicated an inmate who didn't snitch. Inmates shared extra food with their friends. There were no "toughs" or "gorilla" roles, which were present in men's prisons. There was no evidence of adherence to Wheeler's U-shaped curve in reference to conformity to prison rules.

They noted that women resorted to homosexuality. About 50 percent of the women engaged in homosexuality. They believed that homosexuality in the women's prisons was greater than homosexuality in the men's prisons. However, this was not true homosexuality; the true homosexual refrains in prison because of loyalty to her mate on the outside. Homosexuality practiced for enjoyment is considered cheap. The homosexual relationships were temporary and problematic. The staff recognized the functions which homosexuality served in women's prisons, although they might not understand its complexity. Female argot in prison was different from male argot.

The researchers conclude that the structure of the female prison is different from that of the male prison. They believe that inmates bring in part of their prison code from the outside. They believe that the female role and needs of women result in different crimes for women than for men. Women, for example, have had less experience in burglary, robbery, and larceny than men, and they have a history of shorter periods of penal confinement than men. Ward and Kassebaum believe that women's role in society and the psychological needs of women in prison are responsible for differences between male and female prisons.[75]

Hefferman studied the women's prison at Occuquan in the District of Columbia. The inmate social structure was not seen as a closely knit group, but it was not considered to be in a state of anomie either. The inmates were grouped on the basis of offense type and common background. Hefferman delineated three prison types. They were the "square," the "cool," and the "life," reflecting the noncriminal, professional criminal, and the habitual criminal types, respectively. The groups overlapped, however.

The square and the cool were concerned with inmate activities, and the life was concerned with regulations, staff, and control of the prison. There were homosexual relations in prison based on family and kinship ties. The argot found at Alderson didn't exist here. The "bully" or "gorilla" type did exist here. Most inmates violated the inmate codes. Staff also enacted the roles of the cool, the square, and the life, and inmates kept staff in line by threatening to report them for violations of regulations.[76]

Ward and Kassebaum state that there was little evidence found in women's prisons of differentiated female types and the social solidarity reported in men's prisons. There was no evidence of the U-shaped curve found by Wheeler. They found that overinvolvement in criminal activity as measured by age at first arrest seemed to be more important in accounting for attitudes of female inmates than serving time in prison. The term "jailhouse turnout" indicated that most prison love affairs were temporary and situational. More inmates resorted to homosexuality than to psychological withdrawal, rebellion, colonization, or any other type of adaptation.[77]

Ohlin doesn't believe that the theft culture exists in institutions for women or some institutions for juveniles.[78] However, as mentioned, Giallombardo believes that stealing is universal in women's prisons.

Giallombardo also did research in female juvenile institutions. She found that adolescents formed courtships, marriages, and kinship ties with other inmates. She noted that kinship ties in women's prisons were found in other cultures. She found that punitive actions were instituted in some of these institutions, e.g. straight jackets, handcuffs, etc. Some inmates were inexperienced in homosexual relations and had to be socialized into the role. There were some homosexual attacks. There were marriages, marriage ceremonies, divorces, and documents.

The nuclear family formed in these institutions satisfied the inmates' needs for security, mutual aid, and protection. There were social roles, e.g. parents, husband, wife, and children. Very few, if any, girls could withdraw from the kinship ties. Giallombardo concluded that inmates were handled *en masse*.[79]

Giallombardo has been criticized for rejecting any influence of the organizational structure of the prison upon inmate behavior and for attributing all behavior to imported sex-role socialization.[80]

Adjustment in Prison

Many inmates don't consider prison to be too bad. Many inmates consider prison as a second home, and they have more going for them inside prison than outside. Casper interviewed inmates and ex-inmates and found that prison held a mystery and an excitement for younger men and that older men could handle prison. The inmates believed that life on the street was as bad or even worse than life in prison. Prison was an extension of life on the street. Some inmates gained status in prison, and they had someone to talk to.[81]

Toch studied breakdowns in prisons. He found that younger and single inmates were likely to break down more than others. Blacks were less prone to crises than whites or Latins. Blacks broke down less because they were more used to a male-oriented world in which danger was important and the survival process necessary for prison adjustment was prevalent. Latins broke down because their family-oriented worlds were incompatible with prison survival. Women in prison found more support than men, but when they broke down, they did so explosively. Toch concludes that all inmates go through stress in prison.[82]

Goodstein found that prison could be rewarding to some inmates, and that some inmates misbehaved in order to prolong their confinement. Adjustment to prison life was not always associated with adjustment in the outside world. Incarceration didn't affect all inmates equally. Some inmates viewed prison as their home. Most inmates adjusted to the demands of the prison staff.[83]

Mylonas and Reckless, in their study of an Ohio maximum-security penitentiary, found that the better-socialized prisoner and the one with high personal morals had more favorable attitudes toward prison than others. The Negro property offender had less favorable attitudes than the white property offender. The single offender had less favorable attitudes than the married, separated, or divorced offenders, and first offenders had more favorable attitudes than recidivists. They concluded that the longer the correctional experience, the less favorable the attitudes toward prison.[84]

Irwin noted that there was no relation between behavior in prison and behavior on the outside. He found that many men longed for prison, and that prison memories faded with time.[85]

Glaser found that prisoners had unrealistic expectations of very rapid job improvement in their postrelease years. However, they had more realistic perceptions of pay prospects near release or shortly after release. Inmates had an unrealistically pessimistic view of their postrelease prospects for success.[86]

Toch, in his research, found that prison experiences had a differentiated impact on prisoners. All inmates went through adjustment problems in prison. He found that freedom was the most important concern for inmates in prison. Almost equally important were feedback, support, privacy, and safety. Structure was of less concern and activity was the least important. Satisfaction in prison was related to a high value placed on personal rehabilitation, educational or vocational advances, keeping busy, and limited disposition to resent authority. Blacks were less satisfied than whites. However, certain groups valued these variables more than others. Safety, for example, was an issue mainly for younger defendants. Whites were more interested in safety than blacks. The married were more interested in emotional feedback than the single. A stressed person was one who discovered that familiar, customary ways of coping were being challenged.

Toch found that homosexual rape was rare; that rapists and victims were derived from similar background; and that rape victims were disproportionately white and aggressors disproportionately black. This proved the strength of the aggressors and weakness of the victims. Inmates appeared afraid to seek help from the staff. Many inmates sought protection as an adjustment to crises, although protection was not always safe.

Toch concluded that prisons will achieve their objectives if they attempt to match persons with their distinctive patterns of preference and with relevant characteristics of particular surroundings.[87]

Cohen and Taylor, in their study, found that many inmates read extensively or wrote a lot in order to cope with stress. Body building was popular in prison. There was little opportunity for presentation of selves, and there was a lack of privacy. Prisoners lived for the present out of necessity. Inmates distinguished good and bad prisons. Crises in prisons brought out the best and worst in men. Inmates resorted to political devices to deny or mitigate the identity of a convict.[88]

Homosexuality, Homicide

It has been asserted that homosexuality is prevalent in prison. Sacco believes that blacks rape whites as an act of punishment and debasement. Sacco believes that the prison community is conducive to homosexuality, and that guards either look the other way purposely, don't notice it, or actually encourage it. It is impossible, Sacco says, for one aggressor to rape a victim without the help of others; moreover, if the aggressor has others to help they can act as witnesses to the debasement. The blacks are the aggressors and the whites and Puerto Ricans the victims. The whites don't band together to seek revenge for their ill-treatment because of the perceived likelihood of punishment from the staff.[89]

Lockwood, in his research on homosexuality in prison in New York, offers us an alternative theory. He found that 28 percent of the prisoners had been the targets of sexual aggression at least once, 51 percent of the incidents contained physical violence, and that sexual rape was low. He also found that sexual aggression was more prevalent in prisons which had a heterogeneous population compared to prisons which had a homogeneous population.

In a systematic comparison of targets, nontargets, aggressors, and controls, Lockwood found that targets were white and aggressors black. Blacks were more closely tied to groups and thus avoided homosexual attacks more successfully than whites. Targets usually had no criminal history of violence compared to aggressors, but did have a history of mental health problems compared to others. He found that targets and aggressors were more suicide-prone than others. Guards sometimes looked the other way. Targets protected themselves from homosexual attack by isolation. He found victims were only victims once. However, the effects of homosexual rape might last for months.

Lockwood believes that aggressors choose whites because they are weak and sexually attractive. They are an easy mark because they fail the test of masculine strength, assertiveness, and physical aggression. Lockwood believes that if animosity were the main reason for homosexual rape of blacks against whites, black-white rape would occur on the street, outside of prison, and it doesn't. Some aggressors are accepted by most inmates. Lockwood believes that the aggressors are essentially heterosexual. Very few assaults are prosecuted because of fear, lack of witnesses, and the reluctance and inability of staff to observe homosexual incidents.[90]

Bowker studied prison victimization and concludes that prison rape emphasized brutality, dominance, and affirmation of the masculinity of the aggressor. Self-mutilation occurred as a result of victimization or fear of future victimization. Bowker concludes that psychological victimization over time can be just as brutal as physical victimization. He also states that a greater proportion of victimization in women's prisons is psychological and a greater proportion of victimization in men's prisons is physical.[91]

Sylvester and others have studied prison homicide. They found that homicides were common among maximum-security prisoners with a history of violence. Gang conflicts were not the predominant cause of homicide. The lack of witnesses prevented prosecution of homicides, although the conviction rate for homicides was 45 percent. Homicides didn't occur at random. Multiple-assailant homicides were more rational and planned than single-assailant homicides. Guards were more likely to be attacked or killed by groups than by individuals. Stabbing was the most common method of death, because of the easy access to this kind of weapon.

About 5 percent of the homicides involved racial antagonisms. Victims were more likely than assailants to be older, formerly married, Protestant, and to have ten or more years of schooling. Crowding didn't appear to be associated with homicide. Prisons which used reduction of time for good behavior were 26 percent less likely to have had prison homicides. Prisons which housed minimum- , and medium- , and maximum-security prisoners together had more homicides than others, and prisons with single-person cells had less homicides than others.

The most salient feature of these homicides was the extreme brutality and violence associated with them. Most victims were beaten and stabbed more times than was necessary to cause death. A motive could not be found in about one-quarter of the cases.[92]

Custody vs. Treatment

One of the most important theoretical issues in the study of prison is the conflict over the goals of prison as either custody-oriented or treatment-oriented. Carney believes that more staff are employed in custodial functions than in treatment functions.[93] Goodstein believes that inmates have an easier time adjusting to custody-oriented prisons where the rules are unambiguous compared to treatment-oriented prisons where the rules are ambiguous.[94] A 1975 survey indicated that 63 percent of prison administrators still believed in rehabilitation, ignoring the fact that prisons have failed to reduce recidivism.[95] Public opinion polls in the past have shown that Americans accept rehabilitation as the purpose of prison.[96] Irwin believes that no new correctional philosophy will replace the rehabilitation idea.[97]

Zald concludes that conflict is lowest in custody-oriented institutions compared to treatment-oriented institutions or prisons with mixed goals of treatment and custody. This is because treatment-oriented personnel clash with custody-oriented personnel.[98] Giallombardo noted in her study of women's prisons that prisons which attempted to maximize both treatment- and custody-oriented goals will conflict.[99] Guards seem to know the difficulty of enforcing treatment and custody at the same time.[100]

Riots

As mentioned, riots existed in prisons even hundreds of years ago. There are some theories on the causes of riots. Carney believes that prison unrest is related to the freedom permitted inmates.[101] Irwin notes that riots were in exception in the Big House prison because peace was secured.[102] Keve states that sadistic guards, bad food, and other grievances are only superficial causes of riots.[103] Prisoners listed excessive bail and pressure to plead guilty as the causes of the prison riots in the Tombs in New York in 1970.[104] Cohen and Taylor believe that the monotony of prison routine can cause strikes and work stoppages.[105]

Research reveals that collective violence in prison is provoked by the stress and deprivation that inmates experience. Collective violence occurs amidst disorganization and conflict. Violence occurs amidst deprivation, social disintegration, administrative conflict, instability, and pressure and publicity from outside prison walls. Some believe that there are no theories of collective violence in prison.[106]

Some believe that prison architecture and design are related to prison violence.[107] Some believe that unequal sentences for similar offenses can make for unruly prisoners.[108]

Empirical Studies

Vitually all theories of prisons have been based on empirical studies, using such methods as interviews, questionnaires, observation and participant observation, analysis of records, etc. It might be that some researchers had specific hypotheses in mind. In this section a few studies will be discussed which either illuminate some existing or new theory or are interesting in themselves.

Jacobs did a study of Stateville, a maximum-security prison in Chicago. He noted that the prison had become more open, more bureaucratic, and more legalistic. He noted a conflict between administrators and prisoners when reform was introduced. Jacobs noticed a change in the prison as Irwin did.

Jacobs noted that since World War II, the natural and political expectations of prisoners had risen. The prison reform system had gained strength and legitimacy in the late 1960s. He stated that authority had changed from a charismatic concept of authority to a rational-legal form of authority. Wardens, for example, hadn't come up through the ranks, as previously. Now they were appointed on the basis of a college degree.

Jacobs noticed that the prison was marked by organizational strain. Cooperation between guards and inmates was strained because of racial consciousness. Bureaucratization had not reached its limits. He claimed that the civilization of prison had been gaining momentum. He introduced the concept of "mass society" to prove that all members of society including prisoners could now claim "citizenship." Now prisoners had legal rights. There were now many factional interests in prison. There were gangs, and the guards were experiencing fear. Black guards seemed more empathic to inmates than white guards.[109]

A very interesting empirical study was done in a jail on the personal characteristics of prisoners. The study is not cited much in the literature, but this author believes it has great possibilities because of its psychological orientation to prisoner behavior. The researcher concluded that inmates loved to "people watch" and that their faces were sad. Most prisoners lost weight. Food was important to inmates. Fighting among inmates was common. Inmates daydreamed a lot. Many read.

The researcher believed that common psychological traits characterized inmates. These were alienation, anger, anxiety, depression, excessive sleeping, fantasizing, fear of physical injury or sexual assault, frustration, guilt feelings, insecurity, low self-concept, paranoia, shame, and suicide.

Inmates lived day by day. They were preoccupied with the acquisition of money. Inmates acquired a defensive, jail personality to shield their true personality from harm. They rationalized jail life as pleasant.

The researcher stated that the inmate craved attention to gain individuality. He had a need for religious services. The inmates believed that they were less than human. There was a need to express individuality. There was an abundance of talent in jail. Inmates were afraid of guards' unpredictable behavior. They were either average or below average in physical appearance.

Inmates showed a lack of concern for others. They were interested in quick acquisition of money. They desired excitement. They lacked motivation. They lacked patience to delay their goals. They possessed false beliefs about their talents and skills. They resented authority. They couldn't cope. They became easily frustrated. They were emotionally immature. They resorted to extreme measures to solve their problems. They showed faulty reasoning. They didn't perceive themselves as members of the straight society. They engaged in self-deception. They lied. They were loyal to lawbreakers. They were evasive. They were impulsive and couldn't resist tempting offers. They couldn't make sacrifices.

They couldn't manage money. They had no pride in their work. They were sensitive to errors in their work. They were undependable. They couldn't control their impulses. They lacked respect for their property and the property of others. They showed no guilt feelings about their crime(s). They had no long-range plans. They couldn't study. Many needed psychological therapy.

The researcher concluded that inmates want to be treated with humaneness.[110]

Although Ballesteros didn't specify whether these characteristics were prevalent on the outside, his analysis can be considered contrary to those who believe that inmates show no particular personality traits or characteristics different from the general population.[111]

Prison has an effect on the families and relatives of inmates. One empirical study done in England is worth mentioning. The author concludes that family relationships for those in prison will follow a pattern which existed before imprisonment. The family's adjustment will vary with the type of offense and the extent to which families have dealt with criminals.

Many wives lived with their parents while their husbands were imprisoned. They experienced money problems and problems with their children as a result of their husbands' imprisonment. Many wives suffered from loneliness and sexual frustration. Housing was a problem. The wives received a lot of financial and material support from their families.

Wives believed that husbands would change. Many didn't know the extent of their husbands' criminal activities. They resented that their husbands had been caught and imprisoned. They had doubts and fears about the sexual side of their marriage. However, the shame and stigma of their husbands' imprisonment tended to wear off rapidly.

The personality of the wife was very important in adjustment. Wives often made excessive demands both financially and emotionally upon their own or their husbands' families. A prison sentence rarely caused a marriage to break up, but a succession of prison sentences might do so.

Many wives of civil prisoners were concerned about their husbands' indebtedness, because indebtedness was a way of life for them. Many of the families of civil prisoners lived in poverty and squalor, but their marital relations were warm.

The researcher concludes that more attention should be paid to prisoners' families.[112]

Another empirical study was done on American families and friends of prisoners. This researcher found that letters and visits were important for family ties. Children had a difficult adjustment. Wives didn't believe that their marriage had deteriorated.

Family relationships before imprisonment were associated with family relationships during imprisonment. Subjects who experienced bad relationships before imprisonment experienced worse relationships during imprisonment. Relationships which were good before imprisonment either stayed the same or improved. The majority of relationships showed no change. Prisoners who served long periods of time didn't experience any change in relationships. Many spouses and girlfriends drifted away, but some relationships improved.

Prisoners very often received visits from cousins and siblings. Many received visits from female friends, while many male friends held their distance. One group of prisoners had no visits at all. Many letters to relatives were lengthy during the early part of the confinement, but gradually the length decreased. The longer the prison term, the more the prisoners wrote impersonal, detached letters. Long letters were associated with good or improved relationships.

The author concludes that both prisoners and their families experienced anguish, loneliness, suffering, and unhappiness.[113]

Parole

Over 60 percent of adult felons in America are released on parole before completing their time.[114] As of 1973, every state and the federal system used parole.[115] In California and Indiana, once a term has expired, all offenders are automatically placed on parole. Parole has been eliminated in Maine.[116] Parole has been curtailed in California, Indiana and Illinois,[117] and the parole board has been eliminated in Arizona, California, Illinois, Indiana, Maine, and New Mexico.[118] Parole is a state operation everywhere.[119]

Origin and History of Parole

There are various opinions on the origin of parole. Some say it originated with Sir Walter Crofton in Ireland, the ideas of Maconochie, and on the ticket-of-leave system.[120] Some trace parole to as early as 1776, when philanthropic societies began to help ex-prisoners to adapt to society.[121] Glaser believes that parole was first introduced in the United States in 1870, from experiments in Britain, Ireland, and Australia.[122] Some date it to 1900 in the United States.[123] Some date it to Elmira in the 1870s.[124] Some say parole has been in this country for over a century.[125]

Illinois was the first state to enact parole. Parole was first introduced in New York in 1869. Federal parole was first established in 1910.[126] The first parole law was passed in Massachusetts in 1837.[127]

The Parole Board

Although parole boards are politically appointed, and are persons of integrity and good judgment, they possess little knowledge of sociology, psychology, and psychiatry.[128] Members of parole boards in 40 states are appointed by the governor without any regard to qualifications.[129] A national study disclosed that there was no unanimity in granting parole.[130] Parole boards which encourage the use of prison time have little confidence in prediction tables because they give little weight to institutional factors.[131] Parole boards until recently have operated without any explicit guidelines for release decisions.[132]

The hearing process to grant or to deny parole has not been subjected to extensive research; however, the probability of recidivism is very important, and an attitudinal change is an important indicator for the probability of nonrecidivism.[133] Parole hearings are short and unstructured, and prisoners respond minimally to psychologically oriented questions. Many of the parole board members make psychological evaluations although they are not qualified to do so. Some decisions are made prior to the hearing or within the first three minutes.[134] Counselors write reports on prisoners, and these reports influence parole boards.[135] Parole boards also look at presentence reports.[136] Some jurisdictions have provisions for inmates to appeal negative parole board decisions.[137]

Prison and Parole

Goodstein found that inmates who were hostile and rebellious in prison did not always have more unfavorable adjustments on parole than inmates who had good, model behavior in prison. Long-term prison sentences might make for unfavorable parole adjustment.[138] Coe found that factors associated with parole success might not be predictive of good prison adjustment.[139]

Theories of Parole

Under the grace theory, the person's release under supervision is not a right to which he is entitled, but a privilege and a merciful act of the court or the parole board. The fact that parolees must sign forms specifying the conditions of their liberty has initiated the control theory of parole. The custody theory restricts the parolee's status to that of a quasi-prisoner and shields him from judicial review on both constitutional and nonconstitutional grounds. The exhausted rights theory stipulates that the parolee has exhausted all his due process rights during his trial and subsequent sentencing procedures. The *parens patriae* theory assumes that the parole board has identified with the interest of the parolee in fostering his rehabilitation.[140] One cannot develop a single analysis of parole that will hold for all penal philosophies.

Because parole was seen as a privilege and an act of grace, it wasn't necessary to inquire into its fairness.[141]

Adjustment on Parole

When inmates think about parole shortly before release, they tend to think about it in highly oversimplified terms quite remote from reality. The initial period after release is one of confusion, mixed cues, overintense impulses, and embarrassment. Parolees experience conflict as they move as a man in the community and as they try to be model parolees.[142] The transition from prison to parole is stressful for the parolee.[143] The first entry into the street is apt to be painful and accompanied by disappointment, anxiety, and depression.[144] The parolee's adjustment within one month after release is crucial because of his probability of rearrest and eventual incarceration.[145] The first six months are also crucial.[146]

Parolees express optimism about being outside without being brought back. Most releasees have some noncash resources when they leave prison.[147] Parolees who don't return to a girlfriend or wife don't realize the difficulties involved in making their initial sexual contacts.[148]

Very often, parolees are given a change of parole officer, which can be negative for them.[149] Studt concludes that although parole agents see themselves as sensitive to social and psychological problems, parole officers lack an awareness of the problems experienced by the majority of parolees; and they lack the tools for giving the needed help. Parole officers feel tension on the use of their discretion.[150] They are reluctant to use prediction tables because of confusing technical language and because of their distaste for statistics of any kind.[151]

Inmates at Attica had negative attitudes toward the New York parole system.[152] Waller, in his research, found that the majority of parolees believed that parole supervision was of little assistance.[153] Very often, when a parolee is in a tight situation and needs help, he will turn to others rather than to his parole agent.[154]

A federal study revealed that little time was spent on each parolee. A parolee can expect about 7.7 hours of supervision per year, 9 minutes per week, or 38 minutes per month. Face-to-face contacts averaged 3 minutes per week.[155]

Research has shown that parolees who are under the supervision of parole agents who have minimum caseloads don't perform better than parole agents who have regular caseloads.[156] Other research has also indicated that small caseloads don't alter the behavior of parolees. However, changes in caseload size may produce system effects that influence success and failure rates. Adequate supervision should be given in both small and large caseloads.[157]

Parole officers who are treatment-oriented can still be intolerant of deviant behavior of their parolees.[158] Most parole prediction tables are based on zero-order correlations without regard to intercorrelations.[159]

The increasing violation rates of parole eventually decrease with increasing terms of imprisonment.[160] About 90 percent of the parole violations in New York State are based on technical violations rather than on new criminal offenses.[161] A study revealed that parolees who had no associates had a high violation rate, and those who had three or more associates had a low violation rate.[162]

A high violation rate of a particular parole agent could initiate an investigation from above.[163] When a parolee commits a new offense, his parole may be revoked in lieu of prosecution. A study revealed that parole agents' recommendations for revocation of parole are followed 80 to 90 percent of the time. Some believe that equal penalties should be imposed for parolees who commit equally serious infractions.[164] Parole violation rates are more reliable and less ambiguous than crime rates.[165] Parole revocation is an administrative function, not a court function.[166]

Living alone and moving frequently are associated with parole failure.[167] Personality characteristics of parolees are not significantly related to parole success, and counseling has no impact on parole outcomes.[168] Those who are successful on parole have skilled jobs. Lack of skilled work experience is the primary barrier for employment among parolees. Some studies show that regularity of employment, rather than type of work, is related to parole success,[169] but others believe that the quality of work is important to the parolee.[170] There is no relation between parole outcome and promise of a job at the time of parole.[171]

Inmates have strong kinship ties at the time of release.[172] Strong family ties are associated with parole success.[173] Parole failure is associated with a history of crime in the family and the use of aliases.[174]

Female offenders jump parole less often than male offenders, possibly because their role as mother makes them stay in the same geographical area more often than men.[175]

There seems to be little difference in the violation rates of Negro and white parolees; possibly this may be due to the more careful selection of Negro parolees. American Indians have a high violation rate, and Japanese and Chinese have a violation rate lower than others, possibly due to their strong family support.[176] Others have noted little difference in the recidivism rates of whites and blacks.[177]

Lower parole violation rates were found among those with crimes of violence. Homicide and rape have the lowest violation rates on parole.[178] The bigamist makes a good parole risk.[179] A study of the Borstals in England revealed that the most shocking crimes were associated with low parole violations.[180] Assault offenders do well on parole.[181]

Legal Rights of Parolees

In *Morrissey* v. *Brewer* (1974), the United States Supreme Court held that parolees were entitled to due process safeguards. In *Gagnon* v. *Scarpelli* (1975), the court left to each state the task of deciding on a case-by-case basis the right of a parolee or probationer to receive counsel. There is no right to a jury trial in revocation proceedings.[182] The basic question in *Morrissey* was whether due process in any form applies to the parole revocation process.[183] *Morrissey* granted to parolees the right to be provided with the notice of charges, to have disclosure of evidence, to have an opportunity to present a defense, including the right to confront witnesses and to cross-examine present defense witnesses and documents, to have a neutral hearing making the determination, and to have a written statement of the evidence used in making the decision and reasons for revoking parole. *Gagnon* determined that the parolee could be provided counsel if he could not provide adequate defense; voluntary correctional personnel might also act as advocates in such cases.[184]

An Overview of Parole

There have been few systematic studies of parole. Parole has been studied from the narrow viewpoint of success and failure. Parole outcome has been studied only with regard to parole behavior or neglect of the parole officer. The parole system has not been studied as a complex organization.[185] Parole rules vary by state.[186] Some believe that parole rules have remained largely the same as 100 years ago.[187] There is uncertainty whether or not parole will survive, at least in England.[188] Some would like to eliminate parole in the United States.[189] Some believe that a parole board should have the function of releasing parolees prior to sentence expiration and setting standards for release.[190]

Studies found that parolees generally do better than persons discharged without supervision.[191] Once a parolee is off parole, his chances of staying off parole are good. However, many ex-prisoners in their loneliness long for the prison setting.[192]

Probation

Probation is usually given in lieu of incarceration. Probation sometimes has a dual function, namely, investigation and supervision. Probation officers investigate the background of defendants and write a presentence report for the judge, sometimes with a sentencing recommendation. Probation officers supervise a defendant until the expiration of his or her probation. Jurisdictions vary in the functions of probation officers.

History

It has been stated that probation started in the United States in the seventeenth century.[193] The system of apprenticeship, in which children of poor parents were attached to masters who taught them a trade, was an early form of probation.[194] Probation officially started in the United States in Boston, Massachusetts, in 1878.[195] John Augustus was considered the first probation officer in the United States, but he was selective in choosing those whom he placed on probation.[196]

Probation didn't come about automatically and quickly. Judges and lawyers had considerable difficulty in reconciling the system with the existing scheme of things, mainly because of the absence of established legal and procedural precedents.[197]

Probation was not a deliberate creation, but the result of gradual growth and conscious modification of existing legal practices.[198] For centuries, the courts of England occasionally bound over and released minor offenders on their own recognizance, with or without sureties. This practice was also found in the American colonies. The release of offenders seems to have been the first rudimentary stage of probation.[199]

As of 1967, all 50 states and Puerto Rico had passed laws authorizing probation.[200] As of 1966, 35 out of the 50 states had statutory restrictions on who might qualify for probation; 30 of the 50 states combined felony probation and parole for adults, while 13 did so wholly for juveniles.[201] Most jurisdictions have some statutory definition of what is meant by probation supervision.[202]

Most counties have no probation service.[203] In Cook County, Illinois, judges do not require a preliminary investigation of the defendant.[204]

The number of defendants to be placed on probation grows each year, and the number of probation and parole officers has increased each year.[205] A study revealed that the majority of defendants are placed on probation, with a rate of 71 percent to 83 percent in some counties.[206] However, although misdemeanors outnumber felonies, in some of the larger jurisdictions probation is used in less than 2 percent of all dispositions.[207] In many jurisdictions, if the court is small, it is customary for the investigating probation officer to act both as prosecutor and defense counsel, and as the correctional agent as well.[208] Some believe that the trend in probation and corrections is toward centralization.[209]

Presentence Investigation[210]

About one-quarter of the states make presentence reports mandatory for certain classes of offense which are punishable by imprisonment for more than one year. In the remainder of the states, and in the federal system, the trial judge has discretion to request a presentence report. A presentence report by the probation officer will very often prevent a defendant from going to jail.

However, the probation officers don't give enough information to influence judges to make an intelligent sentencing disposition. The probation officers don't observe the defendants long enough to make an intelligent diagnosis. The reports usually contain emotional value judgments and prejudicial errors. Some believe that defendants should have access to these reports so that they can counter inaccurate, arbitrary statements.[211]

John Hagan and others offer a theoretical and empirical viewpoint on the role of the probation officer in presentence recommendations. They state that the myth of individualization has preserved the legal role of the probation officer. In a "loosely coupled" organization, goals, power, decision-making, and outcomes are vague. Probation serves more of a ritualized, mythical, and ideological function in its decision-making.

An empirical study in Seattle, Washington revealed that employment, sex, race, plea, and bail status had direct and indirect effects on sentencing. Prosecutors' recommendations had more weight than probation officers' recommendations, but judges' decisions were uncorrelated with these recommendations. Hagan *et al.* conclude it is possible for prosecutors to become tightly coupled to the judiciary.[212]

The trend in presentence reports is to gather less information. This can be seen as logically connected to the alterations in sentencing trends. Some believe that there will someday be a checklist approach to factors important in presentence investigations.[213]

A study in California revealed that few factors went into decison-making in probation officers' sentencing recommendations. The prior record and current offense were the two most important factors in sentencing recommendations. Most of the presentencing information was not used in sentencing decisions. Disagreement existed among the various recommendations of the probation officers; therefore, risks for imprisonment depended on the particular officer assigned to the case. Judges accepted 86 percent to 96 percent of the probation officers' recommendations. This large agreement between judge and probation officer might be due to the fact that courts trust the probation officers' decisions, but other reasons, such as obvious decisions, probation officers' placing emphasis on the same factors as courts, and probation officers' shaping decisions to suit the court were important.[214]

A study revealed that additional information after a recommendation for a sentence is made had little effect on recommendations, although some modification might result in a few cases.[215] Czajkoski believes that the probation officers' role in sentencing is diminishing. The judge simply certifies the plea-bargaining process, and the probation officer does the same thing. In this sense, the probation officer's role is quasi-judicial.[216]

In some jurisdictions, probation officers have a lot of input in the sentencing decisions, and in other jurisdictions, they have very little input.

The other function of probation officers is supervision of probationers placed by the court. This will now be discussed.

Theories of Probation

There is no agreement on what probation is except in the most general terms.[217] There is no way of discovering what probation is, what it is attempting to do, and what the probation officer does.[218] Probation doesn't have a special body of knowledge. The probation practitioner draws his knowledge from many disciplines, including biology, medicine, psychology, psychiatry, law, sociology, and social work, among others.[219] Social work has no well-defined theory of its own.[220] Supervision is ill-defined.[221] There is no agreement on what "absconding" means.[222] One definition of treatment in the probation setting is "application of resources to the resolution of client problems to the end that behavior is changed sufficiently to enable him to live in the community without distinctive conflict."[223]

It has been stated that prosecutors and judges have little interest in probation.[224] Some believe that probation should be used only in select cases. It requires great skill by experienced personnel. In one county, probation was given automatically to everyone to clear court calendars. This example shows how probation is improperly administered in many jurisdictions.[225]

Luxenburg did a study of probation supervision in the New York Metropolitan area. She states that the probation officer acts to reintegrate the individual into the society from which he deviated. The probation officer intervenes to resocialize the individual and attempts to modify deviant attitudes, behavior, and values toward acceptable societal standards. Probation as Luxenburg sees it involves improving formal educational and vocational skills. She states that there is a continuum between extrinsic and intrinsic behavior; the two types of behavior are not mutually exclusive.

Luxenburg states that probation by the process of resocialization tries to correct deficits in the individuals' knowledge, ability, and motivation for the groups' expected behavior and values. She states that in our society, motivation is considered an internal factor, achieved by the individual by his own decision, but ability and knowledge are considered external factors, because society confers them upon the individual through education. Probation supervision applies rewards and punishment to external mechanisms but is not concerned about internal mechanisms; perhaps this is because external, observable behavior can be measured, but internal behavior cannot.

Luxenburg concludes that probation supervision must instill faith to probationers that behavioral change is possible. Supervision, she says, must rely on observable behavior accomplished through an obedience model. She states that there are many theories of probation and that supervision depends upon the personalities of the individual probation officers.[226]

Theories of probation resemble those of parole. Under the grace theory, probation is a privilege, not a right. Under the control theory, the probationer agrees to the conditions of his or her liberty; the probationer is a quasi-prisoner. Under the exhausted rights theory, the probationer has exhausted all his due process rights during his trial and sentence. Under the *parens patriae* theory, the probationer agrees to rehabilitation.[227]

Sands believes that there is a new emphasis away from deinstitutionalization and toward community-based rehabilitation programs. There may be more need for volunteers. Closely allied to this trend is an emphasis on uniform standards and goals.[228] Meitz, too, believes that a decentralized probation office is a step toward community corrections.[229] Hussey and Duffee believe that probation will move away from social casework and more toward community resources and services.[230] Killinger and others note a shift from the model based on the illness of the probationers to an emphasis on community resources.[231] Carney, too, notes a trend away from institutional commitment to community supervision.[232]

Breer believes that there are few black probation officers in relation to the size of the black caseload. He believes that black probationers know more about blacks in their caseload than the probation officer. He believes that race and black culture should be discussed openly with blacks. The white probation officer doesn't really understand how to rebuild the personality structure of the blacks or improve family life. Blacks cannot be rehabilitated in a "white mold," and probation officers cannot ignore differences between whites and blacks. Breer concludes that blacks have to be channeled into black identities.[233]

Some theories of probation can be inferred from the roles of supervising probation officers. Gibbs believes that probation officers and parole officers tend to play too many roles, causing them to have excessive caseloads.[234]

Carlson and Parks list the following roles of the probation officer.

1. The punitive law enforcement officer, whose primary concern is protection of the community through control of the probationer.

2. The welfare therapeutic officer, whose primary concern is the improved welfare of the probationer.

3. The protective/synthetic officer, who attempts to effect a blend of treatment and law enforcement.

4. The passive/time server officer, who has little concern for the welfare of the community or the probationer, but sees his job merely as a sinecure requiring a minimum amount of effort.

In addition, they list the quasi-judicial, integrative, and counseling roles of the probation officer.[235]

In a similar vein, Klokars lists several types of probation officers. The first type is the officer who stresses legal authority and enforcement aspects of the job. The second type is the time-serving officer who abides by all the rules and meets the job responsibilities minimally and methodically. The third type is the therapeutic officer who emphasizes both treatment and law enforcement.[236]

Czajkoski poses the question of how far probation officers should penetrate into the lives of the probationers. He believes that the trend is in the direction of deeper and deeper involvement. The probation officer may counsel an offender in regard to physical hygiene, education, employment, hobbies, and marital relationships. Because of a single, isolated, criminal act, probationers may have to conform in a number of ways unrelated to their criminal acts. Czajkoski believes that this also applies to parolees.[237]

Van Laningham and others conclude on the basis of empirical evidence that 85 percent of the probation officers considered it inappropriate to order a probationer to attend church, and that 94 percent considered it inappropriate to order a probationer to marry his pregnant girlfriend.[238]

Monger believes that when a probationer is required to see both a probation officer and a psychiatrist, he may be under conflict because of the conflicting personalities and demands of each.[239]

Imlay and Reid believe that probation officers will more and more formalize sentencing and revocation proceedings, which will change the probation officer's role from an objective, judicial advisor to a participant in an adversary proceeding.[240]

Criticism of Probation

Probation and probation officers have been criticized. Czajkoski believes that the conditions for probation are vague, making it difficult for probation officers to pinpoint technical violations.[241] Klokars believes that probation rules are silly, and states that if everyone took them seriously, few probationers would terminate their time without revocation; therefore, probation officers use a lot of discretion in enforcing the rules.[242]

Mangrum believes that probation requirements should be clearly stated so that probationers can act according to expectations. He feels that probation officers are not equipped to deal with psychologically unbalanced offenders. Mangrum recommends that probation officers help probationers make their own decisions, not make decisions for them. Noting that corrections has been too obsessed with achieving a total cure and with bringing the offender into some state of near-perfection, Mangrum recommends accepting the fact that nothing can be done in some cases for probationers.[243]

Van Laningham and others, basing their findings on empirical evidence, concluded that there was lack of agreement among probation officers on the responsibilities of their jobs. There was disagreement about tasks involving psychotherapy, law enforcement, surveillance, environmental manipulation, and use of authority to control disapproved-of but legal behavior. There was agreement, however, on referrals to appropriate helping resources, advice for day-to-day living, and on acting as social consultants to the court. There was lack of agreement over the educational requirements of the job. This lack of agreement results in probation officers' experiencing conflicting demands, in the probationers' not knowing what to expect, and in the public's lack of knowledge on how to evaluate probation.[244]

Koontz, Jr., asks how probationers can receive skilled assistance if probation officers lack the professional ability and skill to assist them. He believes that there are too many problems for a probation officer to be skilled in everything. He recommends that probation officers should be specialists in one or two areas.[245]

The probation officer cannot be all things to all people. There are no theories which relate specified activities to specified results. The making of a probation order may sometimes have more profound effects upon the individual than either the court or the probation officer realizes.[246] It may be impossible for some probationers to abide by the conditions of probation. For example, one appellate court determined that it was unfair to prohibit a chronic alcoholic from drinking as a condition of probation. The court thought it was impossible for this alcoholic to refrain from drinking.[247]

In the 1930s, most probation departments required a high school rather than a college education and only limited social work experience. Now, slightly more than one-third either require a high school education or have no educational requirements at all.[248] Studies have shown that in spite of prior training, probation officers tend to adopt the philosophy of the court by which they are employed.[249]

Bates believes that effective and intelligent supervision is not being employed in many states.[250] Scarpitti and Stephenson believe that probation supervision and guidance have been traditionally superficial, involving infrequent and ritualistic contacts between officer and offender. There are few special programs for intensive treatment.[251] Only about 5 percent of resources go into rehabilitation, while 95 percent go into custody. The move away from rehabilitation and toward punishment might be accounted for by the lack of success in rehabilitation.[252]

Empirical Studies

There have been various studies of probation success. For example, one study found that probation supervision with no special conditions had a revocation rate of 19 percent; probation with one condition, 24.9 percent; probation with two conditions, 39.2 percent; and probation with three conditions, 47 percent.[253]

Beckman notes that the F.B.I. crime reports show a lower rate of recidivism for offenders who receive probation and suspended sentence in conjunction with probation than for those who go to prison. He cites a study in California which showed that 72 percent of adult probationers in a two-year period completed their probation without revocation.[254]

A review of 11 probation studies indicated a success rate from 60 to 90 percent. A 1944 study of juvenile probationers showed that 35 percent failed on probation. A later study of adult probationers revealed that only 24 percent had their probation revoked. The Gluecks, using more stringent standards, reported a probation failure rate of 57.9 percent for youthful offenders and 92.4 percent for adult male offenders. Looking at postrelease nonrecidivism as a measure of success, the review of 11 studies indicated that eight had a success rate between 70 and 90 percent. Other studies for adults and juveniles reported a success rate from 72 to 83 percent.[255]

Sutherland reported a success rate of 75 percent, but success rates varied widely from department to department. A study in the late 1950s revealed a success rate of 63 percent in California, with wide variations among counties. A more recent study revealed a success rate in California of 51 percent. Glaser reported that out of 146 cases receiving a favorable prediction, only 11 percent were unsuccessful. Out of 15 cases receiving probation in spite of an unfavorable prediction, 87 percent were unsuccessful. Out of 29 borderline cases, 55 percent were unsuccessful.[256]

Another study revealed that 75 percent of the probationers completed probation without revocation, and that four or five out of ten completed probation without an arrest, conviction, or revocation.[257] A study was done on a sample released from probation between 1939 and 1944. Only 17.7 percent were reconvicted of a crime after termination of probation, and mainly for minor crimes.[258]

During the years 1956–1958, 56 California counties granted probation to 1,638 defendants. As of December 31, 1962, 62.5 percent had no reported violations, 7.3 percent had one reported violation, 2 percent had three or more violations, and 28.2 percent were revoked. The more heavily populated counties had higher revocation rates. The amount of probation in a county was not correlated with revocation rates. Forgery and check forgers had the highest revocation rates, and manslaughter the lowest rates. Women had a higher success rate than men. There was a significant difference among the rates for blacks, whites, and Mexican-Americans. The older the defendant, the lower the revocation rate. There were significant differences in revocation rates by conditions of probation.[259]

Toby states that probationers placed on probation recidivate less than those incarcerated.[260] Martinson and Wilks found that for first offenders, probation was superior to imprisonment in terms of recidivism, and that for recidivists, probationers did as well as those who received imprisonment regardless of offense category or marital status. Wilks found in England, based on matched samples, that there was no significant difference in the recidivism rate of two courts, one in which probation was used normally and one in which probation was used three times the national average. In one study, based on experimental methods among youths, Martinson and Wilks found that probationers committed more offenses than controls.[261]

One study reported that whites had a lower failure rate than Negroes. The highest recidivism rate took place within six months of probation.[262] In England, it was found that a good marital relationship between parents and a good child-parent relationship were important for probation successes.[263]

Lemert and Dill reported on the effects of a California program which had subsidized counties, which had kept offenders in the community with probation in lieu of incarceration. The results showed that although commitments declined, it was difficult to pinpoint the cause to state-subsidized programs. Perhaps the subsidy program was one cause for the decline of commitments. Prior to the subsidies, the probation departments had reduced commitments anyway.[264]

A study revealed that probation officers did not believe that all probationers should report regularly. Reporting, they felt, should be based on individual needs.[265]

There is agreement that probationers need intensive supervision during the first twelve months. Marital discord is related to failure on probation.[266] A study revealed that the longer the period of supervision, the higher the recidivism rate.[267] A study found that probation officers make decisions according to their background factors[268]; however, other research revealed that the attitudes of probation officers become similar in a short period of time.[269] A study revealed that probationers in treatment displayed improved relations to authority.[270]

Martinson and Wilks found that the violation rate of probation was sometimes higher for those under smaller caseloads compared to those under regular caseloads.[271] Carney believes that smaller caseloads mean more violation rates reported because of added time for surveillance.[272] A study in San Francisco revealed that there was no significant difference in probation success among minimum, ideal, and intensive supervision.[273] Lohman found no difference in the average monthly earnings of those under three types of supervision, namely, intensive, ideal, or minimal.[274] Lemert and Dill found that probationers in intensive caseloads didn't necessarily do any better than those in regular caseloads.[275] Another study revealed that the effect of caseload size is not strictly a function of simple numbers, but the result of various kinds of interactions.[276]

There have been a few studies showing probationers' attitudes toward their probation officer and probation. Masden reported on a questionnaire administered to 50 probationers and parolees selected at random from the caseloads of six probation officers. Thirty-two completed the questionnaires. The respondents saw themselves as suffering from things from which ordinary people were not suffering. They didn't believe they had the ordinary rights of the average man in the street. They believed that their record prevented them from equal treatment by law enforcement officers. The probation officer, although considered a helper, confidant, and friend, still had power over the ex-offender. The respondents saw their families suffering from their crime.

Many believed that their probation officers didn't listen. Blacks and Chicanos had more negative feelings than whites. The unmarried probationers believed that the system was more restrictive than did the married. The property offenders indicated a greater willingness to cooperate than others. The drug offenders had a negative feeling toward probation restrictions. The drug offenders also seemed more suspicious and less well-integrated into all situations. The respondents also perceived definite punitive aspects of supervision.[277]

Research on empirical aspects of probation has been criticized. Carney believes that there have been few studies of the qualitative aspects of probation. He states that most studies measure probation while a probationer is already on probation, rather than evaluating the relationship between treatment and outcome.[278]

Carlson and Parks state that there is no research on the relation between workload perspective and probation effectiveness. They also believe that the female offender has been neglected. They state that there has been no research on standards of probation, on the quality of the relationship between probation officer and client, or on the difference between single probation officers versus the team approach, and that there has been little research on the proper educational requirements of probation officers.[279]

Luxenburg believes that previous research attempting to quantify the effects of probation supervision presents contradictory empirical findings, probably because of the different methods of inquiry.[280] Bates believes that there is a lack of reliable and comparable statistics on probation and parole.[281] Research is not generally a standard tool of probation departments.[282] There is little reference to termination in social work literature.[283] Research has indicated that change of probation officers doesn't affect outcomes, but probation officers insist that it does. The truth is somewhere in between.[284]

Smith and Berlin state that there are no studies revealing to what degree judges follow probation officers' recommendations for termination of probation, although it would appear that there would be a high correlation between probation officers' recommendations and termination after a violation of probation.[285] Very little is known about the whole revocation process.[286] Probation departments can be judged adversely if there are a large number of revocations or a high rate of recidivism.[287] Generally, the court will go along with the probation officers' recommendations to revoke probation.[288]

It might be assumed that probation officers would do a more effective job of predicting success or failure in probation if they were given feedback on the accuracy of their predictions. One study tried to measure this. An experiment was performed in 1974 on probation officers in San Diego. Ten probation officers, the experimental group, were given feedback on the accuracy of their predictions, and another ten probation officers, the control group, were not given any feedback. There was no significant difference between the experimental and the control group in the accuracy of their predictions. Feedback didn't improve the accuracy of probation officers' predictions for success on probation.[289]

Legal Aspects of Probation

The legal rights of probationers have had some limited success. In 1967, the United States Supreme Court, in *Memphis* v. *Shay*, specifically ruled that probationers had a constitutional right to be represented by counsel at revocation hearings, and pointed out that an accused person is entitled to a lawyer at every stage of a criminal proceeding.[290] However, in *Gagnon* v. *Scarpelli* (1975), the court left it to the discretion of the states to decide on a case-by-case basis whether a probationer should have a court-appointed counsel at revocation of probation. There is no right to a jury trial in revocation of probation.[291]

Alternatives in Corrections

In 1816, many homeless children were wandering the streets of New York City. Many children were placed in jails and prisons. By the midnineteenth century, 20 cities had established separate houses of refuge for children. These institutions sometimes indentured children to private employers, who gave them a home, training, and a trade.[292]

Houses of correction were found in Europe as early as 1690. At first, they were clean and tidy. They were combined with orphanages and asylums; they were profit-making.[293]

De Tocqueville noted that the first house of correction originated in New York in 1825 in the United States. Children were sent there, were separated at night, and in the daytime communicated with each other. They received instruction and labor. Boys and girls were separated from each other.[294]

Halfway houses were used for mental patients in Europe as early as 1870. Organizations such as the Salvation Army, St. Vincent De Paul Society, and Alcoholics Anonymous have long operated halfway houses. In 1845, in New York, a group of Quakers opened a halfway house for ex-prisoners, and the House of Industry in Philadelphia was established in 1889.[295] Keve believes that halfway houses did not begin in America until the 1950s, but he is probably talking about the modern halfway house.[296]

For almost 200 years, religious and humanitarian groups have made sporadic attempts to offer temporary shelter and food for the homeless. Until quite recently, private efforts to establish residences for offenders met with hostility. Halfway houses for adults have remained essentially private except for the federal government, a few states, and several counties. The Federal Bureau of Prisons operates community treatment centers. Private groups have been prone to accept adults rather than juveniles because of the greater disciplinary problems of the latter. The turnover rate in halfway houses is slower for juveniles than for adults. Research has shown that crime has not increased because of halfway houses. All halfway houses emphasize employment and recreation, but there has been very little informal action between residents and the community.[297]

Work in lieu of fines as an alternative seems sensible. Work-release programs have not been properly evaluated. Work-release is old; some form of work-release has existed in the United States since the early days of prison. The first work-release law was passed in Wisconsin in 1913.[298] The relation between work-release and recidivism has not been the subject of research.[299]

Foster homes for homeless juveniles are another alternative. However, they are transient, and most couples do not remain foster parents for many years.[300] Alcoholics Anonymous is another alternative in treatment. It has had a well-documented success rate among the middle class, but it fails to address the handicaps of lower-status men.[301]

A study was done on a comparison of delinquent boys at Highfields, New Jersey, an open residence with lax rules, and Annandale, a closed institution.

Boys admitted to Highfields had to be at least 16 years old, with no previous institutionalization. No homosexuals were admitted. The boys worked on the farm and were given furloughs. The results showed, after controlling many variables, that boys at Highfields had a lower recidivism rate after three or four months compared to boys at Annandale, and that boys at Highfields even had a lower recidivism rate after three years compared to others. The Negroes made a more satisfactory adjustment than whites while at Highfields, but they were not able to carry this over to the community.[302]

Highfields accommodated 20 boys. Fourteen variables were used in the study. The chances of succeeding at Highfields were eight out of ten; at Annandale, five out of ten.[303]

The Highfields study has been criticized by Glaser, who says that it had no control group selected by the same process as the treatment group; therefore, it was not truly an experiment. Although Highfields' cases had a better postrelease record than Annandale's cases, questions arise about the findings.[304] Abadinsky, on the other hand, believes that Highfields did have an experimental and control group. He also believes that in spite of the differences in the two groups, and in spite of the fact that some Highfields residents ran away and committed some serious crimes, Highfields was considered a success.[305]

The PICO experiment was another study for alternative treatment. This was a minimum-security juvenile setting in California. The sample consisted of 856 cases, and the results showed that of those released, the treated amenables who were individually counselled had a lower return to prison than others. The untreated amenables, however, did worse than the nontreated controls.[306]

The Cambridge-Somerville Project was another study for an alternative type of treatment. There were two samples consisting of 325 boys each, who were carefully matched. The boys averaged five years of treatment. The results showed that the treatment group generally had committed more offenses, and serious offenses, but there was some proof that the most serious offenders were in the control group. The researchers concluded that although delinquency may not be averted in the first eight or ten years, in later years, the untreated group may commit slightly more serious offenses.[307]

An experiment was conducted in Midcity Project in Boston, in which delinquents, violent members of gangs, resided. There was counselling by workers. The results showed that delinquency was not reduced initially, but later, at age 18 or 20, there was a decrease in delinquency that might have been attributed to the Project.[308]

One hundred reports of correctional treatments were analyzed. Almost one-half of the reports showed that the treatment group improved considerably as a result of the treatment. One-fourth of the reports showed harmful effects or no change. Since some of the research had limitations, the author believes that the evidence supporting treatment is slight, inconsistent, and of questionable reliability.[309]

Conclusions

It appears that various forms of punishment have origins dating back hundreds of years, although the exact origin of any form of punishment is debatable. It also appears that the four functions of punishment, namely, incapacitation, deterrence, retribution, and rehabilitation are imbedded in all forms of punishment either explicitly or implicitly. Sometimes the four functions work, and sometimes they don't. There are many agents involved in the correctional process, e.g. correctional counselors, guards, lawyers, parole officers, probation officers, psychiatrists, social workers, etc. All of these agents are directly or indirectly impinging on the lives of the defendants, sometimes successfully, sometimes unsuccessfully.

The correctional system comprises vast bureaucratic and informal organizations with a great deal of complexity; there are many fields for much-needed research. The results are often contradictory, conflicting, and ambiguous. We haven't reached the point yet where we know definitely whether or not correction works.

In the next chapter, the discussion will involve arguments either supporting or refuting the question posed in Chapter I: Is criminal justice a science? Much of the discussion will depend on familiarity with material in this book.

Chapter VII
The Science of Criminal Justice

It is now time to answer the question posed at the beginning of this book. Is criminal justice a science? As shown in Chapter I, many criminologists do not believe that criminal justice is a science; some do not believe that sociology is a science, and criminal justice is sometimes considered part of sociology. Although no empirical evidence has been gathered, it is the author's impression that the reason why criminologists and sociologists believe that criminal justice is not a science is that one cannot equate certain outcomes with certain decisions or actions. For example, in spite of all our research, one cannot prescribe certain penalties for certain crimes and be sure that offenders are deterred and rehabilitated sufficiently to prevent crime. One cannot say that four years in prison for offenders will deter and rehabilitate them sufficiently so that they won't commit another crime.

Even taking an individual offender into consideration, one cannot determine that a particular penalty within limits will deter and rehabilitate him sufficiently from committing certain crimes. A sentence of probation with conditions of drug therapy will not necessarily relieve a drug problem so that offender "X" won't commit further crimes. Even after much thought has been applied to the problem, and much money, personnel, and resources expended, criminal justice has not reached the point where it is assured of making the right decisions within limits to prevent future crime. This is in spite of the fact that many personnel in criminal justice are college-trained and are professionals, with advanced degrees, with law degrees, willing to use their brains in making appropriate decisions.

Both students of crime and criminologists have hinted to this author that criminal justice is an art, not a science. They have argued that decisions in criminal justice are arbitrary and capricious, made on the basis of expediency and politics or after persuasive arguments by defense lawyers or other legal actors. These decisions, some argue, are not based on scientific principles, theories, or laws; some believe that we don't have any scientific principles, theories, or laws. However, this author believes that they fail to see the crux of the system.

It is this author's opinion that criminal justice is a science, and he will attempt to prove his point. First, restating what has been argued in the beginning of this book, many consider criminal justice a science if it meets the criteria for science in general: i.e., its methods are scientific. Criminal justice has a special language and vocabulary (e.g. adversary system, pretrial status, disposition, etc.). There are also classification schemes (e.g. dangerous versus nondangerous offenders, recidivists versus nonrecidivists, etc.). It has been shown throughout this book that there are many theories on all aspects of criminal justice; some of these theories are competitive and contradictory. There are many theories on the police, the courts, punishment, and corrections. Some of these theories are on a low level, that is, they are not built on a high level of abstraction, but they are considered theories nonetheless.

The methods of criminal justice are scientific. Some of our research methods are based on very advanced techniques, such as path analysis, discriminant analysis, log-linear methods, and mathematical models based on calculus and econometrics. This is in addition to participant observation, interviewing, questionnaires, analysis of records, and experimental methods — the standard tools used in research.

Researchers very often base their findings in light of some relevant theory or theories which they espouse as a theoretical framework. In this sense, some argue that criminal justice, as well as other disciplines, is scientific.

This author has argued that this reasoning isn't sufficient to prove that criminal justice is a science. There must be some other proof. This author believes that one must look deeper into the situation to prove that criminal justice is a science. In spite of all our theories on crime, the causes of crime are not definitely known; therefore, criminal justice may never be proven scientific if it waits until causes of crime are discovered.

This author shall propose his argument in the form of certain assumptions and theorems. The ideal situation would be to prove the theorems mathematically; however, criminal justice has not yet reached the point where mathematical proofs can be formulated for all its knowledge. Intuitive proofs will have to do at this point. It might be that what this author has formulated is nothing more than another theory of criminal justice. As stated in Chapter II, no theory is definite in science; therefore, this author's conclusions shall be considered tentative and subject to disagreement and debate.

Assumptions

This author argues that the criminal justice system starts with two basic assumptions or premises.[1] The first assumption is that members of our society conform to some of the basic values of our society. Some of these values include legitimate employment, legitimate means to reach goals, and elimination of certain forms of deviance (e.g. drug use, mental illness, etc.). Although our society is pervaded with many groups, each group espousing unique values, there must be consensus on some common societal norms if our society is to survive. This is true in all societies and is a basic sociological generalization.

The proof is not difficult to find. Everywhere in criminal justice, personnel try to inculcate these basic values among offenders. Legitimate employment, for example, is a factor which enters into many of our decisions. Employment is considered when making a prognosis in criminal justice. If an offender is employed, his or her chances of gaining a favorable disposition are sometimes better than if he or she is unemployed.

The prior record of a defendant is crucial in criminal justice decisions. A criminal record indicates adherence to illegal norms, values, etc. It indicates that offenders do not adhere to the important values of American society, e.g. legitimate means to reach goals.

An offender who has a drug or psychiatric problem must engage in therapy as part of the conditions of probation or parole because both types of deviance may directly or indirectly lead to crime. Whether therapy helps is beside the point; therapy is a basic value in our society.

The second assumption is that offenders have free will to change their lives. This is the old argument of free will versus determinism. Many have argued that offenders are free to change their lives from crime to legitimate goals. The Classical school of punishment was built on the premise that offenders were entirely responsible for their fate. Monger, for example, states that society can operate only on the premise that the citizen is in control of what he does and that he can make choices in his behavior. He believes that society would be shaken if this premise were abandoned.[2] Gross believes that an offender must be responsible for his criminal act if crime is to be defined as a crime. However, he admits that many criminal acts are engaged in unintentionally by the offender.[3] Forer believes that the law is based on the premise that people are reasonable.[4]

Everywhere in criminal justice there is proof of free will. Criminal justice personnel operate on the assumption that offenders are voluntarily accepting decisions. Plea-bargaining is based on this premise. Defendants are supposed to accept the plea voluntarily without any coercion, although in practice this doesn't happen. Defendants are supposed to accept the conditions of probation volunarily. Defendants are supposed to follow through on job referrals, therapy, restitution, etc. The personnel in criminal justice impose conditions and orders, but the defendant must be actually free to initiate action along these lines.[5]

This doesn't mean that events and situations don't determine a defendant's fate. Certainly many defendants are a product of their environment. They live in poverty conditions, in ghetto areas where broken families, poor housing conditions, and all types of deviant behavior (e.g. drugs, illegal enterprises, crime, etc.) prevail. Who knows how much the environment determines a person's fate? We may never be able to measure its effect on crime. Yet many poverty-stricken people manage to refrain from crime altogether.

Theorems

It is possible to formulate some theorems in criminal justice which can be proven intuitively. Six theorems will be formulated. These theorems are generalizations which hold historically across criminal justice systems. These theorems can be applicable to other societies.

Theorem 1. Many agents and forces, both inside and outside the criminal justice system, are acting to determine the offender's fate both directly and indirectly. Some of these forces are positive, some negative, and some neutral.

This theorem is not too difficult to prove. From the time of arrest to the time of sentencing, and beyond, agents and forces act upon the defendant. The police officer initiates an arrest. His influence can be positive or negative, depending on what he charges and how he acts. Some officers will charge the maximum, and will even use force to display their power. A police officer can influence a prosecutor or a judge either negatively or positively. This author has talked to many police officers who actually wanted to do something positive for a defendant, e.g., help him seek drug therapy. On the other hand, a police officer can look for the defendant on the street even when he is acquitted and watch him for further crime.

Prosecutors certainly have an effect on the defendants' fates. Their charging and sentencing recommendations are certainly significant for the offender's fate. Research has shown that many factors figure into a prosecutor's decisions, but there is still a lot of discretion. If a prosecutor believes an offender's crime is serious, that belief can be negative for the offender; however, if a prosecutor believes that a defendant is trying to rehabilitate himself, he can recommend probation. Prosecutors don't have the time or resources to prosecute all cases. Even if luck is involved, the prosecutor can work positively or negatively for the defendant's case. Prosecutors are also influenced by others both inside and outside the system, e.g. complainants, psychiatrists, ministers, defense attorneys, etc. Any one of these actors can exert a positive or negative influence on the prosecutor, thus indirectly affecting the defendant.

A defense attorney can determine a defendant's fate. If he or she is concerned about a particular defendant, he or she can argue for favorable treatment. He or she can influence the prosecutor to get the best deal. Generally defense attorneys are supposed to exert a positive influence, not a negative influence.

If a presentence report is ordered, the report can have a positive or negative effect on the defendant's fate. Probation officers are supposed to individualize the defendant's case. They are supposed to look at circumstances that have been missed by other legal actors. Their recommendations can have either a positive or negative effect on outcomes.

Judges certainly have power to influence a defendant's fate. This is in spite of the fact that they are influenced by other legal actors, e.g., probation officers, prosecutors, etc. They still have discretion and power to decide a defendant's fate.

The defendant is not finished even after he receives a prison sentence. The personnel inside prison can determine his fate. Chaplains, counselors, guards, psychiatrists, social workers, wardens, and even other inmates can determine whether a defendant can make it successfully in prison. The reports of prison personnel figure in reduction of time for good behavior and in parole boards' decisions.

If a defendant is placed on probation in lieu of prison, his or her supervising probation officer has a great deal of power to determine his or her fate positively or negatively by the power to recommend a favorable or unfavorable termination of probation. If a defendant is placed on parole after prison, the parole officer has similar power.

There are many others who determine an offender's fate. Assistant district attorneys, bail bondsmen, job counselors, psychologists, psychiatrists, and social workers may all have influence on the outcomes.

There are forces outside the criminal system that figure in dispositions. Relatives, through social support systems, can have positive or negative effects. This author has seen many relatives try to direct their sons, daughters, husbands, and wives into right channels. Some relatives exert a negative influence by avoiding or stigmatizing the defendant.

Even if an offender is processed quickly, and skips many steps in the process, agents and forces can still affect outcomes. If an offender is disposed of quickly at arraignment, court policy can determine an offender's fate. For example, for minor crimes, such as driving without a license, gambling, prostitution, etc., the court's policy may be a fine or unconditional discharge.

Some agents exert no influence on a defendant's fate. For example, sometimes lawyers just function to influence a defendant to plead guilty; sometimes lawyers have no effect on outcomes. Judges very often "rubber stamp" a prosecutor's or a probation officer's recommendation. Some police officers have no effect on the disposition. Sometimes the effect is direct and sometimes indirect. For example, if a prosecutor remands a defendant before sentencing and remand status means a negative disposition, then the prosecutor will exert an indirect effect on the defendant's sentence.

What about the defendant himself? Can he influence his own fate? Very often he can. This is based on the assumption of free will proposed here. The defendant can either comply or not comply with the warnings received throughout the system. If he or she purposely makes a conscious effort to comply with orders, no matter how disagreeable, he or she can determine his or her fate, perhaps positively, because cooperation is viewed positively in the system. A lot depends on the influence of outside forces.

The system itself can stigmatize defendants, but it is not known to what extent a particular defendant is stigmatized sufficiently to change to socially acceptable behavior. Perhaps the stigma or negative experience can deter a particular defendant to change to law-abiding behavior. Punishment can deter and rehabilitate, through incapacitation and retribution, but sometimes it does not do so. The extent to which it does or does not deter and rehabilitate is unknown.

What if criminal justice personnel do not perform their role functions properly? What if they don't understand defendants' problems? Can this be negative or positive? It has been seen throughout this book that many criminal justice personnel don't understand the needs of the defendant. This can have both positive and negative effects. If a parole officer violates a defendant's case for one rearrest that is no fault of the defendant, the violation can have negative effects on the defendant. However, if he can afford a lawyer to advise him and to defend him at a revocation hearing, this can be positive for the defendant. If an employer is dissatisfied with a probationer's work, and the probationer knows this will be reported to his or her probation officer, who may violate the defendant's case, even though the employer is unreasonable and strict, the defendant can "shape up" to stay on the job so that he or she can remain on probation.

Many forces, too numerous to mention, directly or indirectly influence a defendant's fate. However, a defendant interacts on the basis of his free will to reciprocate with action which can determine his fate directly or indirectly. The interaction of the defendant with these agents and forces is important. Doing nothing, e.g., accepting a charge in plea-bargaining, is an example of the defendant's interaction with a criminal justice agent.

Theorem 2. Defendants receive individual attention in the processing of their cases.

This author for a long time believed that only certain defendants were lucky enough to receive individual attention instead of mass processing of their cases. After reanalyzing the situation, this author believes that everyone receives both individual attention *and* mass processing of his or her cases.

The proof is not difficult to see. One starts with the fact that discretion pervades the criminal justice system. Very often in research there is a lot of unexplained variation which is not accounted for by the variables in the analysis. This unexplained variance can be caused either by variables not brought into the analysis, or by discretion. This discretion can be equated with individual attention.

Theorem 1 can also indirectly supply the proof. According to Theorem 1, many forces can influence a defendant's fate either positively or negatively. Although court policy can determine if cases are processed in mass production, no two cases receive the same consideration all the time. Prosecutors, for example, will not always recommend identical sentences for two separate homicide cases. It depends on the circumstances. Prosecutors weigh the individual evidence and strength of the case, and this means individual attention.

There is more disparity than equality in the criminal justice system. This disparity can mean individual attention. Even codefendants in a case will receive different sentences. Even if the defendant isn't the focus of attention, but the arresting officer and the complainant are, the defendant is still receiving individual attention. Individual attention doesn't always mean a positive disposition; it can mean a negative disposition. Even if all drunken drivers, regardless of prior record, receive a fine for a disposition, and it appears that this is an example of "assembly-line justice," defendants are receiving individual attention in the sense that judges are not singling out a particular defendant for different punishment.

Theorem 3. An arrest record is a gauge of prognosis in criminal justice.

This theorem is somewhat easy to follow and prove. Although it is believed that many defendants commit crimes for which they don't get arrested, it is almost impossible for the criminal to be unapprehended; somewhere he has to be caught. Even if one assumes an economic theory of crime in the sense that offenders calculate the risks of getting caught, the offenders cannot always be lucky. This author has seen many defendants who failed to appear in court but eventually were arrested for further crime.

Research has shown that it can never be known with certainty that our treatment works. However, criminal justice agents like to believe that their efforts at rehabilitation have been directly or indirectly responsible for a defendant's less frequent contact with the courts. We can never be certain. Outside forces might be responsible for the defendant's reduced criminal activities. According to Theorem 1, forces outside of criminal justice, e.g., a wife or a job, can influence a defendant's fate positively. An analogous situation occurs in psychotherapy. A patient can spend thousands of dollars in psychotherapy, medicine, and hospitalization. Suddenly the patient is "normal"; he is employed, functioning, and needs less and less therapy and medicine. Psychiatrists like to believe that therapy and medication cured their patient. However, they can never really be certain.

It is not always important to know why a defendant commits less crime. It is not always important that he commits crimes for which he doesn't get arrested. We know that his criminal record will tell whether he is conforming to lawful behavior. This is what courts look for.

More evidence is the fact that prior record very often exerts a strong direct or indirect effect on final outcomes. The record is used as a gauge in making decisions on the defendant's fate. The prior record is used by prosecutors, probation officers, and judges. However, this is not the only factor affecting outcomes.

Theorem 4. There are no right or wrong decisions in criminal justice; there are only moral and normative decisions.

The proof is difficult to follow. We like to believe that our decisions are the right ones. Criminal justice personnel are often guided by this assumption. They tend to believe that their decisions are logical. If, for example, a defendant commits assault, has five prior felony convictions, doesn't work, and shows no remorse for his crime, it is logical, so some personnel say, to incarcerate him. They believe this defendant is dangerous.

On the other hand, what about the defendant who commits petit larceny to pay for his rent? He has no prior record, and the amount stolen was only $55. He is steadily employed. He is married with children and is considered a model husband. Is it right to incarcerate him? The consensus of opinion would probably be no; however, the law would permit his incarceration.

Criminal justice personnel sometimes spend a lot of time arguing the pros and cons of their decisions. Certainly these arguments should be continued. These decisions are approved or disapproved by a hierarchy of decision-makers. Yet each of these decisions is just as "right" or "wrong" as any other; one or more arguments can be found to support any decision. Criminal justice agents either can be kind, gentle, and humane, or mean, hostile, and punitive in their personality traits, which are just as "right" or "wrong" as other personality traits. A judge who is punitive and incarcerates defendants with long sentences for relatively minor crimes is just as logical as a judge who gives individual punishments to each defendant.

All decisions throughout the system, from arrest to termination of parole, involve outcomes which are neither right nor wrong. As long as these decisions are legal, then they are justified. All decisions may not satisfy all criminal justice actors, the defendants, or the defendants' peers, and the defendants may try to appeal these decisions, but these decisions are both right and wrong.

Therefore, it is not essential that all criminal justice personnel be good social workers and listen to each defendant. It is not essential that criminal justice personnel be free of prejudice and discrimination. Any decision is justified. Even a lenient disposition for a serious crime is justified because dangerousness can never be predicted with certainty.

We don't presently know if the four functions of punishment work. We cannot equate a certain range of punishments with a certain range in the reduction of crime. Sometimes, as research has shown, deterrence and rehabilitation work, but we cannot be certain who is deterred or rehabilitated, or how much. Therefore, there are no right or wrong answers; there are only normative and moral choices.

These assertions by this author are based on extensive experience, reading, and research. All decisions are moral and normative; they are all justified. There is always an argument justifying an atypical decision. Every criminal justice agent can invent a logical moral argument for every decision.

Norms very often govern decisions. These norms determine court policy. An example of a normative constraint is agreement that prior criminal record is important as a determinant in criminal justice decisions. However, these norms are not necessarily right or wrong.

Therefore, if judges were randomly to select legal punishments without thinking of each individual case, the result would not be a system of right or wrong decisions. All decisions would be just as right or wrong as those made after long deliberation of a particular case.

Decisions, however, must be based on criminal justice variables or parameters, e.g., prior record, seriousness of charge, psychiatric history, cooperation, number of warrants, etc. A judge cannot impose a ten-year prison sentence on a prostitute because her eyes are brown. He or she can, however, impose this sentence if the prostitute robs every client, and it is normative to incarcerate any offender who is a potential danger to the public.

A corollary to Theorem 4 might be, "There are no right or wrong actions in criminal justice which determine a decision." This means that if a criminal justice agent decides to obtain information on six factors for a particular decision and another agent decides on two factors for this decision, each agent is just as right or wrong as the other. For another example, suppose that one probation officer bases his sentencing recommendation on seriousness of the offense plus six other legal and extralegal factors, and another probation officer bases his sentencing recommendation on prior record only. All things being equal, the former probation officer will probably spend more time in making a decision. However, even though the latter probation officer is spending less time on the case compared to the former probation officer, each probation officer is doing the right or wrong thing depending on one's viewpoint. This also includes the quality of the action performed.

These actions, however, may be based on normative or moral considerations. They may be motivated by personal reasons, e.g. desire to please a supervisor, a judge, or fellow-workers; the desire to please a defendant; the desire to morally perform a good day's work.

The proof of this corollary follows from Theorem 4. Since there are no right or wrong decisions, and since decisions must be based on criminal justice variables and parameters, any action is right or wrong which leads to decisions based on norms, morals, and criminal justice variables.

Theorem 5. Uncertainty is essential in the criminal justice system.

This is somewhat difficult to prove. There have been studies showing that certainty of punishment is important and acts as a deterrent in criminal justice compared to uncertainty of punishment, but other studies have shown that certainty doesn't make a difference. Beccaria and Bentham stated that certainty, celerity, and severity of punishment were very important as a deterrent in criminal justice, but they never tested their assertion (see Chapter V).

It is known that discretion pervades the criminal justice system. Discretion cannot be eliminated. This follows from Theorem 2, which states that all defendants receive individual attention in the processing of their cases. Attempts to implement determinate sentencing have not eliminated discretion or disparity in sentencing; sentences are still unequal in order to individualize a defendant. It is essential that discretion be part of the system.

Theorem 5 follows from Theorem 4. It there are no right or wrong decisions in criminal justice, then it isn't essential that equality prevail in criminal justice. If there are no right or wrong answers, then uncertainty can pervade the system. One cannot ever know with certainty, for example, what sentence he will receive for committing a crime.

Uncertainty starts at the very beginning of the system. An offender at the time of arrest doesn't know exactly how the police will react to his crime. The offender doesn't know with certainty whether he or she will be given bail he or she can afford, paroled in his or her own custody, released on recognizance, or remanded before sentencing. There is uncertainty later on in the system. The offender or defendant doesn't know for certain what the prosecutor will charge or recommend or what the judge will do. The defendant is uncertain whether the defense attorney will help him.

The defendant may have some idea from past experience and from prevailing policy what the consequences will be, but he can never know how negatively or positively any criminal justice agent will act. If he thinks he knows exactly how the case will turn out, he is blinding himself or herself to reality. This follows from Theorem 1, that many agents and forces, both positive and negative, interact with the defendant's free will to affect the defendant's fate. Even a single crime like driving without a license may so irritate some emotionally distraught judge that the defendant's sentence is one year in prison instead of a fine.

Uncertainty is essential, for it sometimes represents the defendant's only hope that something positive wil happen to him. This author has interviewed thousands of inmates in remand before sentencing. Generally the remand cases were the worst cases of all. They usually had long prior records and were remanded because both the prosecutor and the judge wanted to give them a prison sentence. In spite of this, many defendants asked if they could get probation. Although they knew of a jail promise and accepted a plea on the basis of this, many still had hope that they would be released.

Although many defendants can calculate the exact time they have to spend in prison, there is uncertainty whether good time will be credited to them. Some incur infractions which will prevent their early release. This uncertainty keeps the prisoners in line.

This doesn't mean that certainty doesn't exist; it does. For example, judges generally adhere to plea-bargains made with the prosecutors and defense attorneys. Certain crimes carry mandatory prison sentences. Very serious charges and a heavy record mean severe dispositions. However, even here there are examples in which certainty is never completely assured.

Theorem 6. The criminal justice system will never break down.

This is difficult to prove, but it follows from theorems 1, 4, and 5. If many forces are at work, if there are no right or wrong decisions, and if uncertainty is essential, then the system is certain not to break down. There is too much flexibility built into it (relative to other cultures and societies). There are too many decisions that can keep the system in balance.

This doesn't mean that there aren't breakdowns in prison or in court; the history of corrections and criminal justice has proven that there were many of these. Attica and Sing Sing are two examples where breakdowns in prison have occurred. There have been riots in prisons for hundreds of years. However, new disturbances in prison or in court can result in new arrests and punishments. Certain key individuals or groups of inmates can be punished for their part in the riots. The system has checks and balances which assure its perpetuation.

As mentioned throughout this book, thousands were arrested during the racial riots of the 1960s in American cities. Still the system managed to survive because the offenders and defendants were processed quickly with light sentences. When jails and prisons get crowded, defendants can be given probation, fines, conditional discharges, or dismissals — because there are no right or wrong decisions in criminal justice. Also, as mentioned, the system has survived for hundreds of years without breaking down. In spite of all the threats that excessive caseloads and excessive court calendars will break the system down, it hasn't happened.

The proof of Theorem 6 is easier to see if we perceive the purpose of criminal justice as punishment. There is a general consensus in society that punishment is essential for the maintenance of our social system. Durkheim and Hobbes recognized this. The public accepts some form of punishment to bring offenders into line (although many segments of American society don't approve of certain acts of punishment, which they perceive as either too lenient or too severe).

The criminal justice system is accepted as one of the necessary institutions in our society. It is necessary to perceive punishment as the staple constant that pervades all action in criminal justice. Our society is too complicated for us to return to a system where private citizens decide among themselves the fate of offenders. This would lead to chaos.

The defendants themselves accept the system. Many defendants are law-abiding citizens themselves between crimes. They realize there must be a system of criminal justice.

All dispositions will be used among the offenders. Capital punishment is the most severe disposition which can be imposed in our society. In spite of the debate to reenact the death penalty in various states, it is being used sparingly today; however, it is still being used. All dispositions will be used if they exist. Judges, for example, cannot help giving prison sentences to some offenders because pressures mount for them to do so. Public opinion and prosecutors will press for prison sentences for criminal career offenders. As long as the alternatives exist, they will be used in some way.

Even the most humane, tolerant criminal justice agent will sometimes use the most severe sanctions. On the other hand, the most severe, punitive criminal justice agent will use the most lenient dispositions at times. He will use them because these alternatives exist. This helps to keep the system intact because it satisfies some criminal justice personnel and some public pressure. The diversity of alternatives, the uncertainty of outcomes, and the fact that all decisions are right or wrong, help to prevent the system from breaking down.

Conclusions

These six theorems essentially characterize the American system of criminal justice. What about other systems of justice? Can these theorems apply historically to all systems? Let's see.

The two assumptions certainly apply. Historically, as mentioned, the Classical school of criminology assumed that offenders had complete free will in committing crimes. Gradually, theorists questioned this, and the Positivist school of criminology believed that the offenders' fate sometimes was caused by conditions beyond their control. Historically, however, the criminal justice system was built and perpetuated upon the assumption that citizens valued a crime-free life, and that citizens abided by the prevailing norms of society, no matter how dissatisfied they were with these norms. This is one reason why vagrancy and witchcraft were punished for hundreds of years.

Even historically many criminal justice agents and forces impinged on an offender's life. There were juries and the Star Chamber in England. There was evidence that in England and Europe during the periods when the most brutal punishments were enacted, judges and others asked advice on methods of punishment from kings and queens. Chambers in England deliberated to enact the most severe punishment.[6]

There was evidence that some offenders escaped punishment. Benefit of clergy and trial by ordeal were two methods for offenders to escape punishment. There was evidence that preferential treatment was shown to women[7] and to various classes of society. Only slaves were tortured in ancient Greece, not citizens.[8] Certain types of punishment were reserved for certain classes of people. Perhaps this was analogous to individual attention to each case.

Very often, in the history of punishment, an offender who stole would be branded or have his ears or legs cut off as a reminder and as a deterrent to others about what would happen to them. There were other instances of warnings given to offenders during the history of the most severe punishments. This can be analogous to a criminal record as a gauge in criminal justice.

Historically, there were no right or wrong answers. All forms of punishment were accepted. The public generally condoned the forms of torture. Men of high esteem deliberated philosophically on the method and type of torture to be used. There were logical reasons to use the most severe forms of punishment. There were no right or wrong decisions or actions.

Historically, there was uncertainty. Although an offender was told of the punishment, no offender knew exactly how he or she would die. Much was left to the individual executioner. No offender knew exactly how he or she would react to the method of death. No offender knew exactly how much suffering would occur in his or her case or how the crowd would react. Some offenders didn't know the punishment until after they were accused of crimes. Some confessed in order to be spared torture and death.

The system maintained itself. There were many critics, of course, but the public saw no harm. The public even treated executions like a wedding, like a spectacle that amused them. The system didn't break down. It was supplemented with more humane forms of punishment. These were moral issues; there were no right or wrong answers.

This author believes that the two assumptions and six theorems can partially apply to other societies, but punishment is culturally and historically determined. Each society's criminal justice system would have to be analyzed historically in depth before any generalizations could be made. Perhaps other theorems would apply. However, this author believes that the six theorems loosely apply to other societies.

This analysis doesn't imply that all offenders receive justice. As mentioned in Chapter I, some criminologists have defined justice, but there is not universal agreement on the definition(s). Some defendants don't receive justice, no matter how it is defined. For example, justice may be defined as punishment for the guilty—but some innocent defendants are punished. If justice means equal dispositions for similar cases, then some defendants are not given justice. If justice means that criminal justice agents are free of prejudice, then some defendants don't receive justice. This doesn't negate Theorem 4, which states that there are no right or wrong decisions in criminal justice. It simply means that some offenders and defendants are going to get hurt according to various definitions of justice, but with no consequences to the system.

Offenders suffered injustice in the past. Parry states that the laws in England never authorized torture, and the common law prohibited it; yet it was administered in England. He states that those tortured in England implicated anyone, even the innocent, in order to gain relief from the agony of torture. Many innocent people were forced to confess under torture.[9]

One may believe that this author's approach is strictly a structural-functionalist approach. One can argue, as mentioned in Chapter I, that since the system is functional to the maintenance of society, it should be continued without question. History tells us that there were critics of the system hundreds of years ago. Bentham, Beccarra, Maconochie, and others were all critics who formulated schemes for improvement. There must have been critics in ancient times when Greeks and Romans tortured slaves, prisoners of war, and some free citizens, etc. There are probably critics of criminal justice in totalitarian and socialist countries today.

Those who criticize the system offer suggestions for reforms, but virtually all these reforms involve changes that keep the system intact. Suggestions for reform involve abolition of the grand jury or regular jury, abolition of plea-bargaining, restrictions of judges' power, shorter sentences, determinate sentencing, abolition of the worst conditions in prison, abolition of the parole board, community involvement in probation and parole, etc. Although new structures and functions are suggested, these suggestions for reform still leave the system intact.

Those who propose abolition of the system often recommend the abolition of our capitalist society. However, those who propose this abolition don't specify if the criminal justice system will be needed or not in the resulting new society. If a criminal justice system is not needed because crime would be entirely eliminated, then perhaps these theorems would not be applicable.

This author believes that perhaps his analysis suggests a new theory in criminal justice. Like all theories, it should be tested empirically. To do so would be a gigantic task. It will be important for others to comment on this theory both theoretically and empirically. As Popper states, no theory is 100 percent probable.[10] Theories must constantly be verified and refuted to make way for new theories. This, after all, is a definition of science.

Notes

Chapter I. The Nature of the Problem

1. Isaac Balbus, *The Dialectics of Legal Repression*, New York: Russell Sage Foundation, 1973.

2. See, for example, Herman and Julia Schwendinger, *Armchair Sociology-Sociology of the Chair*, New York: Basic Books, 1974, who believe that sociologists and criminologists assume the social system as given when analyzing our society.

3. Herman and Julia Schwendinger.

4. Louis P. Carney, *Introduction to Correctional Science*, New York: McGraw-Hill, 1974, 280, 294–295.

5. Harold K. Becker and Jack E. Whitehouse, *Police of America, a Personal View: Introduction and Commentary*, Springfield IL: Charles C. Thomas, 1979, 70.

6. Gordon A. Misner, "Criminal Justice Education — The Unifying Force," in Donald T. Shanahan, *The Administration of Justice System — an Introduction*, Holbrook Press, Boston: 1977, 23, 25.

7. Richard Quinney, *Class, State, and Crime*, New York: McKay, 1977, 114.

8. Misner, 23.

9. See Jack Gibbs, *Crime, Punishment, and Deterrence*, New York: Elsevier, 1975.

10. Milton Heumann, "A Note on Plea-bargaining and Case Pressure," *Law and Society Review*, 1975, 9:515–528.

11. Kenneth Culp Davis, *Discretionary Justice — a Preliminary Inquiry*, Baton Rouge: Louisiana State University Press, 1969; *Discretionary Justice in Europe and America*, Chicago: University of Illinois Press, 1976; and *Police Discretion*, St. Paul MN: West Publishing Co., 1975.

12. Edward Cahn, *The Sense of Injustice*, Bloomington: Indiana University Press, 1949, 12.

13. Ibid., 13–14.

14. Ibid., 19, 21–22.

15. Alfred Cohn and Roy Udolf, *The Criminal Justice System and Its Psychology*, New York: Van Nostrand Reinhold, 1979, 2, 10.

16. Ibid., 17.

17. Herbert L. Packer, *The Limits of the Criminal Sanction*, Stanford CA: Stanford University Press, 1968.

18. See Quinney.

19. Cohn and Udolf, VII.

20. Burton Wright and Vernon Fox, *Criminal Justice and the Social Sciences*, Philadelphia; W.B. Saunders, 1978, 247.

21. Willa Dawson, "The Need for a System Approach to Justice Administration," in Shanahan, 17.

22. J.W. La Patra, *Analyzing the Criminal Justice System*, Lexington MA: Lexington Books, 19, 92.

23. Carney, 65.

24. John F. Galliher and James McCartney, *Criminology, Power, Crime and Criminal Law*, Homewood IL: Dorsey Press, 1977, 122.

25. Howard Abadinsky, *Probation and Parole, Theory and Practice*, New York: Prentice-Hall, 1977, 67.

26. Cesare Beccaria, "On Crimes and Punishment," in Sawyer F. Sylvester, *The Heritage of Modern Criminology*, Cambridge MA: Shenkman Press, 1972, 11–12.

27. Galliher and McCartney, 459.

28. Henry M. Boies, *The Science of Penology — The Defense of Society Against Crime*, New York: Putnam, 1901.

29. Carney, 1, 4.

30. Cohn and Udolf, 212.

31. Roscoe Pound, *Criminal Justice in America*, New York: DaCapo, 1972, 38.

32. La Patra, 8–9.

33. Arthur Niederhoffer, *Beyond the Shield — The Police in Urban Society*, Garden City NY: Doubleday, 1967, 27.

Chapter II. What Is Science?

1. Lon L. Fuller, *The Morality of Law*, New Haven CT: Yale University Press, 1964, 19.

2. Karl Gareis, *Introduction to the Science of Law — Systematic Survey of the Law and Principles of Legal Study*, New York: Augustus M. Kelley, 1968, 13.

3. Ibid., 14.

4. Ernest Nagel, The *Structure of Science — Problems in the Logic of Scientific Explanation*, New York: Columbia University Press, 1961, 3–4.

5. Ibid., 5.

6. Carl G. Hempel, *Aspects of Scientific Explanations and Other Essays in the Philosophy of Science*, New York: Free Press, 1965, 139.

7. Ibid., 488.

8. Max Weber, *The Methodology of the Social Sciences*, New York: Free Press, 1949.

9. Ibid., 13.

10. Weber.

11. See Karl Popper, *Conjectures and Refutations — The Growth of Scientific Knowledge*, London: Routledge and Kegan Paul, 1963; *The Open Society and Its Enemies*, Princeton NJ: Princeton University Press, 1962; *Objective Knowledge — An Evolutionary Approach*, Oxford, At the Clarendon Press, 1972; and *The Logic of Scientific Discovery*, New York: Harper and Row, 1959.

12. Popper, *The Logic of Scientific Discovery*, 317.

13. Max Blatt, "Some Half-baked Thoughts About Induction," in Sidney Morgenbesser, Patrick Suppes and Morton White, eds., *Philosophy, Science and Method*, New York: St. Martin's Press, 1969. 147.

14. Hempel, 424–425.

15. R.B. Braithwaite, "Models in the Empirical Sciences," in Baruch A. Brody, ed., *Readings in the Philosophy of Science*, Englewood Cliffs NJ: Prentice-Hall, 1970. 268.

16. Thomas S. Kuhn, *The Structure of Scientific Revolution*, second edition, Chicago: University of Chicago Press, 1970.

17. Lewis Feuer, *Einstein and the Generation of Science*, New York: Basic Books, 1974.

18. See Quinney; Herman and Julia Schwendinger; and Ian Taylor, Paul Walton and Jock Young, *The New Criminology — For a Social Theory of Deviance*, London: Routledge and Kegan Paul, 1973, New York: Harper and Row, 1973.

19. Edward Shils, "Tradition, Ecology, and Institution in the History of Sociology," in Gerald Holton, *The Twentieth Century Sciences — Studies with Biography of Ideas*, New York: W.W. Norton, 1972, 83–84.

20. Saul Benisin, "The History of Polio Research in the United States — Appraisal and Lesson," in Holton, 327.

21. W.R. Campbell, "What is Theory"? in Brody, 252.

22. Ryan D. Tweney, Michael E. Doherty and Clifford R. Mynatt, *On Scientific Thinking*, New York: Columbia University Press, 1981, 7.

23. Popper, *Conjectures and Refutations*, 5.

24. Popper, *The Open Society and Its Enemies*, 32–33, 67, 286.

25. Noam Chomsky, "Some Empirical Assumptions in Modern Philosophy of Language," in Morgenbesser, Suppes and White, 286, 305.

26. Abraham Edil, "Metaphor, Analogies, Models, and All That in Ethical Theory," in Morgenbesser, Suppes and White, 364.

27. Nagel, 447.

28. Ibid., 471.

29. Hempel, 236, 243.

30. J.D. Bernal, *The Social Function of Science*, Cambridge MA: The M.I.T. Press, 1939, 342.

31. Shils, in Holton, 33.

32. Ibid., 89, 92.

33. Ibid., 91.

Chapter III. Theories of the Police

1. It is true that a witness or complainant sometimes initiates an arrest directly or indirectly, but the police are still the formal agents who have the authority and power to arrest a suspect.

2. That is, provided the case is not dismissed early in the process.

3. See, for example, Jerome Skolnick, *Justice Without Trial — Law-Enforcement in a Democratic Society*, New York: Wiley, 1966, 164.

4. See Niederhoffer, 133.

5. Harlan Hahn, "The Public and the Police — A Theoretical Perspective," in Harlan Hahn, *The Police in Urban Society*, Beverly Hills CA: Sage Publications, 1970, 28.

6. See Davis, *Police Discretion*, 46.

7. United States, *National Advisory Commission on Civil Disorders, The Kerner Report*, New York: Dutton, 1968.

8. Niederhoffer, 21.

9. Allen Silver, "The Demand for Order in Civil Society: A Review of Some Themes in the History of Urban Crime, Police, and Riots," in David Bordua, *The Police — Six Sociological Essays*, New York: Wiley, 1967, 51.

10. Niederhoffer, 22–24.

11. Roger Baldwin, "The Police and the Ex-Convict," *Criminology*, November, 1970, 8:287.

12. James Q. Wilson, *Varieties of Police Behavior — The Management of Law and Order in Eight Communities*, Cambridge MA: Harvard University Press, 1968, 28.

13. David H. Bayley and Harold Mendelsohn, *Minorities and the Police — Confrontation in America*, New York: Free Press, 1969.

14. George Berkley, *The Democratic Policeman*, Boston: Beacon Press, 1969, 11–12.

15. Hahn, in Hahn, 26.

16. John H. McNamara, "Uncertainties in Police Work — The Relevance of Police Recruits' Backgrounds and Training," in Bordua, 199.

17. Peter K. Manning, *Police Work — The Social Organization of Policing*, Cambridge MA: The M.I.T. Press, 1977, 354.

18. Skolnick, for example, believes that a conflict between bureaucratic rules, which emphasize initiative, and laws, which emphasize individual rights and restrain initiative, causes conflict in the police role. See Skolnick.

19. See, for example, William K. Muir, Jr., *Police — Street-Corner Politician*, Chicago: University of Chicago Press, 1977, 247; and Wayne LaFave, *Arrest — The Decision to Take a Suspect into Custody*, Boston: Little, Brown, 1965, 157.

20. Michael K. Brown, *Working the Streets — Police Discretion and the Dilemmas of Reform*, New York: Russell Sage Foundation, 1981, 50, 90, 286.

21. Leonard Savitz, "The Dimensions of Police Legality," in Hahn, 226.

22. See, for example, James I. Alexander, *Blue Coats-Black Skin — The Black Experience in the New York City Police Department Since 1891*, Hicksville NY: Exposition Press, 1978.

23. See, for example, Wilson, 78; and Jonathan Rubinstein, *City Police*, New York: Farrar, Straus and Giroux, 1973, 333, 445.

24. In certain respects, they are still probably a tightly knit group. For example, they may keep silent about informal, illegal practices, and offer mutual aid in time of emergency.

25. W. Boyd Littrell, *Bureaucratic Justice — Police, Prosecutors, and Plea-Bargaining*, Beverly Hills CA: Sage Publications, 1979, 163.

26. Albert J. Reiss, Jr., and David J. Bordua, "Environment and Organization — A Perspective on the Police," in Bordua, 39.

27. See Timothy D. Naegele, "Civilian Complaints Against the Police in Los Angeles," *Issues in Criminology*, Summer, 1967, 3:24. This doesn't mean the statement is accurate.

28. Arthur Niederhoffer and Alexander Smith, *New Directions in Police-Community Relations*, San Francisco: Holt, Rinehart and Winston, 1974, 13.

29. La Fave, 490, 505.

30. H. Goldstein, *Policing in a Free Society*, Cambridge MA: Ballinger, 1977, 217.

31. William A. Westley, *Violence and the Police — A Sociological Study of Law, Custom, and Morality*, Cambridge MA: The M.I.T. Press, 1970.

32. David Burnham, "Police Violence, A Changing Pattern," in Arthur Niederhoffer and Abraham Blumberg, *The Ambivalent Force — Perspectives on the Police*, Hinsdale IL: Dryden Press, 1976, 188.

33. John H. Broderick, *Police in a Time of Change*, Morristown NJ: General Learning Press, 1977, 8.

34. There are some exceptions. See, for example, Herman and Julia Schwendinger; and Taylor, Walton and Young.

35. Skolnick, 6, 10, 15, 241.

36. Manning, 6, 35.

37. Eric Beckman, *Law Enforcement in a Democratic Society*, Chicago: Nelson Hall, 1980, 298.

38. Davis, *Police Discretion*.

39. Jerome H. Skolnick and Richard Woodworth, "Bureaucracy, Information, and Social Control," in Bordua, 112.

40. Adrian Kinnane, *Policing*, Chicago: Nelson Hall, 1979, 154.

41. Richard J. Lundman, "Routine Police Arrest Practices: A Conventional Perspective," *Social Problems*, 1974, 22:127–141.

42. Donald J. Black, *The Manners and Customs of the Police*, New York: Academic Press, 1980.

43. Brown, 170, 212, 214, 218.

44. Wilson.

45. La Fave, 208.

46. Paul Chivigny, *Police Power — Police Abuses in New York City*, New York: Pantheon, 1969.

47. Black, 97.

48. Westley.

49. Lundman.

50. Albert J. Reiss, Jr., *The Police and the Public*, New Haven CT: Yale University Press, 1971, 53.

51. Theodore M. Ferdinand and Elmer G. Luchterhand, "Intercity Youth, the Police, the Juvenile Court, and Justice," *Social Problems*, Spring, 1970, 17:519.

52. Donald J. Black and Albert J. Reiss, Jr., "Police Control of Juveniles," *American Sociological Review*, 1970, 63:63–77.

53. Irving Piliavan and Scott Briar, "Police Encounters with Juveniles," *American Journal of Sociology*, 1964, 70:206–214.

54. La Fave, 76, 82, 144, 155, 227.

55. Littrell, 11.

56. Later, he retracts the statement and says that their higher suicide rate is mythical. See Alexander Smith and Harriet Pollack, *Criminal Justice, An Overview*, 2nd ed., New York: Holt, Rinehart and Winston, 1980, 93.

57. Niederhoffer, *Behind the Shield*.

58. Skolnick, *Justice Without Trial*, 70, 235; and Skolnick, "Research Contribution of the American Bar Association," in Niederhoffer and Blumberg, 219.

59. George L. Kirkham, "From Profession to Patrolman — A Fresh Perspective on the Police," in Niederhoffer and Blumberg, 219.

60. James Q. Wilson, "Police Morale Reform and Citizen Respect, The Chicago Case," in Bordua, 140, 142, 144, 146, 148.

61. McNamara, 194–198, 202, 210–212, 227, 249.

62. Kinnane, 6, 12–13.

63. Muir, Jr., 5, 36, 127, 157, 181, 244, 267, 292.

64. Reiss, *The Police and the Public*, 142, 164.

65. Michael Banton, *The Policeman in the Community*, New York: Basic Books, 1964, 149–150, 170, 267.

66. Broderick, 6, 21.

67. Bayley and Mendelsohn, 15, 18.

68. Brown, 84, Chapter 8.

69. Kinnane, 101.

70. Muir, Jr., 6.

71. Goldstein, 188, 192, 193, 210, 219.

72. Ellwyn R. Stoddard, "The Informal Code of Police Deviance: A Group Approach to Blue-Collar Crime," *Journal of Criminal Law, Criminology and Police Science*, June, 1968, 59:201–213.

73. Julian B. Roebuck, "A Typology of Police Corruption," *Social Problems*, 1974, 21:433–437.

74. Rubenstein, 387–388, 391, 405.

75. Savitz, in Hahn, 220, 221.

76. It is probably true that generally police are still very secretive and will not talk about their fellow officers.

77. Laurence W. Sherman, *Police Corruption—A Sociological Perspective*, New York: Anchor, 1974.

78. Laurence W. Sherman, "Controlling Police Corruption—Scandal and Organizational Reform," unpublished dissertation for the Ph.D., Yale University, 1976.

79. Knapp Commission, *Report on Police Corruption*, New York: George Braziller, 1972.

80. Bayley and Mendelsohn.

81. Edward Green, "Race, Social Status, and Criminal Arrest," *American Sociological Review*, 1970, 35:476–490.

82. Black, *The Manners and Customs of the Police*, 95, 99, 116, 136, 141.

83. Ibid., 123, 140.

84. Alexander.

85. Lundman.

86. Piliavin and Briar.

87. Ferdinand and Luchterhand, 510–527.

88. Robert F. Wintersmith, *Police and the Black Community*, Lexington MA: Lexington Books, 1974, XV, 96, 104.

89. Black and Reiss.

90. La Fave, 470.

91. W. Eugene Groves and Peter H. Rossi, "Perceptions of a Hostile Ghetto—Realism to Projection," in Hahn, 180, 184.

92. Goldstein, 271.

Chapter IV. Theories of the Court

1. Jerome H. Skolnick, "The Police and the Urban Ghetto," in Jack T. Kuykendall and Charles Reasons, *Race, Crime and Justice*, Pacific Palisades CA: Goodyear Publishing Co., 1972, 259.

2. This is true of other parts of the criminal justice system, e.g., the police.

3. James Eisenstein and Herbert Jacob, *Felony Justice: An Organizational Analysis of Criminal Courts*, Boston: Little, Brown, 1977, 9–10, 15–16, 28.

4. Laurence B. Mohr, "Organizations, Decisions, and Courts," *Law and Society Review*, Summer, 1976, 10:621–642.

5. Joseph Hoane, "Strategems and Values—An Analysis of Plea Bargaining in an Urban Court," unpublished dissertation for the Ph.D., New York University, 1978.

6. Roberta Rovner-Pieczenik, *The Criminal Court—How It Works*, Lexington MA: Lexington Books, D.C. Health, 1978, XIII, 2–4; and "Urban Justice: Understanding the Adjudication of Felony Cases in an Urban Criminal Court," unpublished dissertation for the Ph.D., New York University, 1974, 39–40, 202.

7. Malcolm M. Feeley, *The Process Is the Punishment*, New York: Russell Sage Foundation, 1979, 16, 18.

8. Norman Dorsen and Leon Friedman, *Disorder in the Court: Report of the Association of the Bar of the City of New York—Special Committee on Courtroom Conduct*, New York: Pantheon, 1973, 8, 124, 251.

9. Felix Frankfurter and Roscoe Pound, *Criminal Justice in Cleveland, Reports of*

the Cleveland Foundation Survey of the Administration of Justice in Cleveland, Ohio, Montclair NJ: Patterson Smith 1968, 191.

10. Dorsen and Friedman, 16.

11. Whitney North Seymour, Jr., *Why Justice Fails*, New York: Morrow, 1973, 3.

12. Herbert Jacob, *Justice in American Courts, Lawyers and the Judicial Process*, Boston: Little, Brown, 1965, 7.

13. Jerome Frank, *Courts on Trial — Myth and Reality in American Justice*, Princeton NJ: Princeton University Press, 1949, 11.

14. Hans Zeisel, Harry Kalven, Jr. and Bernard Buchholz, *Delay in the Court*, Boston: Little, Brown, 1959, 187, 209, 220.

15. Maureen Mileski, "Courtroom Encounters — Observations of a Lower Criminal Court," *Law and Society Review*, 1971, 5:473–538.

16. Martin A. Levin, "Delays in Five Criminal Courts," *Journal of Legal Studies*, 1975, 4:97.

17. See John H. Reed, *The Application of Operations Research to Court Delay*, New York: Praeger, 1973, 7; and James Eisenstein and Herbert Jacob, "Measuring Performance Outcomes of Urban Criminal Courts," *Social Science Quarterly*, 1974, 54:713–714.

18. See, for example, Neil C. Chamelin, "The Court Administrative Concept — Let the Judges Judge," in Shanahan, 249, 251.

19. Rovner-Pieczenik, *The Criminal Court — How it Works*, 17.

20. Raymond Moley, *Our Criminal Courts*, New York: Minton Batch, 1930, 26.

21. See Arthur J. Rosett and Donald Cressey, *Justice by Consent*, Philadelphia: Lippincott, 1976, 18; and Packer, 207.

22. Lee Silverstein, *Defense of the Poor in Criminal Cases in American State Courts*, Washington DC: American Bar Association, 1965, 125.

23. Lewis R. Katz, Laurence Litwin and Richard Bamberger, *Justice Is the Crime — Pretrial Delays in Felony Cases*, Cleveland: The Press of Case Western University, 1972, 119.

24. Donald Newman, *Conviction — The Determination of Guilt or Innocence Without Trial*, Boston: Little Brown, 1966, 45.

25. Paul Hoffman, *Court House*, New York: Hawthorn Books, 1978, 7.

26. See Abraham Blumberg, *Criminal Justice*, Chicago: Quadrangle Books, 1967.

27. Charles Ares and Herbert Sturz, "Bail and the Indigent Accused," *Crime and Delinquency*, January, 1962, 8:13.

28. Ronald Goldfarb, *Ransom — A Critique of the American Bail System*, New York: Harper and Row, 1965, 2.

29. William A. Landes, "Legality and Reality: Some Evidence in Criminal Procedure," *Journal of Legal Studies*, 1974, 3:333.

30. Goldfarb, 227.

31. Lee Silverstein, "Bail in the State Courts — a Field Study and Report," *Minnesota Law Review*, March, 1966, 50:621.

32. Herbert Packer, "Two Models of the Criminal Process," in John A. Robertson, *Rough Justice — Perspectives in Lower Criminal Courts*, Boston: Little, Brown, 1974, 141.

33. Rosett and Cressey, 22.

34. Stephen Bing and Stephen Rosenfeld, *The Quality of Justice in Lower Criminal Courts of Metropolitan Boston*, Boston: Lawyer's Committee for Civil Rights Under Law, 1970, 5.

35. Goldfarb, 101.

36. Bing and Rosenfeld, 124, 126.

37. Packer, *The Limits of the Criminal Sanction*, 219.

38. Ebbe B. Ebbesen and Vladimir J. Konečni, "An Analysis of the Bail System," in Vladimir J. Konecni and Ebbe B. Ebbesen, *The Criminal Justice System — a Social Psychological Analysis*, San Francisco: Freeman, Cooper, 1982, 202.

39. Silverstein, "Bail in the State Courts — a Field Study and Report," 623.

40. Katz, Litwin and Bamberger, 157.

41. Arthur L. Beeley, *The Bail System in Chicago*, Chicago: University of Chicago Press, 1927, 155.

42. Balbus, 109, 120, 121, 127, 129.

43. F. Philip Colista and Michael Domonkos, "Bail and Civil Disorders," *Journal of Urban Law*, Spring, Summer, 1968, 45:815–839.

44. Ebbesen and Konečni, 198.

45. Beeley, 78.

46. Goldfarb, X.

47. Paul B. Wice, "Bail and Its Reform," unpublished paper, 1973.

48. Goldfarb, 5, 156.

49. Landes, 324.

50. William H. Hewitt, *Administration of Criminal Justice in New York — a Manual for Law Enforcement Officers*, Rochester NY: Aqueduct Books, 1967, 177.

51. Rosett and Cressey, 197.

52. Cohn and Udolf, 163.

53. Frank J. Remington, Donald I. Newman, Edmond L. Kimball, Marygold Milli and Herman Goldstein, *Criminal Justice Administration — Materials and Cases*, New York: Bobbs-Merrill, 1976, 515.

54. Rovner-Pieczenik, "Urban Justice," 78–91.

55. Remington, Newman, Kimball, Milli and Goldstein, 555.

56. Hewitt, 185, 189.

57. Morris J. Bloomstein, *Verdict — The Jury System*, New York: Dodd, Mead, 1972, 124.

58. Harry Kalven, Jr. and Hans Zeisel, *The American Jury*, Boston: Little, Brown, 1966, 3.

59. Pearl Zuchlewski, "Challenging New York — The Grand Jury Composition — Barriers of the Systematic and Intentional Exclusion Requirement," *Fordham Urban Law Journal*, Winter, 1975, 6:332.

60. Littrell, 185.

61. Norbert Kerr, "Trial Participants' Behaviors and Jury Verdicts — An Exploratory Field Study," in Konečni and Ebbesen, 281.

62. Kalven, Jr., Zeisel, 372, 413.

63. William J. Bryan, Jr., *The Psychology of Jury Selection — The Chosen Ones*, New York: Vantage, 1971, Foreword, 16, 358.

64. Donald J. Jackson, *Judges — An Inside View of the Agonies and Exercises of an American Elite*, New York: Atheneum, 1974, 32.

65. Fred L. Strodbeck, Rita M. James and Charles Hawkins, "Social Status in Jury Selection," *American Sociological Review*, December, 1957, 27:713.

66. Kerr, 268, 269, 273, 278, 279, 280, 281.

67. Kalven, Jr. and Zeisel.

68. George J. McCall, *Observing the Law. Study of Crime and the Criminal Justice System*, New York: Free Press, 1978, 113.

69. Bloomstein, 113.

70. The authors, however, note that military background vanished when controls were introduced. That is, military background had no independent effect on the results.

71. Charles Judson, James J. Pandell, Jack B. Owens, James L. McIntosh and Dale L. Matschullat, "A Study of the California Penalty Jury in First Degree Murder Cases," *Stanford Law Review*, 1969, 21: 1247–49.

72. Cahn. Although theoretically this discussion of juries applies to the juries composed of laymen, it is possible for defendants, especially in misdemeanors, to be tried by a panel of three or more judges. In this case, new empirical evidence would have to be analyzed.

73. Mary S. Knudten, "Prosecutor's Role in Plea-Bargaining: Reasons Related to Actions," in Robert Rich, ed., *Essays in the Theory and Practice of Criminal Justice*, Washington DC: University Press of America, 1978, 275.

74. Newman, 234, 237.

75. David W. Neubauer, *Criminal Justice in Middle-America*, Morristown NJ: General Learning Press, 1974, 115.

76. Welsh S. White, "A Proposal for Reform of the Plea-Bargaining Process," *University of Pennsylvania Law Review*, 1970–1971, 119:448.

77. See, for example, Katz, Litwin and Bamberger, 115; and Pierce O'Donnell, Michael J. Churgin and Dennis E. Curtis, *Toward a Just and Effective Sentencing System-Agenda for Legislative Reform*, New York: Praeger, 1977, 169; and Littrell, 38.

78. President's Commission on Law Enforcement and Administration of Justice, *Task Force Report, the Courts*, Washington DC: United States Government Printing Office, 1967, 108.

79. William J. Teitlebaum, "The Prosecutor's Role in the Sentencing Process: A National Survey," *American Journal of Criminal Law*, 1972, 1:75–95.

80. See, for example, Albert W. Alschuler, "Sentencing Reform and Pro-secutorial Power—A Critique of Recent Proposals for 'Fixed and Presumptive' Sentencing," *University of Pennsylvania Law Review*, January, 1978, 126:567; and White, 443.

81. Jonathan D. Casper, *American Criminal Justice—The Defendant's Perspective*, Englewood Cliffs NJ: Prentice-Hall, 1972, 87, 128.

82. John Paul Ryan and James J. Alfini, "Trial Judges Participation in Plea-Bargaining: An Empirical Perspective," *Law and Society Review*, Winter, 1979, 13:478–505.

83. Harry M. More, Jr. and Richard Chang, *Contemporary Criminal Justice*, San Jose CA: Justice System Development, Inc., 1974, 7.

84. Frank Miller, *Prosecution—The Decision to Charge a Suspect with a Crime—Report of the American Bar Foundation's Survey of the Administration of Criminal Justice in the United States*, Boston: Little, Brown, 1969, 240.

85. See, for example, William J. Chambliss and Robert O. Seidman, *Law, Order, and Power*, Reading MA: Addison-Wesley, 1971, 409.

86. President's Commission on Law Enforcement and Administration of Justice, *Task Force Report*, 565.

87. Alschuler, 565.

88. Albert W. Alschuler, "The Prosecutor's Role in Plea-Bargaining," *University of Chicago Law Review*, Fall, 1968, 36:98.

89. Heumann.

90. Eisenstein and Jacob, *Felony Justice*, 238, 239.

91. Hoane, Chapters 2, 3.

92. Rosett and Cressey, 148–158.

93. Miller, 207.

94. Alschuler, "Prosecutor's Role in Plea-Bargaining," 54.

95. Neubauer, 236.

96. Littrell.

97. Newman, 78-79.

98. Rosett and Cressey, 100, 147.

99. William M. Rhodes, "The Economics of Criminal Courts—A Theoretical and Empirical Investigation," *Journal of Legal Studies*, 1976, 5:311.

100. Lois G. Forer, *Criminals and Victims—A Trial Judge Reflects on Crime and Punishment*, New York: W.W. Norton, 1980, 29.

101. Cohn and Udolf, 170, 171.

102. Knudten, 276-287.

103. La Patra, 108.

104. Hyman Gross, *A Theory of Criminal Justice*, New York: Oxford University Press, 1979, 29.

105. Newman, 75, 77.

106. Lief H. Carter, *The Limits of Order*, Lexington MA: Lexington Books, 1974, 19, 29, 42, 63.

107. Newman, 102, 105.

108. Packer, *The Limits of the Criminal Sanction*, 137.

109. Miller, 180, 189, 266, 279, 282-283, 347.

110. Alschuler, "The Prosecutor's Role in Plea-Bargaining," 58.

111. Reed, 187.

112. Newman, 125, 128-129, 174.

113. Neubauer, 202, 204, 218, 221.

114. David Sudnow, "Normal Crimes: Sociological Features of the Penal Code in a Public Defender Office," *Social Problems*, Winter, 1965, 12:255-276.

115. Hoane, 1:14, 4:6.

116. Lynn M. Mather, "Some Determinants of the Method of Case Disposition—Decison-Making by Public Defenders in Los Angeles," *Law and Society Review*, 1973, 8:210.

117. White, 446.

118. Rhoades, 332.

119. Law Enforcement Assistance Administration, *Private and Public Trouble: Prosecutors and the Allocation of Court Resources*, Washington DC: U.S. Government Printing Office, 1978.

120. Hoane, Chapters 3 through 7.

121. McCall, 97, 99.

122. Rovner-Pieczenik, *The Criminal Court—How It Works*, 17, 38, 39.

123. Martha A. Meyers, "The Effects of Victim Characteristics on the Prosecution, Conviction, and Sentencing of Defendants," unpublished dissertation for the Ph.D., Indiana University, 1977. This might be the same study reported earlier. See Law Enforcement Assistance Administration, *Private and Public Trouble*.

124. Littrell, 85, 164-165.

125. Hoffman, 43.

126. Balbus, 51, 112, 118, 142-143, 169.

127. Chambliss and Seidman, 373.

128. Leonard R. Mellon, Joan C. Jacoby and Marion A. Brewer, "The Prosecutor Constrained by His Environment—A New Look at Discretionary Justice in the United States," *Journal of Criminal Law and Criminology*, Spring, 1981, 72:52-81.

129. See Neubauer, 196.

130. Miller, 250-251.

131. Ernest Frieson, "Future Role of Judges, Prosecutors, and Defenders," in More, Jr. and Chang, 211.

132. Arthur M. Campbell, *Law of Sentencing*, New York: Lawyers' Co-operative Publishing Co., 1978, 446.

133. Smith and Pollack, 121.

134. Paul B. Wice and Peter Suwak, "Current Realities of Public Defender Programs — A National Survey and Analysis," *Criminal Law Bulletin*, 1974, 10:161-162.

135. Cohn and Udolf, 3-4, 10.

136. Abraham Blumberg, "The Practice of Law as a Confidence Game — Organizational Cooperation of a Profession," *Law and Society Review*, June, 1967, 1:28.

137. Rosett and Cressey, 126.

138. Ibtihaj Arafat and Kathleen McCatherty, "The Relationship Between Lawyers and Their Clients," in Rich, 194-214.

139. Bing and Rosenfeld, 32-34.

140. Silverstein, *Defense of the Poor*, 46, 55, 73.

141. Dallin H. Oaks and Warren Lehman, "Lawyers for the Poor," in Abraham Blumberg, *The Scales of Justice*, New York: Aldine, 102-103.

142. Albert Alschuler, "The Defense Attorney's Role in Plea Bargaining," *Yale Law Journal*, 1974, 84:1209.

143. Wice and Suwak, 169.

144. Robert Hermann, Eric Single and John Boston, *Counsel for the Poor — Criminal Defense in Urban America*, Lexington MA: Lexington Books, 1977, 43, 154, 159-161.

145. Casper, 113-119, 122-123.

146. Rovner-Pieczenik, *The Criminal Court — How It Works*, 80, 81, 82, 88, 91-92.

147. Meyers, 54.

148. Stuart Nagel, "The Zipped Scales of American Justice," in Blumberg, *The Scales of Justice*, 38.

149. William J. Chambliss, *Crime and the Legal Process*, New York: McGraw-Hill, 1965, 216.

150. Alan J. Lizotte, "Extra-Legal Factors in Chicago's Criminal Courts — Testing the Conflict Model of Criminal Justice," *Social Problems*, June, 1978, 25:564-580.

151. Bing and Rosenfeld, 32-34.

152. Balbus, 124.

153. Cohn and Udolf, VII, 130-131, 154.

154. Seymour, Jr., 23.

155. President's Commission on Law Enforcement and Administration of Justice, 119.

156. Smith and Pollack, 207.

157. Pamuela Samuelson, "Sentence Review and Sentence Disparity — A Case Study of the Sentence Review Division," *Connecticut Law Review*, Fall, 1977, 10:10.

158. William Austin and Thomas A. Williams, "A Survey of Judges' Responses to Simulated Legal Cases — Research Note in Sentencing Disparity," *Journal of Criminal Law and Criminology*, 1977, 68:306.

159. Sol Rubin, "Disparity and Equality of Sentences — A Constitutional Challenge," *Federal Reports Decisions*, 1966, 40:55.

160. Samuelson, 30.

161. Balbus, 84, 170, 203. Of course, as Balbus himself points out, some of these sentences might be normal regardless of the riot situations.

162. Rovner-Pieczenik, *The Criminal Court — How It Works*, 36.

163. Sheldon Messinger and Philip E. Johnson, "California's Determining Sentencing Statute — History and Issues," in National Institute of Law Enforcement

and Criminal Justice, Law Enforcement Assistance Administration, *Determinate Sentencing — Reform or Regression?*, Washington DC: U.S. Department of Justice, 1978, 16–54.

164. April Cassou and Brian Taugher, "Determinate Sentencing in California — The New Numbers Game," *Pacific Law Journal*, 1978, 9:5–106.

165. See Alschuler, "Sentencing Reform and Prosecutorial Power — A Critique for Recent Proposals for 'Fixed and Presumptive' Sentencing," in National Institute of Law Enforcement and Criminal Justice, 80.

166. John O. Newman, "A Better Way to Sentence Criminals," *American Bar Association Journal*, 1977, 63:1563.

167. Joint Committee on Continuing Legal Education of the American Law Institute of the American Bar Association, *The Problem of Sentencing*, New York: American Bar Association, 1962, 29.

168. Thomas J. Bernard, "Individualization vs. Uniformity — The Case of Regulation of Criminal Justice," *Federal Probation*, December, 1970, 40:19–23.

169. Lizotte, 564–565.

170. Marshall B. Clinard and Peter C. Yeager, *Corporate Crime*, New York: Free Press, Macmillan, 1980.

171. Victoria Lynn Swigert and Ronald A. Farrell, *Murder, Inequality, and the Law — Differential Treatment in the Legal Process*, Lexington MA: Lexington Books, 1976; and "Normal Homicides and the Law," *American Sociological Review*, February, 1977, 42:16–32.

172. Lizotte, 564–580.

173. Stuart Nagel, "Disparities in Criminal Procedures," *University of California Law Review*, August, 1964, 14:1271–1305.

174. Theodore G. Chiricos and Gordon Waldo, "Socioeconomic Status and Criminal Sentencing — An Empirical Assessment of a Conflict Proposition," *American Sociological Review*, December, 1975, 40:753–772.

175. Charles Reasons, "On Methodology, Theory, and Ideology," *American Sociological Review*, 1977, 42:177–181.

176. La Patra, 131.

177. See, for example, John Hagan, "The Social and Legal Construction of Criminal Justice — A Survey of Pre-Sentence Process," *Social Problems*, 1975, 38:620–637.

178. See, for example, John Hogarth, *Sentencing As a Human Process*, Toronto: University of Toronto Press, 1971, 373, 376.

179. Newman, *Conviction*, 15.

180. Harry More, Jr., "Disparity in the System," in More, Jr. and Chang, 33.

181. Robert O. Dawson, *Sentencing — The Decision As to Type, Length, and Conditions of Sentencing*, Boston: Little, Brown, 1969, 78.

182. American Bar Association, *Project on Standards for Criminal Justice, Probation*, New York: American Bar Association, 1970, 73.

183. Jeremy S. Williams, *The Law of Sentencing and Correction*, Buffalo NY: William L. Hein, 1974, 1.

184. Casper, 17, 135.

185. For a biography on sentencing, see James R. Davis, *The Sentencing Dispositions of New York City Lower Court Criminal Judges*, Washington DC: University Press of America, 1982.

186. Sometimes these factors are classified in other ways, e.g., legal variables, personal attributes, and relations.

187. Charles E. Silberman, *Criminal Violence, Criminal Justice*, New York: Random House, 1978, 254–255, 266, 290–291, 294.

188. Vladimir I. Konečni and Ebbe E. Ebbesen, "An Analysis of the Sentencing System," in Konečni and Ebbesen, 325.

189. Meyers, 235, 236, 237, 256, 277.

190. Smith and Pollack, 211.

191. Hogarth.

192. Stuart Nagel, "Judicial Backgrounds and Criminal Cases," *Journal of Criminal Law, Criminology, and Police Science*, 1962, 53:33–339.

193. Eisenstein and Jacob, "Measures of Performance and Output in Urban Criminal Courts," 333–339.

194. Austin and Williams, 308.

195. Rufferford B. Campbell, "Sentencing—The Use of Psychiatric Information and Presentence Reports," *Kentucky Law Journal*, 1971-1972, 60:311.

196. Neubauer, 240–243.

197. Rosett and Cressey, 83.

198. Eisenstein and Jacob, *Felony Justice*, 9.

199. Campbell, *Law of Sentencing*, 44.

200. See, for example, George M. Pugh and Hampton Carver, "Due Process of Sentencing—From Mapp to Mempa to McGautha," *Texas Law Review*, 1971, 49:32.

201. Marvin E. Frankel, *Criminal Sentences—Law Without Order*, New York: Hill and Wang, 1972, 13.

202. George E. Dix, "Judicial Review of Sentencing—Implications for Individual Dispositions," *Law and the Social Order*, 1969, 1:373.

203. Eric M. Edmunds, Jr., "Disparity and Discretion in Sentencing—A Proposal for Uniformity," *University of California Law Review*, 1977, 25:327.

204. Friesen, 210–211.

Chapter V. Theories of Punishment

1. The four functions will be defined and operationalized either implicitly or explicitly as the discussion goes on.

2. Francis A. Allen, "Criminal Justice, Legal Values, and the Rehabilitative Ideal," in Stanley E. Grupp, ed., *Theories of Punishment*, Bloomington: Indiana University Press, 1971, 323.

3. Ted Honderich, *Punishment—The Supposed Justification*, London: Hutchinson, 1969, 1.

4. Commission of Canada, *Fear of Punishment and Deterrence*, Montreal: Minister of Supply and Services, 1976, 21.

5. Frank Pakenham Lonford, *The Idea of Punishment*, London: Geoffrey Chapman, 1961, 102.

6. In the Probation Department of New York City where this author has been employed for many years, the staff was told that probation was strictly rehabilitation, not punishment. The probation officers were literally ordered not to think of probation as a form of punishment.

7. Sir Walter Moberly, *The Ethics of Punishment*, Hamden CT: Archon, 1968, 99.

8. Dwight C. Jarvis, *Institutional Treatment of the Offender*, New York: McGraw-Hill, 1978, 13.

9. Allen, 318–319.

10. Jerome Hall, "The Purpose of a System for the Administration of Criminal Justice," in Grupp, 390.

11. Honderich, 4.

12. Anthony J. Manocchio and Jimmy Dunn, *The Time Game — Two Views of Prison*, Beverly Hills CA: Sage Publications, 1970, 249.

13. Moberly, 269.

14. Graeme Newman, *The Punishment Response*, Philadelphia: Lippincott, 1978, 84.

15. J. Thorsten Sellin, *Slavery and the Penal System*, New York: Elsevier, 1976, 13.

16. See, for example, John Monahan, "A Critique of Kozol et al.," *Crime and Delinquency*, 1973, 19:418–420.

17. Herbert Morris, "Persons and Punishment," in Grupp, 79.

18. D.J.B. Hawkins, "Punishment and Moral Responsibility," in Grupp, 14.

19. Gordon Hawkins, "Punishment and Deterrence — The Educational, Moralizing, and Habituative Effects," in Grupp, 168–169.

20. Margaret Wilson, *The Crime of Punishment*, New York: Harcourt, Brace, 1931, 25, 60.

21. Moberly, 92, 134, 141, 232, 233, 343, 381.

22. T.C. Esselstyn, "The Social System of Correctional Workers," in Robert M. Carter and Leslie T. Wilkins, eds., *Probation and Parole — Selected Readings*, New York: Wiley, 1970, 691.

23. Newman, *The Punishment Response*, 8.

24. Moberly, 381.

25. Franklin E. Zimring, "Punishment and Deterrence — Bad Checks in Nebraska — a Study in Complex Threats," in David F. Greenberg, ed., *Corrections and Punishments*, Beverly Hills CA: Sage Publications, 1977, 188.

26. John Freeman, *Prisons Past and Future*, London: Heinemann Educational Books, 1978, 208.

27. Forer, 91.

28. Abadinsky, 17.

29. Raymond Saleilles, *The Individualization of Punishment*, Boston: Little, Brown, 1911, 55, 84, 102, 151.

30. This biography of Beccaria comes from Cesare Beccaria, *On Crimes and Punishment*, Indianapolis: Bobbs-Merrill, 1963; and a review of the literature.

31. Gibbs, 9.

32. Aryeh Neier, *Crime and Punishment — a Radical Solution*, New York: Stein and Day, 1978, 132–133.

33. Newman, *The Punishment Response*, 153.

34. Ibid., 202, 203, 206.

35. This analysis of Bentham is based on the review of the literature.

36. Andrew von Hirsch, *Doing Justice — The Choice of Punishment: Report of the Committee for the Study of Incarceration*, New York: Hill and Wang, 1976, 6, 160.

37. Sir Walter Moberly, "The Ethics of Punishment," in Rudolph J. Gerber and Patrick D. McAnany, eds., *Contemporary Punishment — Views, Explanations and Justifications*, Notre Dame IN: University of Notre Dame Press, 1972, 73.

38. Harry Elmer Barnes, *The Story of Punishment — a Record of Man's Inhumanity to Man*, Montclair NJ: Patterson Smith, 1972, 96.

39. Newman, *The Punishment Response*, 211–214.

40. Enrico Ferri, *Criminal Sociology*, New York: D. Appleton, 1898.

41. John Hospers, "Retribution, the Ethics of Punishment," in Randy E. Barnett and John Hagel, eds., *Assessing the Criminal — Restitution, Retribution, and the Legal Process*, Cambridge MA: Ballinger, 1977, 188.

42. Von Hirsch XXXVII.

43. Abadinsky, 8.

44. Edmund Pincoffs, *The Rationale of Legal Punishment*, New York: Humanities Press, 1966, 98–101.

45. Gustave de Beaumont and Alexis de Tocqueville, *On the Penitentiary System in the United States and Its Application in France*, Philadelphia: Carey, Lea, and Blanchard, 1833.

46. Frank G. Carrington, *Neither Cruel nor Unusual*, New Rochelle NY: Arlington House, 1978, 52.

47. Gibbs, 4, 13, 151, 237–238.

48. Clinand and Yeager, 90.

49. Dorothy Miller, Ann Rosenthal, Don Miller and Cheryl Ruzek, "Public Knowledge of Criminal Penalties—a Research Report," in Grupp, 212.

50. Newman, *The Punishment Response*, 28, 38, 192, 195–198.

51. Norval Morris and Donald Buckle, "The Humanitarian Theory of Punishment—a Reply to C.S. Lewis," in Grupp, 13.

52. Egon Bittner and Anthony Platt, "The Meaning of Punishment," in Gerber and McAnany, 27.

53. Wilson, *The Crime of Punishment*, 146.

54. Barnes, 45–48.

55. Svend Ranulf, *Moral Indignation and Middle-class Psychology—a Sociological Study*, New York: Schocken, 1960. Ranulf never uses "retribution" as the author does. He uses the words "punishment" and "disinterested tendency." However, he has been considered to be talking about retribution. This is implied in his work.

56. Jackson Toby, "Is Punishment Necessary"? in Grupp, 108–109.

57. Larry Charles Berkson, *The Concept of Cruel and Unusual Punishment*, Lexington MA: Lexington Books, 1975, 81.

58. Newman, *The Punishment Response*, 6–7, 54, 263.

59. Many good sources reveal the history of punishment. Three suggested by the author are Newman, *The Punishment Response*; Barnes; and Heinrich Oppenheimer, *The Rationale of Punishment*, London: University of London Press, 1913.

60. Newman, *The Punishment Response*, 104–105.

61. Ibid., 113.

62. Ibid., 123.

63. Carney, 54–55.

64. Ronald Goldfarb and Linda Singer, *After Conviction—A Review of the American Correctional System*, New York: Simon and Schuster, 1973, 142.

65. Andrew A. Bruce, Albert J. Harno, Ernest M. Burgess and John Landesco, *The Workings of the Indeterminate Sentence—Law of the Parole System in Illinois*, Montclair NJ: Patterson Smith, 1968, 14.

66. Task Force on Criminal Sentencing, *Fair and Uncertain Punishment—Report of the Twentieth Century Fund*, New York: McGraw-Hill, 1976, 83.

67. Newman, *The Punishment Response*, 123.

68. Ibid., 5, 32, 36, 60, 94–95, 123, 135, 136, 207.

69. George Rudé, *Protest and Punishment—The Story of Social and Political Protestors. Transportation to Australia, 1778–1868*, Oxford: Clarendon, 1978.

70. Ibid., 47.

71. Hans Von Hentig, *Punishment, Its Origin, Purpose, and Psychology*, Montclair NJ: Patterson Smith, 1973, 73.

72. Ibid., 80, 88.

73. George Rusche and Otto Kirchheimer, *Punishment and Social Structure*, New York: Russell and Russell, 1939, 20.

74. Newman, *The Punishment Response*, 48, 50.

75. Saleilles, 46–47.

76. Newman, *The Punishment Response*, 57.

77. Karl Schuessler, "The Deterrent Influence of the Death Penalty," in Grupp, 191.

78. David D. Cooper, *The Lesson of the Scaffold, The Public Execution Controversy in Victorian England*, Athens: Ohio University Press, 1974, 5.

79. Von Hentig, 48.

80. Janet Harris, *Crisis in Corrections — The Prison Problem*, New York: McGraw-Hill, 1973, 25–26.

81. Rusche and Kirchheimer, 9, 16.

82. Newman, *The Punishment Response*, 210.

83. Sellin, 18, 39, 41.

84. Nicholas N. Kittrie, *The Right to be Different, Deviance and Enforced Therapy*, Baltimore: Johns Hopkins University Press, 1971, 32, 108–109.

85. Newman, *The Punishment Response*, 110, 140.

86. Barnes, 71.

87. Michael Steven Hindus, "Prison and Plantation — Criminal Justice in Nineteenth Century Massachusetts and South Carolina," unpublished dissertation for the Ph.D., University of California, Berkeley, 1975, 283.

88. Kittrie, 19.

89. Phyllis Elperin Clark and Robert Lehrman, *Doing Time — A Look at Criminal Prisons*, New York: Hastings House, 1980, 26.

90. Goldfarb and Singer, 320, 322.

91. Rusche and Kirchheimer, 79.

92. Task Force on Criminal Sentencing, 83–84.

93. Moberly, *The Ethics of Punishment*, 71, 291.

94. Newman, *The Punishment Response*, 111.

95. Michael Ignatieff, *A Just Measure of Pain — the Penitentiary in the Industrial Revolution — 1750-1850*, New York: Pantheon, 1978, 19, 45.

96. Berkson, 21.

97. Newman, *The Punishment Response*, 145, 185.

98. Berkson, 8, 9, 10, 11.

99. Lloyd E. Ohlin, *Prisoners in America — The American Assembly*, Englewood Cliffs NJ: Prentice-Hall, 1973, 50–51.

100. Barnes, 66, 128.

101. Harris, 53–54.

102. Newman, *The Punishment Response*, 181, 183, 185.

103. Cooper, 4, 39.

104. Newman, *The Punishment Response*, 185.

105. Sellin, 109.

106. Rudé, 61, 67, 180, 186, 187.

107. Saleilles, 256–257.

108. Gibbs, 156.

109. La Patra, 77; and Robert Martinson and Judith Wilks, *The Effectiveness of Correctional Treatment Evaluation Studies*, New York: Praeger, 1975.

110. Robert Fishman, *Criminal Recidivism in New York City — An Evaluation of the Impact of Rehabilitation and Diversion Services*, New York: Praeger, 1972.

111. Jessica Mitford, *Kind and Usual Punishment, The Prison Business*, New York: Knopf, 1973, 287.

112. Harry L. Kozol, Richard J. Boucher and Ralph F. Garofolo, "The

Diagnosis and Treatment of Dangerousness," *Crime and Delinquency*, 1972, 18:371–392.

113. Charles E. Weeks, "Evaluation of a Method of Predicting Violence in Offenders," *Criminology*, 1973, 11:427–435.

114. Carrington, 88–90, 199.

115. Leon S. Robertson and Robert J. Rich, "Deterring the Drunk Driver," in Norman Johnston and Leonard Savitz, *Justice and Corrections*, New York: Wiley, 1978, 391–399.

116. Stephen Van Dine, Simon Dinitz and John Conrad, "Incapacitation of Dangerous Offenders," in Johnston and Savitz, 422–432; and *Restraining the Wicked — The Incapacitation of Dangerous Offenders*, Lexington MA: Lexington Books, 1979.

117. Charles R. Tittle, *Sanction and Social Deterrence — The Question of Deterrence*, New York: Praeger, 1980.

118. Barnes, 6.

119. Johannes Andenaes, *Punishment and Deterrence*, Ann Arbor: University of Michigan Press, 1974, 86.

120. Rusche and Kirchheimer, 203.

121. Commission of Canada, 20, 60–62, 86–89, 91.

Chapter VI. Theories of Corrections

1. Daniel Glaser, *The Effectiveness of a Prison and Parole System*, New York: Bobbs-Merrill, 1964, 92.

2. James Jacobs, *Stateville — The Penitentiary in Mass Society*, Chicago: University of Chicago Press, 1977, X.

3. John Irwin, *Prisons in Turmoil*, Boston: Little, Brown, 1980, X.

4. Glaser, 225.

5. Robert Sommer, *The End of Imprisonment*, New York: Oxford University Press, 1976, 104.

6. Jack Newfield, *Cruel and Unusual Justice*, New York: Holt, Rinehart and Winston, 1974, 69.

7. Louis M. Robinson, *Jails — Care and Treatment of Misdemeanant Prisoners in the United States*, Philadelphia: John Winston, 1944, 36.

8. Anthony M. Sacco, *Rape in Prison*, Springfield IL: Charles C. Thomas, 1975, 20.

9. Susan Sheehan, *A Prison and a Prisoner*, Boston: Houghton Mifflin, 1978, 116.

10. L. Goodstein, "Inmate Adjustment to Prison and Post-Release Outcome," unpublished dissertation for the Ph.D., City University of New York, 1977, 22.

11. Donald R. Cressey, "Achievement of an Unstated Organizational Goal — An Observation on Prisons," in Laurence E. Hazelrigg, *Prison and Society — A Reader in Penology*, New York: Doubleday, 1968, 52.

12. Kathryn Waterson Burkhart, *Women in Prison*, Doubleday, 1973, 322.

13. Paul W. Keve, *Prison Life and Human Worth*, Minneapolis: University of Minnesota Press, 1974, 46.

14. Sommer, 159.

15. Ronald Goldfarb, *Jails — The Ultimate Ghetto*, Garden City NY: Anchor, 1975.

16. Ohlin, 148.

17. Newman, *The Punishment Response*, 4, 84.

18. Gordon Hawkins, *The Prison — Policy and Practice*, Chicago: University of Chicago Press, 1976, 44.

19. Barnes, 114; and Sommer, 3.

20. Blake McKelvey, *American Prisons — A Study in American Social History Prior to 1915*, Montclair NJ: Patterson Smith, 1936, XI.

21. Paul Takagi, "The Walnut Street Jail — A Penal Reform to Centralize the Power of the State," *Federal Probation*, 1975, 39:18-26.

22. Anonymous, "The Correctional System," *Crime and Social Justice*, 1974, 2:82-89; and Rusche and Kirchheimer, 68-69.

23. Robert Martinson, "The Paradox of Prison Reform," in Franklin Zimring and Gordon J. Hawkins, eds., *Deterrence — The Legal Threat in Crime Control*, Chicago: University of Chicago Press, 1973, 313.

24. Wilson, *The Crime of Punishment*, 207.

25. Clark and Lehrman, 52.

26. Ignatieff, 29-30.

27. Harris, 76; and Frances C. Gray, *Prison Discipline in America*, Montclair NJ: Patterson Smith, 1973.

28. Ignatieff, 209, 215.

29. Freeman, 9, 21, 70.

30. Donald Cressey, "Contradictory Directions in Complex Organizations: The Case of the Prison," in Hazelrigg, 477.

31. Gresham M. Sykes, *The Society of Captives — A Study of the Maximum-Security Prison*, Princeton NJ: Princeton University Press, 1958, VII.

32. Hawkins, *The Prison*, 1.

33. Glaser, 217-218.

34. Rusche and Kirchheimer, 109.

35. Ignatieff, 52, 85, 89; and Harjit S. Sandhu, *Modern Corrections — The Offenders, Therapy and Community Reintegration*, Springfield IL: Charles C. Thomas, 1974, 126.

36. McKelvey, 183.

37. Gilbert Geiss, "Ethics of Prison Experimentation," in Johnston and Savitz, 618; and Mitford, 140.

38. Ignatieff, 122-123, 154.

39. Clarice Feinmore, "Imprisoned Women — A History of the Treatment of Women Incarcerated in New York City, 1932-1975," unpublished dissertation for the Ph.D., New York University, 50.

40. Carney, 196.

41. Ignatieff, 178-179, 180.

42. Wilson, *The Crime of Punishment*, 246.

43. Wilson, *The Crime of Punishment*, 216.

44. Columbus B. Hopper, "Conjugal Visiting," in Johnston and Savitz, 446; and Neier, 182.

45. Feinmore, 40, 191.

46. De Beaumont and de Tocqueville.

47. Jarvis, 30, 31; Neier, 188; and Marvin E. Wolfgang, *Prisons — Present and Possible*, Lexington MA: Lexington Books, 1979, 27, 28, 42.

48. Barnes, 171.

49. Hawkins, *The Prison*, 42.

50. Howard Levy and David Miller, *Going to Jail — The Political Prisoner*, New York: Marcel Dekker, 1969, 115; and Theodore Davidson, *Chicano Prisoners — The Key to San Quentin*, New York: Holt, Rinehart and Winston, 1974, 159.

51. Brian Glick, "Changes Through the Courts," in Erik Olin Wright, ed., *The Politics of Punishment — A Critical Analysis of Prisons in America*, New York: Harper and Row, 1973, 286.

52. Irwin.

53. Donald Clemmer, *The Prison Community*, Boston: Christopher Publishing Co., 1940.

54. Irwin, 31, 32.

55. Sandhu, 116.

56. Donald L. Garrity, "The Prison as a Rehabilitation Agency," in Donald Cressey, ed., *The Prison—Studies in Institutional Organization and Change*, New York: Holt, Rinehart and Winston, 1961, 362.

57. Daniel Glaser and John R. Stratton, "Measuring Female Change in Prison," in Cressey, 381, 383.

58. James B. Jacobs, "Stratification and Conflict Among Prison Inmates," in Johnston and Savitz, 580.

59. Gene Kassebaum, David A. Ward and Daniel Wilner, *Prison Treatment and Parole Survival—An Empirical Assessment*, New York: Wiley, 1971, 143.

60. Peter G. Garabedian, "Social Roles in a Correctional Community," *Journal of Criminal Law, Criminology and Police Science*, September, 1964, 55:341.

61. Frederick A. Hussey and David C. Duffee, *Probation, Parole and Community Field Services, Policy Structure and Processes*, New York: Harper and Row, 1980, 154.

62. Sykes.

63. Goodstein, 17-18, 20; and Peter J. Garabedian, "Social Role Process and Socialization in the Prison Community," in Norman Johnston, Leonard Savitz and Marvin C. Wolfgang, eds., *The Sociology of Punishment and Correction*, New York: Wiley, 1970, 485-494.

64. Jacobs, *Stateville*, 48-49, 58.

65. Garabedian, "Social Roles in a Correctional Community," 338-347.

66. Charles M. Thomas and Samuel C. Fists, "The Importation Model—Perspectives on Inmate Social Roles—An Empirical Assessment," *Sociological Quarterly*, Spring, 1973, 14:226-234.

67. Clarence Schrag, "Leadership Among Prison Inmates," *American Sociological Review*, February, 1954, 19:37-42.

68. Kassebaum, Ward and Wilner, 144.

69. Gresham Sykes and Sheldon Messinger, "The Inmate Social System," in Richard A. Cloward et al., eds., *Theoretical Studies in the Social Organization of a Prison*, New York: Social Science Research Council, 1960, 12.

70. Esther Hefferman, *Making It in Prison—The Square, the Cool, and the Life*, New York: Wiley, 1972, 25.

71. Sykes and Messinger, in Cloward et al., 9-18.

72. Manocchio and Dunn, 25, 150.

73. Barry C. Feld, *Neutralizing Inmate Violence—Juvenile Offenders in Institutions*, Cambridge MA: Ballinger, 1977, 94-96; and John Irwin and Donald Cressey, "Thieves, Convicts, and the Inmate Culture," *Social Problems*, Fall, 1962, 10:42-55.

74. Rose Giallombardo, *Society of Women—a Study of Women's Prisons*, New York: Wiley, 1966.

75. David A. Ward and Gene G. Kassebaum, *Women's Prisons—Sex and Social Structure*, Chicago: Aldine, 1965.

76. Hefferman.

77. David A. Ward and Gene G. Kassebaum, "Homosexuality in a Women's Prison," in Johnston, Savitz and Wolfgang, 464-477.

78. Ohlin, 137.

79. Rose Giallombardo, *The Social World of Imprisoned Girls—A Comparative Study of Institutions for Juvenile Delinquents*, New York: Wiley, 1974.

80. Feld, 172–173.

81. Casper, 159, 163, 168, 178; and Manocchio and Dunn, 150.

82. Hans Toch, *Men in Crisis — Human Breakdowns in Prison*, Chicago: Aldine, 1975.

83. Goodstein.

84. Anastassios D. Mylonas and Walter C. Reckless, "Prisoners' Attitudes Toward Law and Legal Institutions," *Journal of Criminal Law, Criminology and Police Science*, 1963, 54:479–484.

85. John Irwin, *The Felon*, Englewood Cliffs NJ: Prentice-Hall, 1970, 55, 134, 144.

86. Glaser, *The Effectiveness of a Prison and Parole System*, 313, 315, 486.

87. Hans Toch, *Living in Prison — The Ecology of Survival*, New York: Free Press, 1971.

88. Stanley Cohen and Laurie Taylor, *Psychological Survival — The Experience of Long-term Imprisonment*, New York: Pantheon, 1972.

89. Sacco.

90. Daniel Lockwood, *Prison Sexual Violence*, New York: Elsevier, 1980; and Toch, *Living in Prison*, 143, 145, 166.

91. Lee Bowker, *Prison Victimization*, New York: Elsevier, 1980.

92. Sawyer F. Sylvester, John H. Reed and David Nelson, *Prison Homicides*, New York: Spectrum, 1977.

93. Carney, 183.

94. Goodstein, 136.

95. Irwin, *Prisons in Turmoil*, 214–215.

96. Jacobs, *Stateville*, 7.

97. Irwin, *Prisons in Turmoil*, 216.

98. Mayer N. Zald, "Power, Balance, and Staff Conflict in Correctional Institutions," in Hazelrigg, 403, 405.

99. Giallombardo, *Society of Women*, 57.

100. Davidson, 31.

101. Carney, 180.

102. Irwin, *Prisons in Turmoil*, 26.

103. Keve, 15, 60.

104. American Friends Service Committee, *Struggle for Justice — A Report on Crime and Punishment in America*, New York: Hill and Wang, 1971, 138.

105. Cohen and Taylor, inside flap.

106. Richard M. Wilsnack, "Explaining Collective Violence in Prison: Problems and Possibilities," in Albert J. Cohen, George F. Cole and Robert G. Bailey, eds., *Prison Violence*, Lexington MA: Lexington Books, 1976, 61–72.

107. William G. Nagel, "Prison Architecture and Prison Violence," in Cohen, Cole and Bailey, 105.

108. Bruce, Harno, Burgess and Landesco, 54.

109. Jacobs, *Stateville*.

110. Octavio A. Ballesteros, *Behind Jail Bars*, New York: Philosophical Library, 1979.

111. John Braithwaite, *Inequality, Crime and Public Policy*, London: Routledge and Kegan Paul, 1979, 87.

112. Pauline Morris, *Prisoners and Their Families*, London: George Allen and Unwin, 1965.

113. Stanley L. Brodsky, *Families and Friends of Men in Prison*, Lexington MA: Lexington Books, 1975.

114. Clark and Lehrman, 110.

115. Goldfarb and Singer, 203.

116. Hussey and Duffee, 85, 96.

117. Andrew von Hirsh and Kathleen J. Hanrahan, *The Question of Parole: Retention, Reform, or Abolition*, Cambridge MA: Ballinger, 1978, 1.

118. Forer, 113.

119. Ralph C. Brendes, "Interstate Supervision of Parole and Probation," in Carter and Wilkins, 527.

120. Hussey and Duffee, 67, 72.

121. Bruce, Harno, Burgess and Landesco, 8.

122. Glaser, *The Effectiveness of a Prison and Parole System*, 429.

123. Harvey L. Perlman and Thomas Ballington, *A Symposium on Prisons and Correctional Law*, Lincoln: University of Nebraska Press, 1967, 99.

124. Neier, 188.

125. Louis B. Carney, *Probation and Parole—Legal and Social Dimensions*, New York: McGraw-Hill, 1977, 141.

126. Bruce, Harno, Burgess and Landesco, IV, 9, 48.

127. American Correctional Association, "Development of Modern Correctional Concepts," in Edward Eldefonso, ed., *Issues in Corrections, A Book of Readings*, Beverly Hills CA: Glencoe, 1974, 96.

128. Norman S. Hayner, "Parole Boards' Attitudes Toward Predictive Devices," in Johnston, Savitz, and Wolfgang, 840.

129. Sandhu, 269.

130. Don Gottfredson, Leslie T. Wilkins, and Peter B. Hoffman, "Prediction of Parole Behavior," in Johnston and Savitz, 877–885.

131. Hayner, in Johnston, Savitz and Wolfgang, 841.

132. Von Hirsch and Hanrahan, 3.

133. Hussey and Duffee, 137.

134. Vladimir J. Konečne and Ebbe B. Ebbesen, "An Analysis of the Sentencing System," in Konečne and Ebbesen, 354, 357, 359, 364.

135. Wright and Fox, 66.

136. Paul M. Keve, *The Probation Officer Investigates, a Guide to the Presentence Report*, Minneapolis: University of Minnesota Press, 1960, 65.

137. Abadinsky, 176.

138. Goodstein, 174, 175, 177.

139. Rodney M. Coe, "Characteristics of Well-adjusted and Poorly-adjusted Inmates," *Journal of Criminal Law, Criminology and Police Science*, 1961, 52, 178, 184.

140. H. Richmond Fisher, "Probation and Parole Revocation—the Anomaly of Divergent Practices," *Federal Probation*, September, 1974, 38:23–29.

141. Von Hirsch and Hanrahan, 11, 23.

142. Eliot Studt, *Surveillance and Service in Parole—Report of the Parole Action Study*, Washington DC: U.S. Dept. of Justice, May, 1973, 23, 26, 39.

143. Sandhu, 268.

144. Irwin, *The Felon*, 114.

145. Goodstein, 268.

146. Robert C. Wolin, "After Release—The Parolee in Society," *St. John's Law Review*, October, 1973, 48:15.

147. Glaser, *The Effectiveness of a Prison and Parole System*, 340.

148. Irwin, *The Felon*, 112, 139.

149. Irwin, *The Felon*, 172.

150. Studt, 61, 182.

151. Victor H. Evjen, "Current Thinking on Parole Prediction Tables," in Carter and Wilkins, 624.

152. Wolin, 1.

153. Irvin Waller, *Men Released from Prison*, Toronto: University of Toronto Press, 1974, 124.

154. Davidson, 94.

155. Von Hirsch and Hanrahan, 60.

156. Stuart Adams, "Correctional and Caseload Research," in Johnston, Savitz and Wolfgang, 728, 730.

157. Martinson and Wilks, 112, 114, 115.

158. Irwin, *The Felon*, 165.

159. Alfred C. Schnur, "Some Reflections on the Role of Correctional Research," in Hazelrigg, 378.

160. Daniel Glaser and Vincent O'Leary, *Personal Characteristics and Parole Outcome*, Washington DC: U.S. Department of Health, Education and Welfare, 1966, 10–11.

161. Wolin, 13.

162. Bruce, Harno, Burgess and Landesco, 223.

163. Irwin, *The Felon*, 161.

164. Von Hirsch and Hanrahan, 49, 60, 69.

165. Robert M. Martinson, Gene K. Kassebaum and David A. Ward, "A Critique of Research in Parole," in Carter and Wilkins, 643.

166. Abadinsky, 189.

167. Sandhu, 264.

168. Kassebaum, Ward and Wilner, 263, 279.

169. Glaser, *The Effectiveness of a Prison and Parole System*, 331, 361.

170. Gilbert J. McKee, "Cost Effectiveness and Vocational Training," in Johnston and Savitz, 636.

171. Ohlin, 90.

172. Glaser, *The Effectiveness of a Prison and Parole System*, 362.

173. Brodsky, 17.

174. Von Hirsch and Hanrahan, 141.

175. Carney, *Introduction to Correctional Science*, 223.

176. Glaser and McLeary, 16, 18–19.

177. Glaser, *The Effectiveness of a Prison and Parole System*, 51.

178. Glaser and McLeary, 13, 23.

179. Paul Keve, *Prison, Probation, or Parole — A Probation Officer Investigates*, Minneapolis: University of Minnesota Press, 1954, 62, 123.

180. Herman Mannheim and Leslie T. Wilkins, *Prediction Methods in Relation to Borstal Training*, London: Her Majesty's Stationery Office, 1955, 12.

181. Sandhu, 87.

182. Hussey and Duffee, 53–54.

183. Wolin, 37.

184. Hussey and Duffee, 251–252.

185. Martinson, Kassebaum and Ward, in Carter and Wilkins, 644, 648–649.

186. Glaser and O'Leary, 1.

187. Charles L. Newman, *Sourcebook in Probation, Parole and Pardons*, Springfield IL: Charles Thomas, 1968, 343.

188. Freeman, 123.

189. Neier, 16.

190. Von Hirsch and Hanrahan, 98.

191. Ibid., 62.

192. Irwin, *The Felon*, 134, 189.

193. Mrs. L. Le Mesurier, *A Handbook of Probation and Social Work of the Courts*, London: National Association of Probation Officers, 1935, 20–21.

194. George G. Killinger, Hazel B. Kerper and Paul F. Cromwell, Jr., *Probation and Parole in the Criminal Justice System*, St. Paul MN: West Publishing Co., 1976, 32.

195. D. McGorman, "A Survey of Probation Practices in the United States," unpublished master's thesis, California State University, Long Beach, 1974, 4.

196. John Augustus, *First Probation Officer*, Montclair NJ: Patterson Smith, 1972.

197. Newman, *Sourcebook of Probation and Parole*, 15.

198. United Nations, "The Legal Origins of Probation," in Carter and Wilkins, 4.

199. Ibid., 6, 8.

200. Alexander Smith and Louis Berlin, *Introduction to Probation and Parole*, St. Paul MN: West Publishing Co., 1976, 81.

201. *President's Commission on Law Enforcement and Administration of Justice*, "Probation," in Carter and Wilkins, 32.

202. Al Havenstrite, "Case Planning in the Probation Supervision Process," *Federal Probation*, June, 1980, 44:57.

203. Perlman and Ballington, 32.

204. Bruce, Harno, Burgess and Landesco, 97.

205. American Bar Association, *Probation*, New York: American Bar Association Project, 1970, 27–28.

206. Hussey and Duffee, 328.

207. Ohlin, 79.

208. Ibid., 34.

209. Eric Carlson and Evelyn C. Parks, *Critical Issues in Adult Probation*, Washington DC: U.S. Department of Justice, 1979, 17.

210. For some empirical studies on presentence investigation, see James R. Davis.

211. Goldfarb and Singer, 147–148, 154–155.

212. John Hagan, John J. Hewitt and Duane Falwin, "Ceremonial Justice — Crime and Punishment in a Loosely Coupled System," *Social Forces*, December 1979, 58:506–527.

213. Hussey and Duffee, 50, 122.

214. James Robison, Leslie Wilkins, Robert M. Carter and Albert Wahl, *The San Francisco Project — A Study of Federal Probation and Parole*, San Francisco: National Institute of Mental Health, 1969.

215. Robert M. Carter, "The Presentence Report and the Decision-making Process," in Carter and Wilkins, 136.

216. Eugene H. Czajkoski, "Exposing the Quasi-judicial Role of the Probation Officer," *Federal Probation*, September, 1973, 37:10.

217. Edwin M. Lemert and Forrest Dill, *Offenders in the Community*, Lexington MA: Lexington Books, 1978, 14.

218. Edward M. Taylor and Alexander M. McEachern, "Needs and Directions in Probation Training," in Carter and Wilkins, 673.

219. Claude T. Mangrum, *The Professional Practitioner in Probation*, Springfield: Charles C. Thomas, 1975, 52.

220. Louis Diana, "What Is Probation"? in Carter and Wilkins, 51–52.

221. Carter, in Carter and Wilkins, 136.

222. Robert H. Vasoli, "Some Reflections in Measuring Probation Outcomes," in Carter and Wilkins, 332.

223. Mangrum, 189.

224. Stein H. Clark, "What Is the Purpose of Probation and Why Do We Revoke It"? *Crime and Delinquency*, October, 1979, 25:411.

225. Sanford Bates, "When Is Probation Not Probation"? *Federal Probation*, 1960, 24:14, 15, 16.

226. Joan Luxenburg, "The Probation Supervision Process and Its Conformity to Models of Socialization: A Descriptive Analysis," unpublished dissertation for the Ph.D., Columbia University, 1978.

227. Fisher.

228. E. Eliot Sands, "New Directions in Probation in the U.S.A.," *International Journal of Offender Therapy and Comparative Criminology*, 1976, 26:33-40.

229. Gary Meitz, "The Bakery: Probation Reaches the Inner City," *Federal Probation*, March, 1978, 42:50-52.

230. Hussey and Duffee, 57, 123, 263.

231. Killinger, Kerper and Cromwell, 99.

232. Carney, *Probation and Parole*, 111.

233. William M. Breer, "Probation Supervision of the Black Offender," *Federal Probation*, June, 1972, 36:31-26.

234. Gibbs, 67.

235. Carlson and Parks, 455-459.

236. Carl B. Klokars, Jr., "A Theory of Probation Supervision," *Journal of Criminal Law, Criminology, and Police Science*, 1972, 63:550-557.

237. Eugene H. Czajkoski, "The Need for Philosophical Direction in Probation and Parole," *Federal Probation*, September, 1965, 24:24-28.

238. Dale E. Van Laningham, Merlin Taber and Rita Dimants, "How Adult Probation Officers View Their Job Responsibilities," *Crime and Delinquency*, April, 1966, 12:106.

239. Mark Monger, *Casework in Probation*, London: Butterworth, 1972, 167.

240. Carl H. Imlay and Elsie L. Reid, "The Probation Officers' Sentencing and the Winds of Change," *Federal Probation*, December, 1975, 39:17.

241. Czajkoski, "Exposing the Quasi-Judicial Role of the Probation Officer," 12.

242. Klokars, Jr., 554-555.

243. Mangrum, 8, 11, 105, 237, 339.

244. Van Laningham, Taber, Dimants, 97-108.

245. John F. Koontz, Jr., "Change vs. Probation Management," *Federal Probation*, March, 1978, 42:25-34.

246. Hussey and Duffee, 55, 242 and Monger, 78.

247. Hussey and Duffee, 254.

248. American Bar Association, *Probation*, 93.

249. Ohlin, 105.

250. Bates, 19.

251. Frank Scarpitti and Richard M. Stephenson, "A Study of Probation Effectiveness," *Journal of Criminal Law, Criminology, and Police Science*, 1968, 59:362.

252. Hussey and Duffee, 321-322.

253. Goldfarb and Singer, 239-240.

254. Beckman, 146.

255. Scarpitti and Stephenson, 361-362.

256. Rex M. Warburton, "The Effect of Information Feedback on the Prediction Capabilities of Probation Officers," unpublished thesis, United States International University, 1974, 7-10.

257. Hussey and Duffee, 328-329.

258. Ralph M. England, "Post-probation Recidivism," in Johnston, Savitz and Wolfgang, 680, 692.

259. George F. Davis, "A Study of Probation Violation Rates by Means of the Cohort Approach," *Journal of Criminal Law, Criminology, and Police Science*, 1964, 55:70-85.

260. Jackson Toby, "Is Punishment Necessary"? in Gerber and McAnany, 225; and La Patra, 104.

261. Martinson and Wilks, 53, 56, 334, 576.

262. Scarpitti and Stephenson, 365, 367.

263. Monger, 113.

264. Lemert and Dill.

265. Paul Keve, *Imaginative Programs in Probation and Parole*, Minneapolis: University of Minnesota Press, 1967, 5, 7.

266. Sandhu, 250.

267. Bruce, Harno, Burgess and Landesco, 232.

268. John F. Reed and Charles E. King, "Factors in the Decision-making of North Carolina Probation Officers," *Journal of Research in Crime and Delinquency*, 1966, 3:126-132.

269. Carlson and Parks, 467.

270. Alexander Bassin, "Effect of Group Therapy Upon Certain Attitudes and Perceptions of Adult Offenders on Probation," unpublished dissertation for the Ph.D., New York University, 1957.

271. Martinson and Wilks, 516.

272. Carney, *Probation and Parole*, 15.

273. Robison, Wilkins, Carter and Wahl, 6-7.

274. Martinson and Wilks, 334.

275. Lemert and Dill, XIV, 148.

276. Adams, 722.

277. Daniel Masden, "Diversified Opinions Gathered from Sampling of Ex-Offenders," *American Journal of Corrections*, March, 1978, 40:22-24.

278. Carney, *Introduction to Correctional Science*, 306.

279. Carlson and Parks, 139, 186, 401, 461, 467.

280. Luxenburg, 20.

281. Bates, 18.

282. Taylor and McEachern, in Carter and Wilkins, 163.

283. Monger, 142.

284. Ibid., 151.

285. Smith and Berlin, 139.

286. Vasoli, in Carter and Wilkins, 334.

287. Killinger, Kerper and Cromwell, Jr.

288. Steven Clark, 412.

289. Warburton.

290. Smith and Berlin, 2.

291. Hussey and Duffee, 54.

292. Goldfarb and Singer, 52.

293. Rusche and Kirchheimer, 48, 64, 84, 85.

294. De Beaumont and de Tocqueville, 108, 114, 117.

295. Carney, *Introduction to Correctional Science*, 353.

296. Keve, *Imaginative Program in Probation and Parole*, 222.

297. Goldfarb and Singer, 552-578.

298. Ibid., 129, 446, 528, 547.

299. Von Hirsch and Hanrahan, 32.

300. Goldfarb and Singer, 567.

301. Goldfarb, *Jails*, 252–253.

302. Lloyd M. McCorkle, Albert Elias and F. Lowell Bixby, *The Highfields Story — An Experimental Treatment Project for Youthful Offenders*, New York: Henry Holt, 1958.

303. Howard E. Freeman, "The Prediction of Recidivism Among Youthful Offenders in the Highfields Treatment Program," unpublished dissertation for the Ph.D., New York University, 1955.

304. Daniel Glaser, "Correctional Research: An Elusive Paradise," in Carter and Wilkins, 540.

305. Abadinsky, 50.

306. Glaser, *The Effectiveness of a Prison and Parole System*, 186; and Stuart Adams, "The Pico Project," in Johnston, Savitz, and Wolfgang, 548–559.

307. Edwin Powers and Helen Witmer, "The Cambridge-Somerville Study," in Johnston, Savitz, and Wolfgang, 587–600.

308. Walter B. Miller, "The Midcity Delinquency Control Project," in Johnston, Savitz and Wolfgang, 635–651.

309. Walter C. Bailey, "An Evaluation of 100 Studies of Correctional Outcomes," in Johnston, Savitz, and Wolfgang, 733–744.

Chapter VII. The Science of Criminal Justice

1. A third assumption implicit is that a legal system exists.

2. Monger, 70, 112.

3. Gross, 60, 71, 94.

4. Forer, 163.

5. Criminal justice personnel may believe, however, that offenders comply with the conditions of the court, no matter how disagreeable these conditions are to the offender, in order to avoid prison.

6. See L.A. Parry, *The History of Torture in England*, Montclair NJ: Patterson Smith, 1975.

7. This included witchcraft, because burning for women was considered more humane than quartering, for example.

8. Parry, 26.

9. Parry, xii, 3.

10. Popper, *Conjectures and Refutations*, 192–193.

Bibliography

Abadinsky, Howard. *Probation and Parole—Theory and Practice*. New York: Prentice-Hall, 1977.

Adams, Stuart. "Correctional and Caseload Research." In Norman Johnston, Leonard Savitz, and Marvin E. Wolfgang, eds. *The Sociology of Punishment and Correction*. New York: Wiley, 1970, 721–732.

_____. "The Pico Experiment." In Johnston, Savitz and Wolfgang, 548–559.

Alexander, James I. *Blue Coats—Black Skin—The Black Experience in The New York City Police Department Since 1891*. Hicksville NY: Exposition Press. 1978.

Allen, Francis A. "Criminal Justice, Legal Values, and the Rehabilitative Ideal." In Stanley C. Grupp, ed. *Theories of Punishment*. Bloomington: Indiana University Press, 1971, 317–325.

Alschuler, Albert. "Sentencing Reform and Prosecutorial Power—A Critique of Recent Proposals for 'Fixed and Presumptive Sentencing.'" *University of Pennsylvania Law Review*. January, 1978, 126:550–577.

_____. "Sentencing Reform and Prosecutorial Power—A Critique of Recent Proposals for 'Fixed and Presumptive Sentencing.'" In National Institute of Law Enforcement and Criminal Justice, Law Enforcement Assistance Administration. *Determinate Sentencing—Reform or Regression?* Washington DC: U.S. Department of Justice, 1978, 80–107.

_____. "The Defense Attorney's Role in Plea-Bargaining." *Yale Law Journal*, 1974, 84:1179–1314.

_____. "The Prosecutor's Role in Plea-Bargaining." *University of Chicago Law Review*, Fall, 1968, 36:50–112.

American Bar Assocation. *Project on Standards for Criminal Justice—Probation*. New York: American Bar Association, 1970.

American Correctional Association. "Development of Modern Correctional Concepts." In Edward Eldefonso, ed. *Issues in Corrections—A Book of Readings*. Beverly Hills CA: Glencoe, 1974, 76–100.

American Friends Service Committee. *Struggle for Justice—A Report on Crime and Punishment in America*. New York: Hill and Wang, 1971.

Andenaes, Johannes. *Punishment and Deterrence*. Ann Arbor: University of Michigan Press, 1974.

Anonymous. "The Correctional System." *Crime and Social Justice*, 1974, 2:82–89.

Arafat, Ibtihaj, and McCaherty, Kathleen. "The Relation Between Lawyers and Their Clients." In Robert M. Rich, ed. *Essays in the Theory and Practice of Criminal Justice*. Washington DC: University Press of America, 1978, 194–214.

Ares, Charles, and Sturz, Herbert. "Bail and the Indigent Accused." *Crime and Delinquency*, January, 1962, 8:12–20.

Augustus, John. *First Probation Officer*. Montclair NJ: Patterson Smith, 1972.

Austin, William, and Williams, Thomas A. "A Survey of Judges' Responses to Simulated Legal Cases—Research Notes on Sentencing Disparity." *Journal of Criminal Law and Criminology*, 1977, 68:306–310.

Bailey, Walter C. "An Evaluation of 100 Studies of Correctional Outcomes." In Johnston, Savitz, and Wolfgang, 733–744.

Balbus, Isaac. *The Dialectics of Legal Repression*. New York: Russell Sage Foundation, 1973.

Baldwin, Roger. "The Police and the Ex-Convict." *Criminology*, November, 1970, 8:279–294.

Ballesteros, Octavio A. *Behind Jail Bars*. New York: Philosophical Library, 1979.

Banton, Michael. *The Policeman in the Community*. New York: Basic Books, 1964.

Barnes, Harry Elmer. *The Story of Punishment—A Record of Man's Inhumanity to Man*. Montclair NJ: Patterson Smith, 1972.

Barnett, Randy E., and Hagel, John, eds. *Assessing the Criminal—Restitution, Retribution, and the Legal Process*. Cambridge MA: Ballinger, 1977.

Bassin, Alexander, "Effect of Group Therapy Upon Certain Attitudes and Perceptions of Adult Offenders on Probation." Unpublished dissertation for the Ph.D., New York University, 1957.

Bates, Sanford. "When Is Probation Not Probation"? *Federal Probation*, 1960, 24:13–20.

Bayley, David H., and Mendelsohn, Harold. *Minorities and the Police—Confrontation in America*. New York: Free Press, 1969.

Beaumont, Gustave de, and Tocqueville, Alexis de. *On the Penitentiary System in the United States and Its Application in France*. Philadelphia: Carey, Lea, and Blanchard, 1833.

Beccaria, Cesare. *On Crimes and Punishment*. Indianapolis IN: Bobbs-Merrill, 1963.

————. "On Crimes and Punishment." In Sawyer F. Sylvester, ed. *The Heritage of Modern Criminology*. Cambridge MA: Shankman Press, 1972, 11–26.

Becker, Harold K., and Whitehouse, Jack. *Police of America—A Personal View—Introduction and Commentary*. Springfield IL: Charles C. Thomas, 1979.

Beckman, Eric. *Law Enforcement in a Democratic Society*. Chicago: Nelson Hall, 1980.

Beeley, Arthur L. *The Bail System in Chicago*. Chicago: University of Chicago Press, 1927.

Benisin, Saul. "The History of Polio Research in the United States—Appraisal and Lesson." In Gerald Holton, ed. *The Twentieth Century Sciences—Studies in the Biography of Ideas*. New York: Norton, 1972, 308–333.

Berkley, George E. *The Democratic Policeman*. Boston: Beacon Press, 1964.

Berkson, Larry Charles. *The Concept of Cruel and Unusual Punishment*. Lexington MA: Lexington Books, 1975.

Bernal, J.D. *The Social Function of Science*. Cambridge MA: The M.I.T. Press, 1939.

Bernard, Thomas J. "Individualization vs. Uniformity—The Case of Regulation in Criminal Justice." *Federal Probation*, December, 1976, 40:19–23.

Bing, Stephen, and Rosenfeld, Stephen. *The Quality of Justice in the Lower Criminal Courts of Metropolitan Boston*. Boston: Lawyers' Committee for Civil Rights Under Law, 1970.

Bittner, Egon, and Platt, Anthony. "The Meaning of Punishment." In Rudolph J. Gerber and Patrick D. McAnany, eds. *Contemporary Punishment—Views, Explanations, and Justifications*. Notre Dame IN: University of Notre Dame Press, 1972, 25–30.

Black, Donald. *The Manners and Customs of the Police*. New York: Academic Press, 1980.

————, and Reiss, Albert J., Jr. "Police Control of Juveniles." *American Sociological Review*, 1970, 63:63–77.

Blatt, Max. "Some Half-Baked Thoughts About Induction." In Sidney

Morgenbesser, Patricia Suppes, and Morton White, eds. *Philosophy, Science and Methods*. New York: St. Martin's, 1969, 146–148.

Bloomstein, Morris J. *Verdict — The Jury System*. New York: Dodd, Mead, 1972.

Blumberg, Abraham. *Criminal Justice*. Chicago: Quadrangle Books, 1967.

_____. "The Practice of Law as a Confidence Game — Organizational Cooperation of a Profession." *Law and Society Review*, June, 1967, 1:15–39.

_____, ed. *The Scales of Justice — Law and Order*. New York: Aldine, 1970.

Boies, Henry M. *The Science of Penology — The Defense of Society Against Crime*. New York: Putnam, 1901.

Bordua, David, ed. *The Police — Six Sociological Essays*. New York: Wiley, 1967.

Bowker, Lee. *Prison Victimization*. New York: Elsevier, 1981.

Braithwaite, John. *Inequality, Crime, and Public Policy*. London: Routledge and Kegan Paul, 1979.

Braithwaite, R.B. "Models in the Empirical Sciences." In Baruch A. Brody, ed. *Readings in the Philosophy of Science*. Englewood Cliffs NJ: Prentice-Hall, 1970, 268–289.

Breer, William M. "Probation Supervision of the Black Offender." *Federal Probation*, June, 1972, 31–36.

Brendes, Ralph C. "Interstate Supervision of Parole and Probation." In Robert M. Carter and Leslie T. Wilkins, eds. *Probation and Parole — Selected Readings*, First Edition. New York: Wiley, 1970, 524–528.

Broderick, John J. *Police in a Time of Change*. Morristown NJ: General Learning Press, 1977.

Brodsky, Stanley. *Families and Friends of Men in Prison*. Lexington MA: Lexington Books, 1975.

Brody, Baruch A., ed. *Readings in the Philosophy of Science*. Englewood Cliffs NJ: Prentice-Hall, 1970.

Brown, Michael. *Working the Streets — Police Discretion and the Dilemmas of Reform*. New York: Russell Sage Foundation, 1981.

Bruce, Andrew A.; Harno, Albert J.; Burgess, Ernest W.; and Landesco, John. *The Workings of the Indeterminate Sentence — Law of the Parole System in New York*. Montclair NJ: Patterson Smith, 1968.

Bryan, Jr., William J. *The Psychology of Jury Selection — The Chosen Ones*. New York: Vantage, 1971.

Burkhart, Kathryn Waterson. *Women in Prison*. Garden City NY: Doubleday, 1973.

Burnham, David. "Police Violence — A Changing Pattern." In Arthur Niederhoffer and Abraham Blumberg, eds. *The Ambivalent Force — Perspectives on the Police*. Hinsdale IL: Dryden Press, 1976, 188–191.

Cahn, Edward. *The Sense of Injustice*. Bloomington: Indiana University Press, 1949.

Campbell, Arthur M. *Law of Sentencing*. New York: Lawyers' Cooperative Publishing Co., 1978.

Campbell, Rufferford B. "Sentencing — The Use of Psychiatric Information and Presentence Reports." *Kentucky Law Journal*, 1971–1972, 60:285–321.

Campbell, W.R. "What Is Theory"? In Brody, 252–262.

Carlson, Eric W., and Parks, Evelyn C. *Critical Issues in Adult Probation*. Washington DC: United States Department of Justice, 1979.

Carney, Louis P. *Introduction to Correctional Science*. New York: McGraw-Hill, 1974.

_____. *Probation and Parole — Legal and Social Dimensions*. New York: McGraw-Hill, 1977.

Carrington, Frank. *Neither Cruel nor Unusual*. New Rochelle NY: Arlington House, 1978.

Carter, Lief. *The Limits of Order*. Lexington MA: Lexington Books, 1974.

Carter, Robert M. "The Pre-Sentence Report and the Decision-Making Process." In Carter and Wilkins, 128–137.

————, and Wilkins, Leslie T., eds. *Probation and Parole — Selected Readings*. First Edition. New York: Wiley, 1970.

Casper, Jonathan D. *American Criminal Justice — The Defendant's Perspective*. Englewood Cliffs NJ: Prentice-Hall, 1972.

Cassou, April Kestell, and Taugher, Brian. "Determinate Sentencing in California — The New Numbers Game." *Pacific Law Journal*, 1978, 9:5–106.

Chambliss, William J. *Crime and the Legal Process*. New York: McGraw-Hill, 1965.

————, and Seidman, Robert B. *Law, Order, and Power*. Reading MA: Addison-Wesley, 1971.

Chamelin, Neil C. "The Court Administrator Concept — Let the Judges Judge." In Donald T. Shanahan, ed. *The Administration of Justice System — An Introduction*. Boston: Holbrook Press, 1977.

Chevigny, Paul. *Police Power — Police Abuses in New York City*. New York: Pantheon, 1969.

Chiricos, Theodore G., and Waldo, Gordon P. "Socioeconomic Status and Criminal Sentencing — An Empirical Assessment of a Conflict Proposition." *American Sociological Review*, December, 1975, 40:753–772.

Chomsky, Noam. "Some Empirical Assumptions in Modern Philosophy of Language." In Morgenbesser, Suppes, and White, 285–321.

Clark, Phyllis, and Lehrman, Robert. *Doing Time — A Look at Criminal Prisons*. New York: Hastings House, 1980.

Clark, Steven H. "What Is the Purpose of Probation and Why Do We Revoke It"? *Crime and Delinquency*. October, 1979, 25:409–424.

Clemmer, Donald. *The Prison Community*. Boston: Christopher Publishing Co., 1940.

Clinard, Marshall, and Yeager, Peter C. *Corporate Crime*. New York: Free Press, 1980.

Cloward, Richard, et al., eds. *Theoretical Studies in the Social Organization of a Prison*. New York: Social Science Council, 1960.

Coe, Rodney M. "Characteristics of Well-Adjusted and Poorly-Adjusted Inmates." *Journal of Criminal Law, Criminology, and Police Science*, 1961, 52:178–184.

Cohen, Albert J.; Cole, George F.; and Bailey, Robert G., eds. *Prison Violence*. Lexington MA: Lexington Books, 1976.

Cohen, Stanley, and Taylor, Laurie. *Psychological Survival — The Experience of Long-Term Imprisonment*. New York: Pantheon, 1972.

Cohn, Alfred, and Udolf, Roy. *The Criminal Justice System and Its Psychology*. New York: Van Nostrand Reinhold, 1979.

Colista, F. Philip, and Domonkos, Michael. "Bail and Civil Disorders." *Journal of Urban Law*, Spring, Summer, 1968, 45:815–839.

Commission of Canada. *Fear of Punishment and Deterrence*. Montreal: Minister of Supply and Services, 1976.

Cooper, David D. *The Lesson of the Scaffold — The Public Execution Controversy in Victorian England*. Athens: Ohio University Press, 1974.

Cressey, Donald R. "Achievement of an Unstated Organizational Goal — An Observation on Prison." In Laurence E. Hazelrigg, ed. *Prison and Society — A Reader in Penology*. New York: Doubleday, 1968, 50–52.

————. "Contradictory Directions in Complex Organizations — The Case of Prison." In Hazelrigg, 477–496.

————, ed. *The Prison — Studies in Institutional Organization and Change*. New York: Holt, Rinehart and Winston, 1961.

Czajkoski, Eugene H. "Exposing the Quasi-Judicial Role of the Probation Officers." *Federal Probation*, September, 1973, 37:9–13.

_____. "The Need for Philosophical Direction in Probation and Parole." *Federal Probation*, September, 1965, 24:24–28.

Davidson, Theodore. *Chicano Prisoners — The Key to San Quentin*. New York: Holt, Rinehart and Winston, 1974.

Davis, George F. "A Study of Probation Violation Rates by Means of the Cohort Approach." *Journal of Criminal Law, Criminology, and Police Science*, 1964, 55:70–85.

Davis, James R. *The Sentencing Dispositions of New York City Lower Court Criminal Judges*. Washington DC: University Press of America, 1982.

Davis, Kenneth Culp. *Discretionary Justice — A Preliminary Inquiry*. Baton Rouge: Louisiana State University Press, 1969.

_____. *Discretionary Justice in Europe and America*. Chicago: University of Illinois Press, 1976.

_____. *Police Discretion*. St. Paul MN: West Publishing Co., 1975.

Dawson, Robert O. *Sentencing — The Decision As to Type, Length, and Conditions of Sentencing*. Boston: Little, Brown, 1969.

Dawson, Willa. "The Need for a System Approach to Justice Administration." In Shanahan, 6–18.

Diana, Lewis. "What Is Probation"? In Carter and Wilkins, 51–57.

Dix, George E. "Judicial Review of Sentencing — Implications for Individual Dispositions." *Law and Social Order*, 1969, 1:369–418.

Dorsen, Norman, and Friedman, Leon. *Disorder in the Court: Report of the Association of the Bar of the City of New York — Special Committee on Courtroom Conduct*. New York: Pantheon, 1973.

Ebbesen, Ebbe B., and Konečni, Vladimir J. "An Analysis of the Bail System." in Vladimir J. Konečni and Ebbe B. Ebbesen, eds. *The Criminal Justice System — A Social Psychological Analysis*. San Francisco: Freeman, Cooper, 1982, 196–231.

Edel, Abraham. "Metaphor, Analogies, Models, and All That in Ethical Theory." In Morgenbesser, Suppes, and White, 364–377.

Edmunds, Jr., Eric M. "Disparity and Discretion in 'Sentencing'— A Proposal for Uniformity." *University of California Law Review*, December, 1977, 25:323–364.

Eisenstein, James, and Jacob, Herbert. *Felony Justice — An Organizational Analysis of Criminal Courts*. Boston: Little, Brown, 1977.

_____, and _____. "Measuring Performance and Outcomes of Urban Criminal Courts." *Social Science Quarterly*, 1974, 54:713–724.

Eldefonso, Edward, ed. *Issues in Corrections — A Book of Readings*. Beverly Hills CA: Glencoe, 1974.

England, Ralph W. "Post-Probation Recidivism." In Johnston, Savitz, and Wolfgang, 684–691.

Esselstyn, T.C. "The Social System of Correctional Workers." In Carter and Wilkins, 684–693.

Evjen, Victor H. "Current Thinking in Parole Prediction Tables." In Carter and Wilkins, 615–625.

Feeley, Malcolm M. *The Process Is the Punishment*. New York: Russell Sage Foundation, 1979.

Feinmore, Clarice. "Imprisoned Women — A History of the Treatment of Women Incarcerated in New York City, 1932–1975." Unpublished dissertation for the Ph.D., New York University, 1976.

Feld, Barry C. *Neutralizing Inmate Violence — Juvenile Offenders in Institutions*. Cambridge MA: Ballinger, 1977.

Ferdinand, Theodore M., and Luchterhand, Elmer G. "Intercity Youth, the Police, the Juvenile Court, and Justice." *Social Problems*, Spring, 1970, 17:510–527.

Ferri, Enrico. *Criminal Sociology*. New York: D. Appleton, 1898.

Feuer, Lewis. *Einstein and the Generation of Science*. New York: Basic Books, 1974.

Fisher, H. Richmond. "Probation and Parole Revocation—The Anomaly of Divergent Practices." *Federal Probation*, September, 1974, 38:23-24.

Fishman, Robert. *Criminal Recidivism in New York City—An Evaluation of the Impact of Rehabilitation and Diversion Services*. New York: Praeger, 1972.

Forer, Lois G. *Criminals and Victims—A Trial Judge Reflects on Crime and Punishment*. New York: Norton, 1980.

Frank, Jerome. *Courts on Trial—Myth and Reality*. Princeton NJ: Princeton University Press, 1949.

Frankel, Marvin E. *Criminal Sentences—Law Without Order*. New York: Hill and Wang, 1972.

Frankfurter, Felix, and Pound, Roscoe. *Criminal Justice in Cleveland—Reports of the Cleveland Foundation Survey of the Administration of Justice in Cleveland, Ohio*. Montclair NJ: Patterson Smith, 1968.

Freeman, Howard. "The Prediction of Recidivism Among Youthful Offenders in the Highfields Treatment Program." Unpublished dissertation for the Ph.D., New York University, 1955.

Freeman, John C. *Prisons—Past and Future*. London: Heinemann Educational Books, 1978.

Friesen, Ernest C. "Future Roles of Judges, Prosecutors, and Defenders." In Harry W. More, Jr. and Richard Chang, eds. *Contemporary Criminal Justice*. San Jose: Justice System Development, 1974, 200-218.

Fuller, Lon L. *The Morality of Law*. New Haven CT: Yale University Press, 1964.

Galliher, John F., and McCartney, James. *Criminology, Power, Crime, and Criminal Law*. Homewood IL: Dorsey, 1977.

Garabedian, Peter G. "Social Roles in a Correctional Community." *Journal of Criminal Law, Criminology, and Police Science*, September, 1964, 55:338-347.

————. "Social Role Process and Socialization in the Prison Community." In Johnston, Savitz, and Wolfgang, 485-494.

Gareis, Karl. *Introduction to the Science of Law—Systematic Survey of the Law and Principles of Legal Study*. New York: Augustus M. Kelley, 1968.

Garrity, Donald L. "The Prison As a Rehabilitative Agency." In Cressey, 362-378.

Geiss, Gilbert. "Ethics of Prison Experimentation." In Norman Johnston and Leonard Savitz, eds. *Justice and Corrections*. New York: Wiley, 1978, 617-620.

Gerber, Rudolph J., and McAnany, Patrick D., eds. *Contemporary Punishment—Views, Explanation, and Justifications*. Notre Dame IN: University of Notre Dame Press, 1972.

Giallombardo, Rose. *Society of Women—A Study of a Woman's Prison*. New York: Wiley, 1966.

————. *The Social World of Imprisoned Girls—A Comparative Study of Institutions for Juvenile Delinquents*. New York: Wiley, 1974.

Gibbs, Jack. *Crime, Punishment, and Deterrence*. New York: Elsevier, 1975.

Glaser, Daniel. "Correctional Research—An Elusive Paradise." In Carter and Wilkins, 531-544.

————. *The Effectiveness of a Prison and Parole System*. New York: Bobbs-Merrill, 1964.

————, and O'Leary, Vincent. *Personal Characteristics and Parole Outcomes*. Washington DC: U.S. Department of Health, Education, and Welfare, 1966.

————, and Stratton, John R. "Measuring Female Change in Prison." In Cressey, 381-392.

Glick, Brian. "Change Through the Courts." In Erik Ohlin Wright, ed. *The Politics of Punishment—A Critical Analysis of Prisons in America*. New York: Harper and Row, 1973, 286–309.

Goldfarb, Ronald. *Jails— The Ultimate Ghetto*. Garden City NY: Anchor, 1975.

_____. *Ransom—A Critique of the American Bail System*. New York: Harper and Row, 1965.

_____, and Singer, Linda. *After Conviction—A Review of the American Correctional System*. New York: Simon and Schuster, 1973.

Goldstein, Herman. *Policing in a Free Society*. Cambridge MA: Ballinger, 1977.

Goodstein, Lynn. "Inmate Adjustment to Prison and Post-Release Outcome." Unpublished dissertation for the Ph.D., City University of New York, 1977.

Gottfredson, Don; Wilkins, Leslie T.; and Hoffman, Peter B. "Prediction of Parole Behavior." In Johnston and Savitz, 877–885.

Gray, Francis. *Prison Discipline in America*. Montclair NJ: Patterson Smith, 1973.

Green, Edward. "Race, Social Status, and Criminal Arrest." *American Sociological Review*, 1970, 35:476–490.

Greenberg, David F., ed. *Corrections and Punishment*. Beverly Hills CA: Sage Publications, 1977.

Gross, Hyman. *A Theory of Criminal Justice*. New York: Oxford University Press, 1979.

Groves, Eugene, and Rossi, Peter H. "Perceptions of a Hostile Ghetto—Realism to Projection." In Harlan Hahn, ed. *The Police in Urban Society*. Beverly Hills CA: Sage Publications, 1970, 176–186.

Grupp, Stanley C., ed. *Theories of Punishment*. Bloomington: Indiana University Press, 1971.

Hagan, John. "The Social and Legal Construction of Criminal Justice—A Survey of Pre-Sentence Process." *Social Problems*. 1975, 38:620–637.

_____; Hewitt, John D.; and Falwin, Duane. "Criminal Justice—Crime and Punishment in a Loosely Coupled System." *Social Forces*, December, 1979, 58: 506–527.

Hahn, Harlan, ed. *The Police in Urban Society*. Beverly Hills CA: Sage Publications, 1970.

_____. "The Public and the Police—A Theoretical Perspective." In Hahn, 12–38.

Hall, Jerome. "The Purpose of a System for the Administration of Justice." In Grupp, 379–401.

Harris, Janet. *Crisis in Corrections— The Prison Problem*. New York: McGraw-Hill, 1973.

Havenstrite, Al. "Case Planning in the Probation Supervision Process." *Federal Probation*, June, 1980, 44:57–66.

Hawkins, D.J.B. "Punishment and Moral Responsibility." In Grupp, 13–18.

_____. *The Prison— Policy and Practice*. Chicago: University of Chicago Press, 1976.

Hawkins, Gordon. "Punishment and Deterrence—The Educative, Moralizing, and Habituative Effects." In Grupp, 168–176.

Hayner, Norman S. "Parole Boards' Attitudes Towards Predictive Devices." In Johnston, Savitz, and Wolfgang, 840–842.

Hazelrigg, Laurence E. ed. *Prison and Society—A Reader in Penology*. New York: Doubleday, 1968.

Hefferman, Esther. *Making It in Prison—The Square, the Cool, and the Life*. New York: Wiley-Interscience, 1972.

Hempel, Carl G. *Aspects of Scientific Explanations and Other Essays in the Philosophy of Science*. New York: Free Press, 1965.

Hermann, Robert; Single, Eric; and Bostin, John. *Counsel for the Poor—Criminal Defense in Urban America*. Lexington MA: Lexington Books, 1977.

Heumann, Milton. "A Note on Plea-Bargaining and Case Pressure." *Law and Society Review*, 1975, 9:515–528.

Hewitt, William H. *Administration of Criminal Justice in New York — A Manual for Law Enforcement Officers*. Rochester NY: Aqueduct Books, 1967.

Hindus, Michael Stephen. "Prison and Plantation — Criminal Justice in Nineteenth Century Massachusetts and South Carolina." Unpublished dissertation for the Ph.D., University of California, Berkeley, 1975.

Hoane, Joseph. "Strategems and Values — An Analysis of Plea-Bargaining in an Urban Court." Unpublished dissertation for the Ph.D., New York University, 1978.

Hoffman, Paul. *Court House*. New York: Hawthorne, 1978.

Hogarth, John. *Sentencing as a Human Process*. Toronto: University of Toronto Press, 1971.

Holton, Gerald, ed. *The Twentieth Century Sciences — Studies in the Biography of Ideas*. New York: Norton, 1972.

Honderich, Ted. *Punishment — The Supposed Justification*. London: Hutchinson, 1969.

Hopper, Columbus B. "Conjugal Visiting." In Johnston and Savitz, 446–449.

Hospers, John. "Retribution — The Ethics of Punishment." In Barnett and Hagel, 181–209.

Hussey, Frederick A., and Duffee, David C. *Probation, Parole, and Community Field Services — Policy, Structure, and Processes*. New York: Harper and Row, 1980.

Ignatieff, Michael. *A Just Measure of Pain — The Penitentiary in the Industrial Revolution — 1750-1850*. New York: Pantheon, 1978.

Imlay, Carl H., and Reid, Elsie. "The Probation Officers' Sentencing and the Winds of Change." *Federal Probation*, December, 1975, 9–17.

Irwin, John. *Prisons in Turmoil*. Boston: Little, Brown, 1980.

_____. *The Felon*. Englewood Cliffs NJ: Prentice-Hall, 1970.

_____, and Cressey, Donald. "Thieves, Convicts, and the Inmate Culture." *Social Problems*, Fall, 1962, 10:42–55.

Jackson, Donald J. *Judges — An Inside View of the Agonies and Exercises of an American Elite*. New York: Atheneum, 1974.

Jacob, Herbert. *Justice in American Courts — Lawyers and the Judicial Process*. Boston: Little, Brown, 1965.

Jacobs, James B. *Stateville — The Penitentiary in Mass Society*. Chicago: University of Chicago Press, 1977.

_____. "Stratification and Conflict Among Prison Inmates." In Johnston and Savitz, 580–587.

Jarvis, Dwight C. *Industrial Treatment of the Offender*. New York: McGraw-Hill, 1978.

Johnston, Norman, and Savitz, Leonard, eds. *Justice and Corrections*. New York: Wiley, 1978.

_____; _____; and Wolfgang, Marvin. *The Sociology of Punishment and Correction*. New York: Wiley, 1970.

Joint Committee on Continuing Legal Education — The American Law Institute of the American Bar Association. *The Problem of Sentencing*. New York: American Bar Association, 1962.

Judson, Charles J.; Pandell, James J.; Owens, Jack B.; McIntosh, James L.; and Matschullat, Dale L. "A Study of the California Penalty Jury in First-Degree Murder Cases." *Stanford Law Review*, 1969, 21:1297–1497.

Kalven, Harry, Jr., and Zeisel, Hans. *The American Jury*. Boston: Little, Brown, 1966.

Kassebaum, Gene G.; Ward, David; and Wilner, Daniel. *Prison Treatment and Parole Survival — An Empirical Assessment*. New York: Wiley, 1971.

Katz, Lewis R.; Litwin, Laurence; and Bamberger, Richard. *Justice Is the Crime—Pretrial Delays in Felony Cases*. Cleveland OH: The Press of Case Western University, 1972.

Kerr, Norbert L. "Trial Participants' Behavior and Jury Verdicts—An Exploratory Field Study." In Konečni and Ebbesen, 264–282.

Keve, Paul W. *Imaginative Program in Probation and Parole*. Minneapolis: University of Minnesota Press, 1967.

_____. *Prison Life and Human Worth*. Minneapolis: University of Minnesota Press, 1974.

_____. *Prison, Probation and Parole—The Probation Officer Investigates*. Minneapolis: University of Minnesota Press, 1954.

_____. *The Probation Officer Investigates—A Guide to the Presentence Report*. Minneapolis: University of Minnesota Press, 1960.

Killinger, George G.; Kerper, Hazel; and Cromwell, Paul E. *Probation and Parole in the Criminal Justice System*. St. Paul MN: West Publishing Co., 1976.

Kinnane, Adrian. *Policing*. Chicago: Nelson-Hall, 1979.

Kirkham, George L. "From Professor to Patrolman—A Fresh Perspective on the Police." In Niederhoffer and Blumberg, 330–331.

Kittrie, Nicholas N. *The Right to Be Different—Deviance and Enforced Therapy*. Baltimore: Johns Hopkins University Press, 1971.

Klokars, Carl B., Jr. "A Theory of Probation Supervision." *Journal of Criminal Law, Criminology, and Police Science*, 1972, 63:550–557.

Knapp Commission. *Report on Police Corruption*. New York: George Braziller, 1972.

Knudten, Mary S. "Prosecutor's Role in Plea-Bargaining: Reasons Related to Actions." In Rich, 275–288.

Konečni, Vladimir, and Ebbesen, Ebbe B. "An Analysis of the Sentencing System." In Konečni and Ebbesen, 296–325.

_____, and _____. *The Criminal Justice System—A Social Psychological Analysis*. San Francisco: Freeman, Cooper, 1982.

Koontz, John F. "Change vs. Probation Management." *Federal Probation*, March, 1978, 42:25–34.

Kozal, Harry L.; Boucher, Richard J.; and Garofolo, Ralph F. "The Diagnosis and Treatment of Dangerousness." *Crime and Delinquency*, 1972, 18:371–392.

Kuhn, Thomas S. *The Structure of Scientific Revolution*. Chicago: University of Chicago Press, 1970.

Kuykendall, Jack L., and Reasons, Charles. *Race, Crime, and Justice*. Pacific Palisades CA: Goodyear Publishing Co., 1972.

La Fave, Wayne. *Arrest—The Decision to Take a Suspect Into Custody*. Boston: Little, Brown, 1965.

Landes, William M. "Legality and Reality—Some Evidence in Criminal Procedure." *Journal of Legal Studies*, 1974, 3:287–337.

La Patra, J.W. *Analyzing the Criminal Justice System*. Lexington MA: Lexington Books, 1978.

Law Enforcement Assistance Administration. *Private and Public Trouble—Prosecutors and the Allocation of Court Resources*. Washington DC: U.S. Government Printing Office, 1978.

Lemert, Edwin M., and Dill, Forrest. *Offenders in the Community*. Lexington MA: Lexington Books, 1978.

Le Mesurier, Mrs. L. *A Handbook of Probation and Social Work of the Courts*. London: National Association of Probation Officers, 1935.

Levin, Martin A. "Delays in Five Courts." *Journal of Legal Studies*, 1975, 4:83–131.

Levy, Howard, and Miller, David. *Going to Jail — The Political Prisoners*. New York: Marcel Dekker, 1969.

Littrell, Boyd. *Bureaucratic Justice — Police, Prosecutors, and Plea-Bargaining*. Beverly Hills CA: Sage Publications, 1979.

Lizotte, Alan J. "Extra-Legal Factors in Chicago's Criminal Courts — Testing the Conflict Model of Criminal Justice." *Social Problems*, June, 1978, 25:564–580.

Lockwood, Daniel. *Prison Sexual Violence*. New York: Elsevier, 1980.

Lonford, Frank Pakenham. *The Idea of Punishment*. London: Geoffrey Chapman, 1961.

Lundman, Richard J. "Routine Police Arrest Practices: A Conventional Perspective." *Social Problems*, 1974, 22:127–141.

Luxenburg, Joan. "The Probation-Supervision Process and Its Conformity to Models of Socialization: A Descriptive Analysis." Unpublished dissertation for the Ph.D., Columbia University, 1978.

McCall, George. *Observing the Law — Study of Crime and the Criminal Justice System*. New York: Free Press, 1978.

McCorkle, Lloyd W.; Ellis, Albert; and Bixby, Lowell. *The Highfields Story — An Experimental Treatment Project for Youthful Offenders*. New York: Henry Holt, 1958.

McGorman, D. "A Survey of Probation Practices in the United States." Unpublished master's thesis, California State University, Long Beach, 1974.

McKee, Gilbert J. "Cost Effectiveness and National Training." In Johnston and Savitz, 633–652.

McKelvey, Blake. *American Prisons — A Study in American Social History Prior to 1915*. Montclair NJ: Patterson Smith, 1936.

McNamara, John H. "Uncertainties in Police Work — The Relevance of Police Recruits' Backgrounds and Training." In Bordua, 181–249.

Mangrum, Claude T., Jr. *The Professional Practitioner in Probation*. Springfield IL: Charles C. Thomas, 1975.

Mannheim, Herman, and Wilkins, Leslie T. *Prediction Methods in Relation to Borstal Training*. London: Her Majesty's Stationery Office, 1955.

Manning, Peter K. *Police Work — The Social Organization of Policing*. Cambridge: M.I.T. Press, 1977.

Manocchio, Anthony J., and Dunn, Jimmy. *The Time Game — Two Views of Prison*. Beverly Hills CA: Sage Publications, 1970.

Martinson, Robert M. "The Paradox of Prison Reform." In Franklin Zimring and Gordon J. Hawkins, eds. *Deterrence — The Legal Threat to Crime Control*. Chicago: University of Chicago Press, 1973, 313–317.

————, Kassebaum, Gene, and Ward, David A. "A Critique of Research in Parole." In Carter and Wilkins, 643–649.

————, and Wilks, Judith. *The Effectiveness of Correctional Treatment Evaluation Studies*. New York: Praeger, 1975.

Masden, Daniel. "Diversified Opinions Gathered from Sampling of Ex-Offenders." *American Journal of Corrections*, March, 1978, 40:22–24.

Mather, Lynn M. "Some Determinants of the Method of Case Disposition — Decision-Making by Public Defenders in Los Angeles." *Law and Society Review*, 1973, 8:187–216.

Meitz, Gary. "The Bakery — Probation Reaches the Inner City." *Federal Probation*, March, 1978, 42:50–52.

Mellon, Leonard; Jacoby, Joan; and Brewer, Marion. "The Prosecutor Constrained by His Environment — A New Look at Discretionary Justice in the United States." *Journal of Criminal Law and Criminology*, Spring, 1981, 72:52–81.

Messinger, Sheldon, and Johnson, Philip E. "California's Determinate Sentencing Statute—History and Issues." In National Institute of Criminal Justice, 16-54.

Meyers, Martha A. "The Effects of Victim Characteristics on the Prosecution, Conviction, and Sentencing of Defendants." Unpublished dissertation for the Ph.D., Indiana University, 1977.

Mileski, Maureen. "Courtroom Encounters—Observation of a Lower Criminal Court." *Law and Society Review*, 1971, 5:473-538.

Miller, Dorothy; Rosenthal, Ann; Miller, Don; and Ruzek, Sheryl. "Public Knowledge of Penalties—A Research Report." In Grupp, 205-225.

Miller, Frank. *Prosecution—The Decision to Charge a Subject with a Crime—Report of the American Bar Foundation's Survey of Justice in the United States*. Boston: Little, Brown, 1969.

Miller, Walter B. "The Midcity Delinquency Control Project." In Johnston, Savitz, and Wolfgang, 635-651.

Misner, Gordon A. "Criminal Justice Education—The Unifying Force." In Shanahan, 23-29.

Mitford, Jessica. *Kind and Usual Punishment—The Prison Business*. New York: Knopf, 1973.

Moberly, Sir Walter. "The Ethics of Punishment." In Gerber and McAnany, 73-76.

_____. *The Ethics of Punishment*. Hamden CT: Archon, 1968.

Mohr, Laurence. "Organizations, Decisions, and Courts." *Law and Society Review*, Summer, 1976, 10:621-642.

Moley, Raymond. *Our Criminal Courts*. New York: Minton Batch, 1930.

Monahan, John. "A Critique of Kozol et al." *Crime and Delinquency*, 1973, 19:418-420.

Monger, Mark. *Casework in Probation*. London: Butterworth, 1972.

More, Harry W., Jr. "Disparity in the System." In More, Jr. and Chang, 32-43.

_____, and Chang, Richard, eds. *Contemporary Criminal Justice*. San Jose: Justice System Development, 1974.

Morgenbesser, Sidney; Suppes, Patrick; and White, Morton, eds. *Philosophy, Science, and Methods*. New York: St. Martin's, 1969.

Morris, Herbert. "Persons and Punishment." In Grupp, 79-92.

Morris, Norval, and Buckle, Donald. "The Humanitarian Theory of Punishment—A Reply to C.S. Lewis." In Grupp, 310-316.

Morris, Pauline. *Prisoners and Their Families*. London: George Allen and Unwin, 1965.

Muir, William K., Jr. *Police—Street Corner Politicians*. Chicago: University of Chicago Press, 1977.

Mylonas, Anastassios D., and Reckless, Walter C. "Prisoners' Attitudes Toward Law and Legal Institutions." *Journal of Criminal Law, Criminology, and Police Science*, 1963, 54:479-484.

Naegele, Timothy J. "Civilian Complaints Against the Police in Los Angeles." *Issues in Criminology*, Summer, 1967, 3:7-34.

Nagel, Ernest. *The Structure of Science—Problems in the Logic of Scientific Explanation*. New York: Columbia University Press, 1961.

Nagel, Stuart. "Disparities in Criminal Procedures." *University of California Law Review*, August, 1964, 14:1271-1305.

_____. "Judicial Backgrounds and Criminal Cases." *Journal of Criminal Law, Criminology, and Police Science*, 1962, 53:333-339.

_____. "The Zipped Scales of American Justice." In Blumberg, *The Scales of Justice*, 33-49.

Nagel, William G. "Prison Architecture and Prison Violence." In Cohen, Cole, and Bailey, 105-106.

National Institute of Law Enforcement and Criminal Justice, Law Enforcement Assistance Administration. *Determinate Sentencing — Reform or Regression?* Washington DC: U.S. Department of Justice, 1978.

Neier, Aryeh. *Crime and Punishment — A Radical Solution.* New York: Stein and Day, 1978.

Neubauer, David W. *Criminal Justice in Middle-America.* Morristown NJ: General Learning Press, 1974.

Newfield, Jack. *Cruel and Unusual Justice.* New York: Holt, Rinehart and Winston, 1974.

Newman, Charles. *Sourcebook on Probation and Parole.* Springfield IL: Charles C. Thomas, 1968.

Newman, Donald. *Conviction — Determination of Guilt or Innocence Without Trial.* Boston: Little, Brown, 1966.

Newman, Graeme. *The Punishment Response.* Philadelphia: Lippincott, 1978.

Newman, Jon O. "A Better Way to Sentence Prisoners." *American Bar Association Journal*, 1977, 63:1563.

Niederhoffer, Arthur. *Beyond the Shield — Police in Urban Society.* Garden City NY: Doubleday, 1967.

————, and Blumberg, Abraham. *The Ambivalent Force — Perspectives on the Police.* Hinsdale IL: Dryden, 1976.

————, and Smith, Alexander. *New Directions in Police Community Relations.* San Francisco: Holt, Rinehart and Winston, 1974.

Oaks, Dallin H., and Lehman, Warren. "Lawyers for the Poor." In Blumberg, *The Scales of Justice*, 91–112.

O'Donnell, Pierce; Churgin, Michael; and Curtis, Dennis E. *Toward a Just and Effective Sentencing System — Agenda for Legislative Reform.* New York: Praeger, 1977.

Ohlin, Lloyd E. *Prisoners in America — The American Assembly.* Englewood Cliffs NJ: Prentice-Hall, 1973.

Oppenheimer, Heinrich. *The Rationale of Punishment.* London: University of London Press, 1913.

Packer, Herbert L. *The Limits of the Criminal Sanction.* Stanford CA: Stanford University Press, 1968.

————. "Two Models of the Criminal Process." In John A. Robertson, ed. *Rough Justice — Perspectives in Lower Criminal Courts.* Boston: Little, Brown, 1974, 138–143.

Parry, L.A. *The History of Torture in England.* Montclair NJ: Patterson Smith, 1975.

Perlman, Harvey S., and Ballington, Thomas B. *The Tasks of Penology — A Symposium on Prisons and Correctional Law.* Lincoln: University Press of Nebraska, 1967.

Piliavin, Irving, and Briar, Scott. "Police Encounters with Juveniles." *American Journal of Sociology*, 1964, 70:206–214.

Pincoffs, Edmund L. *The Rationale of Legal Punishment.* New York: Humanities Press, 1966.

Popper, Karl. *Conjectures and Refutations — The Growth of Scientific Knowledge.* London: Routledge and Kegan Paul, 1963.

————. *The Logic of Scientific Discovery.* New York: Harper and Row, 1959.

————. *Objective Knowledge — An Evolutionary Approach.* Oxford: Clarendon Press, 1972.

————. *The Open Society and Its Enemies.* Princeton NJ: Princeton University Press, 1962.

Pound, Roscoe. *Criminal Justice in America.* New York: Da Capo, 1972.

Powers, Edwin, and Witmer, Helen. "The Cambridge-Sommerville Study." In Johnston, Savitz, and Wolfgang, 587–600.

President's Commission on Law Enforcement and Administration of Justice. "Probation." In Carter and Wilkins, 20–37.

————. *Task Force Report—The Courts*. Washington DC: U.S. Printing Office, 1967.

Pugh, George W., and Carver, Hampton. "Due Process of Sentencing—From Mapp to Mempha to McGautha." *Texas Law Review*, 1971, 49:20–49.

Quinney, Richard. *Class, State, and Crime*. New York: McKay, 1977.

Ranulf, Svend. *Moral Class Indignation and Middle-Class Psychology—A Sociological Study*. New York: Schocken, 1960.

Reasons, Charles. "On Methodology, Theory, and Ideology." *American Sociological Review*, February, 1977, 42:177–181.

Reed, John H. *The Application of Operations Research to Court Delay*. New York: Praeger, 1973.

Reed, John P., and King, Charles E. "Factors in the Decision-Making of North Carolina Probation Officers." *Journal of Research in Crime and Delinquency*, 1966, 3:126–132.

Reiss, Albert J., Jr. *The Police and the Public*. New Haven CT: Yale University Press, 1971.

————, and Bordua, David J. "Environment and Organization—A Perspective on the Police." In Bordua, 29–54.

Remington, Frank J.; Newman, Donald J.; Kimball, Edward L.; Melli, Marygold; and Goldstein, Herman. *Criminal Justice Administration—Materials and Cases*. New York: Bobbs-Merrill, 1976.

Rhodes, William M. "The Economics of Criminal Courts—A Theoretical and Empirical Investigation." *Journal of Legal Studies*, 1976, 5:311–340.

Rich, Robert M., ed. *Essays in the Theory and Practice of Criminal Justice*. Washington DC: University Press of America, 1978.

Robertson, John A., ed. *Rough Justice—Perspectives in Lower Criminal Courts*. Boston: Little, Brown, 1974.

Robertson, Leon S., and Richard, Robert F. "Deterring the Drunk Driver." In Johnston and Savitz, 391–399.

Robinson, Louis M. *Jails—Care and Treatment of Misdemeanant Prisoners in the United States*. Philadelphia: John Winston, 1944.

Robison, James; Wilkins, Leslie T.; Carter, Robert M.; and Wahl, Albert. *The San Francisco Project: National Institute of Mental Health*, 1969.

Roebuck, Julian B. *"A Typology of Police Corruption." Social Problems*, 1974, 21:423–437.

Rosett, Arthur J., and Cressey, Donald. *Justice by Consent*. Philadelphia: Lippincott, 1976.

Rovner-Pieczenik, Roberta. *The Criminal Court—How It Works*. Lexington MA: Lexington Books, D.C. Heath, 1978.

————. "Urban Justice: Understanding the Adjudication of Felony Cases in an Urban Criminal Court." Unpublished dissertation for the Ph.D., New York University, 1974.

Rubenstein, Jonathan. *City Police*. New York: Farrar, Strauss and Giroux, 1973.

Rubin, Sol. "Disparity and Equality of Sentences—A Constitutional Challenge." *Federal Reports Decisions*, 1966, 40:50–78.

Rudé, George. *Protest and Punishment—The Story of the Social and Political Protestors' Transportation to Australia: 1778–1868*. Oxford: Clarendon, 1978.

Rusche, George, and Kirchheimer, Otto. *Punishment and Social Structure*. New York: Russell and Russell, 1939.

Ryan, John Paul, and Alfini, James J. "Trial Judges' Participation in Plea-

Bargaining — An Empirical Perspective." *Law and Society Review*, Winter, 1979, 13:478-508.

Sacco, Anthony. *Rape in Prison*. Springfield IL: Charles C. Thomas, 1975.

Saleilles, Raymond. *The Individualization of Punishment*. Boston: Little, Brown, 1911.

Samuelson, Pamela. "Sentence Review and Sentence Disparity — A Case Study of the Sentence Review Division." *Connecticut Law Review*, Fall, 1977, 10:5-89.

Sandhu, Harjit S. *Modern Corrections — The Offenders, Therapy, and Community Reintegration*. Springfield: Charles C. Thomas, 1974.

Sands, Eliot. "New Directions in Probation in the United States." *International Journal of Offender Therapy and Comparative Criminology*, 1976, 26:33-40.

Savitz, Leonard. "The Dimensions of Police Loyalty." In Hahn, 217-238.

Scarpitti, Frank R., and Stephenson, Richard M. "A Study of Probation Effectiveness." In Johnston and Savitz, 831-839.

_____, and _____. "A Study of Probation Effectiveness." *Journal of Criminal Law, Criminology, and Police Science*, 1968, 59:361-369.

Schnur, Alfred C. "Some Reflections on the Role of Correctional Research." In Hazelrigg, 378-386.

Schrag, Clarence. "Leadership Among Prison Inmates." *American Sociological Review*, February, 1954, 19:37-42.

Schuessler, Karl F. "The Deterrent Influence of the Death Penalty." In Grupp, 184-194.

Schwendinger, Herman and Julia. *Armchair Sociology — Sociology of the Chair*. New York: Basic Books, 1974.

Sellin, Thorsten. *Slavery and the Penal System*. New York: Elsevier, 1976.

Seymour, Whitney North, Jr. *Why Justice Fails*. New York: Morrow, 1973.

Shanahan, Donald T., ed. *The Administration of Justice System — An Introduction*. Boston: Holbrook, 1977.

Sheehan, Susan. *A Prison and a Prisoner*. Boston: Houghton Mifflin, 1978.

Sherman, Laurence W. "Controlling Police Corruption — Scandal and Organizational Reform." Unpublished dissertation for the Ph.D., Yale University, 1976.

_____. *Police Corruption — A Sociological Perspective*. New York: Anchor, 1974.

Shills, Edward. "Tradition, Ecology, and Institution in the History of Sociology." In Holton, 33-93.

Silberman, Charles. *Criminal Violence, Criminal Justice*. New York: Random House, 1978.

Silver, Allen. "The Demand for Order in Civil Society: A Review of Some Themes in the History of Urban Crime, Police, and Riot." In Bordua, 14-54.

Silverstein, Lee. "Bail in the State Court." *Minnesota Law Review*, March, 1966, 50:621-650.

_____. *Defense of the Poor in Criminal Cases in American State Courts*. Washington DC: American Bar Association, 1965.

Skolnick, Jerome H. *Justice Without Trial — Law Enforcement in a Democratic Society*. New York: Wiley, 1966.

_____. "The Police and the Urban Ghetto." In Kuykendall and Reasons, 246-261.

_____. "Research Contribution of the American Bar Association." In Niederhoffer and Blumberg, 218-230.

_____, and Woodworth, Richard. "Bureaucracy, Information, and Social Control." In Bordua, 110-129.

Smith, Alexander, and Berlin, Louis. *Introduction to Probation and Parole*. St. Paul MN: West Publishing Co., 1976.

_____, and Pollack, Harriet. *Criminal Justice — An Overview*, Second Edition. New York: Holt, Rinehart and Winston, 1980.

Sommer, Robert. *The End of Imprisonment*. New York: Oxford University Press, 1976.

Stoddard, Ellwyn. "The Informal Code of Police Deviance: A Group Approach to Blue-Collar Crime." *Journal of Criminal Law, Criminology and Police Science*, June, 1968, 59:201-213.

Strodbeck, Fred; James, Rita M.; and Hawkins, Charles. "Social Status in Jury Selection." *American Sociological Review*, December, 1957, 27:713-719.

Studt, Eliot. *Surveillance and Service in Parole — Report of the Parole Action Study*. Washington DC: U.S. Department of Justice, May, 1973.

Sudnow, David. "Normal Crimes: Sociological Features of the Penal Code in a Public Defender Office." *Social Problems*, Winter, 1965, 12:255-276.

Swigert, Victoria Lynn, and Farrell, Ronald A. *Murder, Inequality, and the Law — Differential Treatment in the Legal Process*. Lexington MA: Lexington Books, 1976.

_____, and _____. "Normal Homicides and the Law." *American Sociological Review*, February, 1977, 42:16-32.

Sykes, Gresham M. *The Society of Captives — A Study of the Maximum Security Prison*. Princeton NJ: Princeton University Press, 1958.

_____, and Messinger, Sheldon. "The Inmate Social System." In Cloward et al., 9-18.

Sylvester, Sawyer F. *The Heritage of Modern Criminology*. Cambridge MA: Shenkman Press, 1972.

_____; Reed, John H.; and Nelson, David. *Prison Homicides*. New York: Spectrum, 1977.

Takagi, Paul. "The Walnut Street Jail — A Penal Reform to Centralize the Power of the State." *Federal Probation*, 1975, 39:18-26.

Task Force on Criminal Sentencing. *Fair and Certain Punishment — Report of the Twentieth Century Fund*. New York: McGraw-Hill, 1976.

Taylor, Edward M., and McEachern, Alexander W. "Needs and Directions in Probation Training." In Carter and Wilkins, 672-683.

Taylor, Ian; Walton, Paul; and Young, Jock. *The New Criminology — For a Social Theory of Deviance*. London: Routledge and Paul Kegan, 1973; and New York: Harper and Row, 1973.

Teitlebaum, William J. "The Prosecutor's Role in the Sentencing Process: A National Survey." *American Journal of Criminal Law*, 1972, 1:75-95.

Thomas, Charles W., and Fists, Samuel C. "The Importation Model — Perspectives on Inmate Social Roles — An Empirical Assessment." *Sociological Quarterly*, Spring, 1973, 14:226-234.

Tittle, Charles R. *Sanction and Social Deterrence — The Question of Deterrence*. New York: Praeger, 1980.

Toby, Jackson. "Is Punishment Necessary"? In Gerber and McAnany, 219-227; and in Grupp, 102-114.

Toch, Hans. *Living in Prison — The Ecology of Survival*. New York: Free Press, 1971.

_____. *Men in Crisis — Human Breakdowns in Prison*. Chicago: Aldine, 1975.

Tweney, Ryan D.; Doherty, Michael E.; and Mynatt, Clifford R., eds. *On Scientific Thinking*. New York: Columbia University Press, 1981.

United Nations. "The Legal Origins of Probation." In Carter and Wilkins, 4-8.

United States. *National Advisory Commission on Civil Disorders — The Kerner Report*. New York: Dutton, 1968.

Van Dine, Stephen; Dinitz, Simon; and Conrad, John. "Incapacitation of Dangerous Offenders." In Johnston and Savitz, 422-432.

_____, _____, and _____. *Restraining the Wicked — The Incapacitation of Dangerous Offenders*. Lexington MA: Lexington Books, 1979.

Van Laningham, Dale; Taber, Merlin; and Dimants, Ruta. "How Adult Probation Officers View Their Job Responsibilities." *Crime and Delinquency*, April, 1966, 12:97–108.

Vasoli, Robert H. "Some Reflections on Measuring Probation Outcomes." In Carter and Wilkins, 332–341.

Von Hentig, Hans. *Punishment — Its Origin, Purpose, and Psychology*. Montclair NJ: Patterson Smith, 1973.

Von Hirsch, Andrew. *Doing Justice — The Choice of Punishment — Report of the Committee for the Study of Incarceration*. New York: Hill and Wang, 1976.

_____, and Hanrahan, Kathleen. *The Question of Parole: Retention, Reform, or Abolition*. Cambridge MA: Ballinger, 1978.

Waller, Irvin. *Men Released from Prison*. Toronto: University of Toronto Press, 1974.

Warburton, Rex M. "The Effect of Information Feedback on the Predictive Capabilities of Probation Officers." Unpublished thesis, United States International University, 1974.

Ward, David A., and Kassebaum, Gene G. "Homosexuality in a Women's Prison." In Johnston, Savitz, and Wolfgang, 464–477.

_____, and _____. *Women's Prisons — Sex and Social Structure*. Chicago: Aldine, 1965.

Weber, Max. *The Methodology of the Social Sciences*. New York: Free Press, 1949.

Weeks, Charles E. "Evaluation of a Method of Predicting Violence in Offenders." *Criminology*, 1973, 11:427–435.

Westley, William A. *Violence and the Police — A Sociological Study of Law, Custom, and Morality*. Cambridge MA: The M.I.T. Press, 1970.

White, Walsh S. "A Proposal for Reform of the Plea-Bargaining Process." *University of Pennsylvania Law Review*, 1970–1971, 119:439–465.

Wice, Paul B. "Bail and Its Reform." Unpublished paper, 1973.

_____, and Suwak, Peter. "Current Realities of Public Defender Programs — A National Survey and Analysis." *Criminal Law Bulletin*, 1974, 10:161–183.

Williams, Jerry S. *The Law of Sentencing and Corrections*. Buffalo NY: William S. Hein, 1974.

Wilsnack, Richard W. "Explaining Collective Violence in Prison — Problems and Possibilities." In Cohen, Cole, and Bailey, 61–72.

Wilson, James Q. "Police Morale, Reform, and Citizen Respect — The Chicago Case." In Bordua, 139–159.

_____. *Varieties of Police Behavior — The Management of Law and Order in Eight Communities*. Cambridge MA: Harvard University Press, 1968.

Wilson, Margaret. *The Crime of Punishment*. New York: Harcourt, Brace, 1931.

Wintersmith, Robert F. *Police and the Black Community*. Lexington MA: Lexington Books, 1974.

Wolfgang, Marvin E. *Prisons — Past and Possible*. Lexington MA: Lexington Books, 1979.

Wolin, Robert E. "After Release — The Parolee in Society." *St. John's Law Review*, October, 1973, 48:1–47.

Wright, Burton, and Fox, Vernon. *Criminal Justice and the Social Sciences*. Philadelphia: Saunders, 1978.

Wright, Erik Ohlin, ed. *The Politics of Punishment — A Critical Analysis of Prisons in America*. New York: Harper and Row, 1973.

Zald, Mayer N. "Power, Balance, and Staff Conflict in Correctional Institutions." In Hazelrigg, 403–419.

Zeisel, Hans; Kalven, Harry, Jr.; and Buchholz, Bernard. *Delay in the Court*. Boston: Little, Brown, 1959.

Zimring, Franklin E. "Punishment and Deterrence — Bad Checks in Nebraska — A Study in Complex Threats." In Greenberg, 176-193.

_____, and Hawkins, Gordon J. *Deterrence — The Legal Threat to Crime Control*. Chicago: University of Chicago Press, 1973.

Zuchlewski, Pearl. "Challenging New York — The Grand Jury Composition — Barriers of the Systematic and Intentional Exclusion Requirement." *Fordham Urban Law Journal*, Winter, 1975, 6:317-332.

Index

Note: The indexed name of an author may refer to the location of that author's research, without mention (except in reference notes) of his or her name, on the page cited. For instance, "Adams, Stuart, 103, 113" refers the reader to two pages on which Adam's research is mentioned, although his name does not appear on either page. In the event of multiple authorship, only the first author has been indexed.